GUARDIANS *of* IDOLATRY

GUARDIANS *of* IDOLATRY

GODS, DEMONS, *and* PRIESTS in Hernando Ruiz de Alarcón's *Treatise on the Heathen Superstitions*

Viviana Díaz Balsera

UNIVERSITY OF OKLAHOMA PRESS : NORMAN

Publication of this book is made possible through the generosity of Edith Kinney Gaylord.

Parts of the introduction and chapter 2 in this book were previously published as "Nombres que conservan el mundo: los *nahualtocaitl*, el *Tratado* sobre idolatrías de Hernando Ruiz de Alarcón," by Viviana Díaz Balsera, in *Colonial Latin American Review* 16.2 (2007), 159–78.

Part of chapter 3 in this book was previously published as "Voicing Mesoamerican Identities on the Roads of Empire: Alarcón and the *Nahualtocaitl* in Seventeenth-Century Mexico," by Viviana Díaz Balsera, in *To Be Indio in Colonial Spanish America*, edited by Mónica Díaz (Albuquerque: University of New Mexico Press, 2017), 169–90.

Part of chapter 6 in this book was previously published as "Atando dioses y humanos: Cipactónal y la cura por adivinación en el Tratado sobre idolatrías de Hernando Ruiz de Alarcón," by Viviana Díaz Balsera, in *Estudios coloniales latinoamericanos en el siglo XXI: Nuevos itinerarios*, edited by Stephanie Kirk (Pittsburgh: Instituto Internacional de Literatura Iberoamericana, Serie Nueva América, 2011), 321–49.

Library of Congress Cataloging-in-Publication Data

Name: Díaz Balsera, Viviana, 1957– author.

Title: Guardians of idolatry : gods, demons, and priests in Hernando Ruiz de Alarcón's treatise on the heathen superstitions / Viviana Díaz Balsera.

Other titles: Gods, demons, and priests in Hernando Ruiz de Alarcón's treatise on the heathen superstitions

Description: First edition. | Norman : University of Oklahoma Press, 2018 | Includes bibliographical references and index.

Identifiers: LCCN 2018011942 | ISBN 978-0-8061-6040-5 (hardcover : alk. paper)

Subjects: LCSH: Tratado de las supersticiones y costumbres gentílicas que oy viven entre los indios naturales desta Nueva España.—History and criticism. | Aztecs—Religion. | Aztecs—Medicine. | Indians of Mexico—Religion. | Indians of Mexico—Medicine.

Classification: LCC F1219.76.R45 D538 2018 | DDC 299.7/8452—dc23

LC record available at https://lccn.loc.gov/2018011942

The paper in this book meets the guidelines for permanence and durability of the Committee on Production Guidelines for Book Longevity of the Council on Library Resources, Inc. ∞

1 2 3 4 5 6 7 8 9 10

In memory of my mother, Lilita Balsera Díaz,
and of my true friend of many decades, Mr. Shahpoor Arjomand

Contents

Illustrations

Acknowledgments

A book is a long journey of discovery. In order to give it full and rightful closure, one must look back to express thanks to the many people and fellow travelers who helped to carry it to completion. My deep gratitude goes to Louise M. Burkhart for her generosity and warmth in sharing with me her authoritative knowledge of all things Nahua. I am indebted to Kris E. Lane for his support and encouragement of many ideas in this book and for inviting me to present them at the Colonial Latin American Review's 20th Anniversary Symposium. Many thanks to Raquel Chang-Rodríguez for endorsing that invitation and for her affectionate introduction at the event in which she recalled—and graciously excused once again—my delay in turning in an article to CLAR; I had just given birth to my son and could not manage to send off the revisions quite on time. I am grateful to Rolena Adorno for having read a related article to this book, for her conscientious comments written in beautiful longhand, and for her true care. Thank you to Margarita Zamora for her support of this project and to Aída Beaupied and Gladys Rivera Ocasio for their unwavering belief in it. A lot of sincere gratitude goes to Anne J. Cruz for all her good advice and firm encouragement to keep working hard. Very special thanks to Maria Elena Díaz, sister and colleague who, with her invaluable readings and critiques, helped me take this book to a higher level. Thank you to my colleagues and to my graduate and undergraduate students at the University of Miami, who have nourished me throughout the years with their enthusiasm, ideas, and insights.

I also wish to acknowledge the financial support from a Provost's Research Award and a Max Orovitz award from the University of Miami. They afforded me precious time for research and writing. My recognition to the Faculty Research

Fellowship at the University of Miami Center for the Humanities directed by Mihoko Suzuki, which provided one full semester course release, and to the great colleagues who read my work during our tenure as fellows at the center. I thank the UM College of Arts and Sciences for their book fund support. I also thank the UM Animal Studies and Environmental Humanities Research Group for their interest and critiques of the chapter on the nahualli. My gratitude extends to Alessandra J. Tamulevich, acquisitions editor at the University of Oklahoma Press, for her support and to my readers for their valuable comments and observations. Special thanks to Kirsteen E. Anderson, my eagle-eyed copy editor, for her inestimable effort in helping me improve the flow and accuracy of my Spanish-accented prose while always conserving my voice. I also thank Emily J. Schuster, my manuscript editor, for her kindness and forbearance with my questions and requests. My recognition to the staff of Special Collections of the Richter Library at the University of Miami for their help in providing the great image of Chicomecoatl for the dust jacket of the book.

Lastly, and most importantly, my deep, heartfelt gratitude to my husband Alberto Jorge Carol for his resolute and inspiring belief in my work, his endless patience, and for his careful, insightful readings. Without his support this book would not have been possible. And many, many thanks to my son Dylan Carol for having always been there for me, who as I wrote and completed this book became an upright and trustworthy high schooler, ready to take on his responsibilities as an adult and global citizen in a world that needs him and the likes of him so much.

GUARDIANS *of* IDOLATRY

Introduction

One hundred years after the cataclysmic fall of Tenochtitlan in 1521, the Nahuas of Central Mexico and its surroundings had adopted the practices and beliefs of the globalizing discourses of Christianity. The grand-scale, time-conserving ritual practices that had served the pre-Hispanic gods and ruled the people had been criminalized and abolished by the Spanish intruders. Innumerable temples, or *teocallis*, had been destroyed, and the *tlamacazque*, or Nahua priests, who formerly maintained them, had devolved from highly esteemed, principal figures in the city to deluded, ignorant agents of the devil. Legions of Nahuas were baptized, and thousands of them followed the friars for weeks in order to confess their sins (Motolinía 1951, 178–83; Mendieta 1993, 258–67). The indigenous peoples built impressive churches and monasteries, and lobbied tenaciously to have friars permanently assigned to their towns, or *altepetl* (Mendieta 1993, 321–58; Gibson 1964, 98–135; Lockhart 1992, 203–60). The natives presented evangelizing plays of epic dimensions, in which they showed off their acceptance and competent understanding of Christianity, and thousands walked in procession on Holy Thursday, whipping themselves and "singing the Pater Noster, the Ave Maria, the Credo and the Salve Regina" (Motolinía 1951, 144), the cardinal prayers that proclaimed the Christian faith—making many Spaniards cry from joy and remorse over their own sins.

And yet, even with the modern city of Mexico sitting securely over the ruins of Tenochtitlan and the Indian peoples showing all mandatory devotion, maintaining the requisite Christian appearance, and conducting public observances with pomp and circumstance, many Spanish and creole priests and friars were apprehensive. They suspected that the slowly recuperating populations of Central Mexico were still calling forth imperceptible Mesoamerican Postclassic entities to intercede in the private spheres of their lives.[1] One of these worried priests was Hernando Ruiz de Alarcón, brother of the famous playwright Juan Ruiz de Alarcón. In the pueblo of Atenango del Río, 125 miles southwest of modern Mexico City, in the mountainous province of Chilapa, he lived and wrote his bilingual *Tratado de las supersticiones y costumbres gentilicas que oy viuen entre los indios naturales desta Nueva España* (henceforth the *Treatise*). The work was part of a commission from Archbishop of Mexico Juan Pérez de la Serna to document backsliding and idolatrous practices among the indigenous peoples of the region. Finished in 1629, the *Treatise* contained a collection of sixty-plus incantations, or *nahualtocaitl*, conjuring a few salient, translocal deities in Central Mexico, some of them harking back centuries to at least the Mesoamerican Postclassic period (circa 900 C.E.–1519 C.E.), or even earlier. Ruiz de Alarcón's work is one of the most significant and valuable records from seventeenth-century Mexico about postconquest indigenous daily subsistence practices that kept alive an important link with a Mesoamerican worldview from the Late Postclassic period (1325–1519 C.E.).

Nahualtocaitl means "language or names that wizards use" (Ruiz de Alarcón 1984, 148). This was the term indigenous people of the region used to denominate a specialized speech for addressing an array of non-ordinary, nonhuman Mesoamerican powers they presumed to exist. These powers were invoked with the expectation that they would produce concrete, perceptible results in the world.[2] They were asked to manifest themselves in the context of culturally marked activities to which they were related in Mesoamerican cosmogonies. In this way, the nahualtocaitl were deemed to help humans achieve success in a wide array of endeavors.

For Ruiz de Alarcón calling forth non-Christian, nonhuman, non-ordinary entities was idolatrous. However, even though he glossed the nahualtocaitl in denunciatory language with the explicit objective of their extirpation, Ruiz de Alarcón carefully transcribed them in the original Nahuatl and translated them into Spanish. Consequently, the *Treatise* is a unique document, a salient original source offering direct, firsthand information about indigenous cosmological beliefs; discourses; and medical, agricultural, and hunting practices in the context of a wide array of actual users and ritual specialists in an extended region to the south and southwest of the Valley of Mexico. Ruiz de Alarcón's work has rightly been compared in importance to Bernardino de Sahagún's monumental, sixteenth-century, also bilingual *Florentine Codex* (Coe and Whittaker 1982, 1). Indeed, Ruiz de Alarcón's *Treatise* and Jacinto de la Serna's later *Manual for Ministers* both documented translocal circulation of the nahualtocaitl.[3] The semantics of the incantations, their internal coherence and consistency; and their recurrent, carefully contextualized images all testify to a robust, prestigious Mesoamerican Postclassic discursive presence coexisting alongside the colonizing discourse of Christianity in the viceroyalty of New Spain.

Foundational editions of both works were released in Mexico in 1892 and 1953, and two major scholarly translations and critical editions of the *Treatise* came out in the United States in 1982 and 1984. In addition, frequent mentions of these texts, and many articles and book chapters dedicated to them, particularly to the *Treatise*, evince their importance in scholarship on Mesoamerican ethnohistory, religion, and colonial studies.[4] There are, however, no book-length monographs devoted to exploring in depth the full richness of either the *Treatise* or the *Manual*. Although in this volume I focus on the *Treatise*, I expand the interdisciplinary scholarship on both cardinal texts in Latin American colonial studies. I delve into the Postclassic Mesoamerican knowledge contained in the nahualtocaitl and recorded in the *Treatise* and the *Manual*. I also examine the relationship of both texts with the early modernization processes unleashed by a universalizing European Christian epistemology, itself also deeply engaged with world spirits.

Indeed, both the *Treatise* and the *Manual* were written from the realization that many indigenous peoples had not completely left behind their pre-Hispanic past despite one hundred years of indoctrination in Christianity.[5] Hence, these texts can be approached from postcolonial, historical, ethnographical, and cultural studies points of view. They allow us to look at how early modern Spanish creole colonial culture recorded and classified, read and misread extant Mesoamerican Late Postclassic indigenous practices one century after contact. Claiming religious truth and epistemological superiority, Hernando Ruiz de Alarcón and Jacinto de la Serna harshly denounced the indigenous peoples of Mexico as recalcitrant backsliders. Serna asserted that "after so much light, so much preaching and works," the indigenous peoples of Mexico still did not shine with deeds of true Christians (Serna 1892, 279; all translations mine). No longer neophytes, they were not ignorant, backward indigenous peasants, but hypocritical, cunning idolaters, who slyly and "maliciously" mixed their old "superstitious" practices with pious

Christian ceremonies (272, 277, 282, 449). Indians believed in the Christian God, but kept turning to their idols for help with their immediate, temporal needs (283). For Ruiz de Alarcón and Serna, this untroubled shift from the Mesoamerican superhuman pantheon to the Christian one and back—not outright rejection of either—was clearly scandalous and incompatible with true Christianity. But such shifts also speak to us about how the indigenous peoples negotiated their relations with the intrusive Christian powers in the land. I will now turn to explore various interdisciplinary perspectives from which the *Treatise* and the *Manual* can be considered.

1

One approach to a postcolonial reading of Ruiz de Alarcón and Serna's texts is to examine their conspicuous strategies of "othering" the indigenous peoples, or portraying them as standing alone among the peoples of the world. One instance of this maneuvering was to single them out as if they were the only people still drawn to superhuman entities not authorized by the Church. Ruiz de Alarcón and Serna ignored the significant degree of Christianization that (for good or ill) had been accomplished among the indigenous population (Andrews and Hassig 1984, 21). They accused the native people of clinging to uniquely Mesoamerican nonhuman super beings such as Tezcatlipoca, Xochiquetzal, Quetzalcoatl, and Centeotl—already denounced by the Church as entities of diabolical origin. From a more transcontinental perspective, however, both authors would have been forced to realize—or acknowledge—that non-Indian populations throughout Europe, in Spain, and in Mexico City itself—cutting across races, social classes, and genders—could also be accused of having recalcitrant, "illicit" dealings with spiritual beings. An extensive bibliography supports the point that the natives of Central Mexico were not the only people whose deeds did not always shine with the light of Christianity.[6]

Another salient instance of othering in these texts is portraying the conflation of medicine and sorcery as something unique to indigenous peoples' practices. According to Ruiz de Alarcón and Serna, in Nahuatl *ticitl* denoted not only doctor, but also "seer and sorcerer, or, perhaps, one who has a pact with the Devil" (Ruiz de Alarcón 1984, 157; Serna 1892, 304).[7] Indigenous peoples took for granted that these *ticitl* had "knowledge of the illness, no matter how serious, occult or unknown, and could apply the convenient remedy to cure it" (Serna 1892, 304).[8] The religious, however, decried native medicine as part of a constellation of practices that dealt with the devil and his superior, dangerous knowledge of the occult. These claims have significant implications for the construction of indigenous idolatry in the *Treatise* and the *Manual*.

Indeed, Nahuas thought that many, though not all, ailments had preternatural or out-of-the-ordinary, superhuman causes. Serious illnesses were viewed as either punishment from the gods or the result of sorcery (Aguirre Beltrán 1963, 36–54; López Austin 1970b; Ortiz de Montellano 1990, 129–49; Lockhart 1992, 259). Cures incorporating both empirical and occult elements were applied even when the malady was diagnosed as having an essentially proximate, "natural" etiology (Ortiz de Montellano 1990, 161). Yet, and very importantly, the Nahua belief in the superhuman or preternatural origin of illness was not totally unlike the mindset of European theologians and many physicians of the early modern period, who thought that many ailments could be caused by witches or the devil. In their infamous *Malleus maleficarum* of 1486, for instance, Heinrich Kramer and James Sprenger wrote about cases in the town of Innsbruck where witches inflicted all sorts of maladies on people, such as "grievous pains in the head," sharp stomachaches, blindness, and lameness (Kramer and Sprenger 1971, 137–40). Martín del Río (1991, 138) declared in his *Disquisitiones magicae* of 1599 that the devil could introduce into and extract from the body various strange objects, such as needles, knives, and nails. The French theologian André Valladier preached in 1612 that the devil could command all powers and humors of the human body so as to alter their normal function (Clark 1999, 187). In 1699 Fray Froilán Díaz—confessor of the unhappy Charles II, nicknamed "El Hechizado" (The Bewitched)—declared he had discovered that the king and queen wore little bags containing spells they erroneously thought were relics. These spells, he alleged, were what had been impeding conception of an heir for the throne of Spain (Caro Baroja 1967, 1:87). As late as 1703, Friedrich Hoffman published the dissertation of Gottfried Büching, entitled *De potentia diaboli in corpora*, in which he argued that the devil could interfere with the imagination and with mental and physical functions, and could induce illusions and trances (Diethelm 1970, 8). All these learned European authors attest to the belief in demonic origins of illness before, during, and after the period in which Ruiz de Alarcón and Serna's treatises were written. Thus, the strong Nahua belief in the presence of preternatural agencies in illnesses was not as uniquely deluded as Ruiz de Alarcón and Serna portrayed it, although the delicate boundary separating natural from preternatural or non-natural causes of illnesses was not identical in the two cultures.

In addition, book 11 of the *Florentine Codex* contains descriptions of about 150 medicinal plants and their practical applications for cures. It documents that Nahua herbalists and healers had vast empirical knowledge of the natural curative properties of indigenous plants in their environment. A few decades earlier, in 1552, Nahua physician Martín de la Cruz had produced the *Codex Cruz–Badianus* in the Franciscan Colegio de Tlatelolco, a manuscript expounding on the medicinal properties of numerous plants used by Nahua herbalists and healers. It is possible, albeit very unlikely, that Ruiz de Alarcón and Serna never heard of the existence and contents of book 11 or the *Codex Badianus,* since both manuscripts admittedly had a limited circulation in Mexico and Spain. However, they could not have been totally unaware of the publication in Mexico in 1615 of Francisco Hernández's *Cuatro libros de la naturaleza y virtudes de las plantas y animales que están recibidos en uso de medicina en la Nueva España.*[9] Hernández's book about medicinal plants and animals, and their properties, was composed in consultation with indigenous healers. Even though Ruiz de Alarcón and Serna sometimes recorded limited information about the plants and physical activities involved in the cures they documented, they usually dismissed them as completely inefficacious in order to underscore that demoniacal forces must have illicitly intervened whenever any positive result was achieved.

Finally, regarding natives' "idolatrous" consultations with diviners, they were not all that different from non-indigenous people consulting local healers and astrologers in sixteenth- and seventeenth-century Europe. According to Keith Thomas, English people from all backgrounds consulted folk practitioners "of very different degrees of learning and honesty" (Thomas 1971, 300). The reasons for seeking their services were very much the same as those Serna mentions for the Nahuas: to find lost objects or goods, to discover the origin of or cure for illnesses when doctors could not determine them, and for fortune-telling (Serna 1892, 304; Thomas 1971, 305–22). All three functions were linked to divination and the pursuit of information "no other agency would provide" (Thomas 1971, 318). One cannot help but observe, then, how similar in relational structures these services, practices, and beliefs were to the ones provided by Nahua sorcerers or ritual specialists in seventeenth-century New Spain, as revealed by Ruiz de Alarcón's and Serna's linkage of medicine, sorcery, and divination and by their collection of nahualtocaitl. Such an observation is supported by French sociologist Jean Delumeau's renowned hypothesis that "on the eve of the Reformation, the average westerner was but superficially Christianized" and "the average European of the early seventeenth century was largely imbued with an animist mentality" (Delumeau 1977, 161, 163).

Clearly then, Ruiz de Alarcón and Serna's attribution of belief in a link between medicine, healing, and divination to Indian simple-mindedness, ignorance, and tendency to deception blatantly overlooked the long history and strong presence of these beliefs in early modern Europe.[10] Because this omission produced a deeply biased representation of indigenous cultural difference, it exemplifies the arbitrary, exclusionary, and conceptually inadequate colonialist mindset deployed in these texts. By focusing on otherness, failing to acknowledge related widespread practices among non-indigenous social groups, and dismissing native populations' ability to acquire Christian competence, Ruiz de Alarcón and Serna produced tendentious, disparaging representations of indigenous difference that in turn promoted discursive strategies that justified ongoing domination.

Reiterating this point, Carmelo Sáenz de Santa María observes that an anonymous Spaniard scribbled a note in the margin of a manuscript copy of Serna's *Manual*, expressing surprise at the Mexican cleric's consternation over the form-changing sorcerer called *nahual* or *nahualli* (who will be examined in chapter 2). According to Sáenz, the Spaniard wrote that if Serna lived in Spain, he would still see casters of spells and *loberos* (werewolves) after 1768 years of Spaniards being Christians, along "with other superstitions and heathenisms that I saw in that Kingdom [of Spain] after such a continuous and legitimate teaching in their language and by their parents and grandparents, etc. . . . and [yet] it has not been enough" (quoted in Sáenz de Santa María 1969, 551–52; translation is mine).

—— 2 ——

Dismantling Hernando Ruiz de Alarcón's and Jacinto de la Serna's strategic, discriminatory account of the indigenous knowledge deployed in the nahualtocaitl does not exhaust the interest of these texts for scholars using postcolonial interdisciplinary approaches. The epistemic jockeying between Christian and Mesoamerican worldviews, especially in the *Treatise* is another important topic. Here it is pertinent that Ruiz de Alarcón was appointed ecclesiastical judge in 1617 (Coe and Whittaker 1982, 15). The creole priest had been denounced in 1613 to the Inquisition in Mexico City for having conducted unauthorized *autos de fe* (public penances) in his parish of Atenango del Río against Indians who had engaged in idolatrous practices.[11] Following the investigation, however, he was not censured for overstepping his pastoral authority (Greenleaf 1965, 146–47; Tavárez 2011, 74–76). On the contrary, Ruiz de Alarcón's fluency in Nahuatl most likely impressed Archbishop Juan Pérez de la Serna (1613–1627; no relation to Jacinto de la Serna). The archbishop allowed the zealous priest to keep investigating pagan practices and even granted him a special commission to order legal proceedings against idolaters in his parish. Subsequently, it is clear from the *Treatise* that Ruiz de Alarcón had the power to order the arrest of and to interrogate indigenous subjects who were suspected of being backsliders.[12]

No declaration of the nahualtocaitl is known to have been extracted under torture.[13] Nonetheless, it is not unreasonable to posit that the declarants gave their testimony anticipating or already facing a hostile, repressive response from their less-than-sympathetic listener. That is, Ruiz de Alarcón's informants did not declare the words of the nahualli (or fragments thereof) in a sociocultural discursive vacuum. Although no record of a trial conducted or mandated by Ruiz de Alarcón has yet been found in the archives (Tavárez 2011, 76), declarants must have been aware that their testimonies were being documented and that they could be prosecuted as a result. In his prologue to the *Treatise*, Ruiz de Alarcón himself comments that his best informants were crafty "offenders" unwilling to reveal all their knowledge (Ruiz de Alarcón 1984, 40).[14] Thus, the priest's interlocutory location as suspicious ecclesiastical judge most likely elicited very alert dialogical utterances of the ritual genre of the nahualtocaitl in the best sense of a Bahktinian tradition *avant la lettre*.[15]

Taking these factors into account, we can plausibly reconstruct a scenario of border epistemology in defendants' quasi-legal, unwilling utterances of the nahualtocaitl to Ruiz de Alarcón. This figure of liminal epistemology, proposed by Walter Mignolo, is useful for thinking theoretically about how Mesoamerican (Late Postclassic) practices, knowledge, and cosmologies shifted with the arrival of the alien colonial forces and imaginaries of the Spaniards. Walter Mignolo links border epistemology with the theoretical concepts of double consciousness and subaltern reason. He argues that the diminished "subaltern epistemic position" that the Spaniards forced the Amerindians to occupy generated an "'impurity' that established the foundation for border epistemology in the modern/colonial world system, [and] gave an epistemological potential to the Amerindians that the Spaniards could not reach and had to repress" (Mignolo 2002, 470–71). For Mignolo, the decentering, redefinition, and reterritorialization forced upon indigenous beliefs via the imposed contact with Christianity did not necessarily cause a debilitating epistemological loss and fracture. It introduced "impurity" but also a double consciousness and border epistemology that enabled indigenous subjects to move into and out of different worlds. Indeed, the subaltern position of colonial Amerindians generated an epistemological suppleness for carving out strategic spaces of coexistence in what José Rabasa (1998) has called "plural world dwelling." In contrast, Christianity, as a colonialist, asymmetrical discourse of revealed truth, could not allow any practice of dwelling in worlds other than its own.

I propose then that Ruiz de Alarcón's native informants may have deployed border epistemology and double consciousness when they were forced to recite the nahualtocaitl. Even though they had limited access to subject positions of authority, the confessants could still produce images of themselves that they believed would best accommodate the colonizer's hegemonic discourse. In other words, while they could not have the same agency as Ruiz de Alarcón, the indigenous confessants still had discursive wiggling room. For one thing, although several legal mechanisms enabled Ruiz de Alarcón, as commissioned judge, to extract what approximated an ecclesiastical confessional discourse, these mechanisms could not force people to say all they knew about or did relative to precontact practices.[16]

I now turn to another aspect of the withholding of information that is closely related to the form of agency that emerges from a border epistemology or double consciousness. The well-respected editors and translators of the *Treatise*, J. Richard Andrews and Ross Hassig (1984, 8), argue that this text should not be considered a comprehensive ethnographic study of native religion and medicine in seventeenth-century Central Mexico. Ruiz de Alarcón's explicit, openly adversarial position vis-à-vis his indigenous parishioners led him to be selective in the nahualtocaitl he included in the text. Andrews and Hassig propose that his selection was biased, deliberately distorted, "carefully sifted to present what Ruiz de Alarcón felt to be the most egregious abuses" (1984, 8). Undoubtedly, Ruiz de Alarcón despised his flock and the *Treatise* does not record the full repertoire of nahualtocaitl that were in use in Atenango del Río and surrounding pueblos. Most likely, he chose the conjurations he felt could best prove that "idolatry" was still rampant among the indigenous people.

Yet, perhaps Ruiz de Alarcón was not the only agent who selected which nahualtocaitl ended up in the *Treatise*. Hardly any of the nahualtocaitl he recorded can be considered socially criminal, violent, or malefic. Almost all of them invoked the agency of Mesoamerican super or non-ordinary, nonhuman entities to intervene in a wide array of daily subsistence and medical activities, in order to attain the desired, anticipated outcomes inscribed in the spells.[17] Such desired outcomes usually involved overcoming obstacles in order to achieve health, fertility, and well-being in this life (W. Taylor 1996, 66). When deities were called upon to help destroy or defeat an opponent, it was to protect the invoker from attackers, not to take advantage of another or to cause harm through acts of hate and revenge. As Andrews and Hassig (1984, 26) eloquently (although somewhat dualistically) write, "the underlying situation in most of the incantations in the corpus involves the interplay of a benevolent agent against a malevolent one, seeking to superimpose benefit over harm."

If this is true, why would Ruiz de Alarcón have chosen the nahualtocaitl that struggled against harm and evil as the "most egregious abuse" he could find in this ritual linguistic practice? If the priest believed the nahualtocaitl he had recorded were the "most injurious to the paganism he sought to eradicate" (Andrews and Hassig 1984, 8), what topics did he avoid as not sufficiently detrimental to the native? Andrews and Hassig (1984, 26) suggest there may have been other nahualtocaitl "for . . . making a confession or expressing praise or thanksgiving," but that Ruiz de Alarcón was "primarily interested in those incantational circumstances in which chance and uncertainty played a predominant role." Consequently, he did not record nahualtocaitl that did not make petitions or command courses of action. This claim implies that for Ruiz de Alarcón the nahualtocaitl that were instrumental were far more alarming than those that gave thanks or praised Mesoamerican deities. Yet the practice of praying, confessing, celebrating, or giving thanks to Mesoamerican nonhuman super entities would have been at least as transgressive of the First Commandment as soliciting their intervention for a pragmatic end. For if the practical aims of the nahualtocaitl involved reverent invocations to forbidden spiritual entities, non-instrumental prayers could entail adoration of these entities. The absence of nahualtocaitl praising and giving thanks to Mesoamerican deities does not necessarily indicate Ruiz de Alarcón was disinterested in finding them, as Andrews and Hassig suppose. More likely, expressions of worship were not the intent of the nahualtocaitl, and this is why no such varieties were recorded. For Alarcón, praying to or thanking a Mesoamerican god would have been at least as serious an offense as soliciting their intervention, and he would have been interested in recording both types of examples.[18]

Andrews and Hassig are however correct in pointing out that the conjuros which do appear in the text were derogatory to the confessants insofar as the spells fit the category of popular, superstitious magical practices condemned by Christian theologians in Europe since the medieval era and particularly in early modern times. Ruiz de Alarcón's greater focus on the language of the conjurations compared to the supporting material practices foregrounded the superstitious nature of the former according to early modern demonological theory in Europe (see chapter 1). In brief, demonological theory, closely aligned with early modern European natural philosophy, posited that words were insufficient to produce concrete, physical effects in the world. Following this basic tenet of demonology, Ruiz de Alarcón and Serna both held that if nahualtocaitl sometimes achieved actual, marvelous results through invoking the Mesoamerican deities of the land, this outcome would have involved at least an implicit pact with the universal, Christian devil who ruled over all of them.

Consider, then, that Ruiz de Alarcón, like preachers, pastors, and theologians all over Europe, railed against beneficial magical incantations and transactions because they required the concrete, superhuman intervention of demons in order to achieve their desired protective or curative ends. As Pedro Ciruelo wrote in his renowned *Reprobación de las supersticiones y hechicerías* (Reprobation of Superstitions and Sorceries): "Any man or woman who seeks a cure through spells tacitly accepts a return to health with the aid of the devil and thus makes a pact of friendship with the enemy of God and men" (Ciruelo 1978, 83–84; translation is mine).[19] However, when affliction, illness, and misfortune descended upon the people, Ciruelo's stern admonitions often fell on deaf ears among the non-indigenous Christian populations of the Old and New Worlds—men and women; peninsular, creole, and mestizo; and all the castas, peasants, emerging elites, and established nobility. It should come as no surprise then that in the disastrous circumstances of a demographic catastrophe brought on by forced globalization, Ruiz de Alarcón's indigenous parishioners held on to the nahualtocaitl passed down from their ancestors, which seemingly had procured health, welfare, and prosperity for the people in good and bad times.

Albeit this unyielding attachment to nahualtocaitl for seeking benevolent ends could have been worrisome to Ruiz de Alarcón, surely other things would have been more disquieting. There is evidence that harmful ritual specialists existed in both pre-Hispanic and colonial Mexico. In book 4 of the *Florentine Codex*, Sahagún's informants talk about those born under Ce Ecatl, which was the day-sign for sorcerers and wizards: "one who had spells to cast. . . . He breathed (evil) on people, or cast the evil eye on them, or said spells over them, brought harm on them, or invoked the god [to do evil] to one" (Sahagún 1950–82, 4:101). The most common term for an evil sorcerer was *tlacatecolotl*, or "human owl" (López Austin 1966, 98; Nicholson 1971, 441). Other specialized categories of sorcerers were *tetlacatecolohuiyani*, who caused harm by bleeding on their victims (Nicholson 1971, 442); *tetlepanquetzqui*, "preparer of fire" for victims; *teyollocuani*, or "heart-eaters" (López Austin 1967a, 91–92); and *temacpalitotique*, who dismembered and stole the left arm of *mocihuaquetzque*, or women who had died in their first childbirth (López Austin 1966, 100–103). Ruiz de Alarcón himself acknowledges the existence of *texoxqui*, "one who has bewitched someone"; teyollocuani, "one who has eaten someone at the heart" or who sucks blood; and *tetlachihuiani*, "a malevolent sorcerer who bewitches people" (Andrews and Hassig 1984, 247). However, he complains that he had never been able to make any of these kinds of sorcerers confess anything about their doings, even if there was evidence against them (47).[20]

Taking all the above into account, I propose that when forced to declare nahualtocaitl, the indigenous confessants complied, but did so from the site of their border epistemology as colonial bicultural subjects. I suggest that from this decentered, diatopic position they only declared those incantations they considered, interpreted, or imagined would be less unacceptable, less incriminating, or less incompatible with the hegemonic, colonialist early modern discourse of Christianity brandished by the *juez comisionado*. Namely, they mostly confessed or declared the nahualtocaitl they attributed to benevolent *nanahualtin* (sorcerers).[21] Ruiz de Alarcón did not record any nahualtocaitl where sorcerers impersonated Mesoamerican deities in order to obtain riches, or asked for powers to destroy or exploit people. Nor did he reference any that invoked the traditional gods to ridicule Christianity or aid in its demise. On several occasions when indigenous suspects discovered their confession was too incriminating, they denied what they had said.[22] This suggests that the confessants were aware of how their practice of the nahualtocaitl was being redefined and relocated by the hegemonic culture of Christianity embodied by the creole priest and his power to make them speak.

Admittedly, it is very difficult to unravel the extent of a politics of savvy self-censorship in utterances or confessions of nahualtocaitl. Even so, the images of the indigenous users of the nahualtocaitl that emerge in the *Treatise* do not represent dominated, powerless, panicked, or depressed indigenous peoples. Neither do these images depict confrontational, defiant, resisting subjects who refused to interact with the often frightening, globalizing power of Christianity. Although Ruiz de Alarcón and Jacinto de la Serna sought to portray their Indian flocks in the worst possible light as users of the nahualtocaitl, other representations of their indigenous charges come to the fore. They can be seen as lucid agents at work, managing at least two worlds with competence, aptitude, and sophistication. They can be viewed as diligent subjects carving out and negotiating spaces where they could deploy their decentered local knowledge as not being contrary to the tenets of hegemonic Christianity.[23] They can be understood as firm believers in the efficacy of their traditional knowledge, holding it up to the cura comisionado as having proven benefit for the people.

Of course, Ruiz de Alarcón's contemptuous exegeses and commentaries on the incantations make it clear that his indigenous confessants did not succeed in obtaining a sympathetic response from him, even though they only confessed nahualtocaitl that invoked Mesoamerican gods and priests to provide sustenance, health, and protection. However, Archbishop of Mexico Francisco de Manso y Zúñiga was not nearly as distressed by Ruiz de Alarcón's supposedly incontrovertible evidence of idolatrous abjection. Even though Alarcón repeatedly boasts in his *Treatise* that he had many of his informants arrested and incarcerated after they confessed to using the proscribed nahualtocaitl, no corresponding trial records have been found to date. Nor was Ruiz de Alarcón able to advance his less-than-stellar ecclesiastical career by investigating and recording idolatrous activity in the Chilapa province and adjacent jurisdictions.[24] Moreover, the *Treatise*, finished in 1629, remained unpublished until the late nineteenth century. In order to explain the episcopal indifference to this text, Coe and Whittaker point out that Juan Pérez de la Serna, who had commissioned the work, was succeeded by Manso y Zúñiga in 1629.[25] The newly arrived archbishop—to whom Alarcón actually dedicated the *Treatise*—would have had little time to peruse it because in that very year a terrible flood struck Mexico City, followed by an epidemic among the indigenous population there. Understandably, these events must have consumed all of Manso y Zúñiga's energy and attention (Coe and Whittaker 1982, 19). After that calamitous year, however, the archbishop's time in office seems to have been relatively uneventful (Sosa 1877, 71; Israel 1975, 186–87), until he got in trouble with Viceroy Marquis Cerralvo in 1635 and requested to be removed from office. It seems he would have had four or five full years to browse through the *Treatise*.[26]

Furthermore, Jacinto de la Serna's much more scholarly (albeit derivative) *Manual for Ministers* also remained unpublished during the colonial era, even though he was undoubtedly a figure of notable prestige. He was three times rector of the University of Mexico, three times curate of the Cathedral of Mexico, and three times visitador general to the archbishops of Mexico, in addition to serving as parish priest of the Sagrario Metropolitano (Sáenz de Santa María 1969, 533–34; Coe and Whittaker 1982, 53).[27] Ruiz de Alarcón's and Serna's texts were neither mentioned in extant colonial works nor influential in later extirpation campaigns in the Archdiocese of Mexico (Gruzinski 1993, 148–49; Tavárez 2011, 92–93). Both works were eventually published in 1892 by the Mexican scholar and *nahuatlato* (scholar of Nahuatl) Francisco de Paso y Troncoso.[28]

I conclude that if archbishops Manso y Zúñiga (1629–35) or Mateo Sagade y Bugueiro (1656–61) ever read these two treatises, the contents did not lacerate their Christian consciences sufficiently to motivate them to launch expensive, time-consuming extirpation campaigns to free the Archdiocese of Mexico from the reported idolatrous practices.[29] The archbishops would have surely agreed with Ruiz de Alarcón and Serna that the recorded nahualtocaitl explicitly addressed and engaged Mesoamerican superhuman entities forbidden to Christians by the Church. However, they may have had sufficient reasons not to plunge into whatever effort was necessary "to erase them, and even to scrape them from the memory of men" as Ruiz de Alarcón urged (1984, 39). As was said, the nahualtocaitl did not seek marvelous interventions, inordinate riches, or malevolent superhuman effects. They did not entail adoration of the invoked entities, nor were they heretical in the sense of a "transgression against the articles of the Faith or the sacraments of the Church" (Mentzer 1984, 38). In addition, not all the incantations were technically superstitious, because many were pronounced along with concrete, rational physical actions necessary to accomplish the desired ends.[30] Both archbishops may have considered that the spells were invoked for the accomplishment of ordinary, beneficial activities, and they were used in the private sphere not in open, public spaces. Thus, Manso y Zúñiga and Sagade Bugueiro's silence vis-à-vis the *Treatise* and the *Manual* may signify that they figured the heathen nahualtocaitl would eventually be rooted out by the priests' continuous, merciful preaching of the word and vigilant, patient correction of their "new plants of the Church"—a frequently repeated phrase in ecclesiastical circles (Poole 1987, 153). In fact, the only (and somewhat disconcertingly tame) remedies Jacinto de la Serna himself proposes in the last chapters of his *Manual* involved more of the same, business-as-usual, pastoral care and supervision (Serna 1892: 457–75). Serna even recommended that the parish priests themselves—not commissioned judges as decreed by the Third Mexican Provincial Council (Llaguno 1963, 272)—should be in charge of investigating and punishing transgressions having to do with idolatry (Serna 1892: 466–67). This would result in more efficient, compassionate, and cunning, and less scandalous and expensive, remedial action appropriate to the kind of "offenses" he had been denouncing, which "require a lot of time to investigate, and to be discovered" (Serna 1892: 470).[31] Finally, the archbishops' silence could also very well mean that the works were simply considered unimportant in the busy courts of the archbishopric, or at least not threatening enough to justify investing time in reading them.

All these possibilities are compatible with the point Richard Greenleaf made some decades ago about the tolerance of the Church and viceregal government toward indigenous cultural practices "in spite of protests from individual clergy" (Greenleaf 1978, 316). More recent arguments also underscore the lack of uniformity among bishops in disciplining indigenous peoples for idolatrous practices

(Bernand and Gruzinski 1992, 152; Zaballa Beascoechea 2005, 59–61; Tavárez 2011, 277; Lara Cisneros 2015, 160–61). Specifically, bishops and archbishops acted against superstition and idolatry in their sees according to their judgment and discretion.

In sum, there are theoretical, textual, and historical reasons to posit that the nahualtocaitl recorded in the *Treatise* were not the only ones circulating in the areas where Ruiz de Alarcón did his investigations. Andrews and Hassig believe Ruiz de Alarcón himself conveniently left some out of the text because they were not sufficiently disparaging to the image of their indigenous users. Even if this were the case, when one considers the near-absence of maleficent nahualtocaitl in the *Treatise* and the priest's own acknowledgment that evil sorcerers refused to confess their ways, it is likely that indigenous confessants may have practiced diatopic, selective, self-censoring, self-representing agency in providing or withholding information. One felicitous consequence of such indigenous agency may have been that Ruiz de Alarcón's condemnatory *Treatise* (like Serna's subsequent *Manual*) did not trigger much extirpative action. Indeed, the silence of the archbishops toward the denunciations of Ruiz de Alarcón and Serna may be interpreted as at least a partial victory of cultural negotiation for the indigenous informants in the mish-mash of colonial modernity in Mexico.[32] For even if they were strategically confessed, the nahualtocaitl in the *Treatise* clearly did invoke, enact, and preserve a robust Late Postclassic Mesoamerican cohort of superhuman entities.

— 3 —

The struggles of powerful Spanish ecclesiastics to control, suppress, or negotiate coexistence with Mesoamerican cosmologies, along with the dialogical agency of bicultural, colonial indigenous subjects who resisted or circumvented colonialist intervention, are compelling tracks for postcolonial interdisciplinary inquiries. However, such inquiries do not exhaust the significance of Ruiz de Alarcón's *Treatise*. For despite the mediations and manipulations likely to have been involved in its production, the *Treatise* is a major primary source recording a relatively organized, indigenous worldview extant in nearly thirty Nahuatl-speaking communities in the regions of Coixcatlalpan and Tlalhuicatlalpan one hundred years after the Conquest (López Austin 1967b, 1–4; Coe and Whittaker 1982, 23–29; Andrews and Hassig 1984, 25; Tavárez 2011, 76).

The prominent Mexican anthropologist and nahuatlato Alfredo López Austin (1967b, 2), has argued that nahualtocaitl were "a firm tradition" in the extended geographical area where Ruiz de Alarcón conducted his investigations. He points out that the style, language, terminology, calendrical names, and even rules of construction of the nahualtocaitl are consistent throughout the *Treatise,* even though the incantations were collected from numerous individuals (López Austin, 1967b, 2–5). Andrews and Hassig meanwhile underscore the regularities of vocabulary, the standardized or marked ways of organizing the verbal structures of the conjurations, and "a repetition of the basic symbolic situations and rhetorical tactics" (1984, 27). Coe and Whittaker emphasize the structural principle of parallel semantic couplets and triplets, which they consider integral to the thought deployed in the nahualtocaitl (1982, 40–41).[33] None of these scholars doubts that the nahualtocaitl were "used in a context of action" (Andrews and Hassig 1984, 28). These conjurations were intended to accomplish numerous and varied activities, most of them traditional (Gruzinski 1993, 155). They encode and compress cultural information in highly distinctive linguistic and tropological patterns, and express rhetoric and epistemic certainty of their efficacy. All these features point to an established pre-Hispanic oral genre, not one originating during a century of extreme duress under colonization. Granted, the *Treatise* does not provide us with indigenous oral knowledge freely expressed and impermeable to contact with Christianity. But the decentered, bicultural, dialogic conjurations nonetheless bear the indelible imprint of a sophisticated precontact Mesoamerican epistemology with cultural historical resonance prior to and outside the text.

Bearing these considerations in mind, I engage in discursive, rhetorical, and cultural close readings of the nahualtocaitl to probe the knowledge that they contain. I examine the different aspects of how they are constructed and posited in order to accomplish what they say they intend. I hope to show that, independent of what the actual users of the conjuros may have known, the structures and figures of the nahualtocaitl reveal an impressively nuanced, operative self-awareness. These oral texts constantly focus on the moment of their enunciation, on their performativity or enacting powers, and on their open intention to produce concrete effects in the world. Recall that nahualtocaitl (names sorcerers use) refer to linguistic usages that embody or reproduce culturally marked processes of transformation, condensation, or substitution. Ruiz de Alarcón (1984, 40) constantly describes this language as a string of very difficult metaphors. My readings will examine these complex, tropological processes in the nahualtocaitl. Via substitutions and condensations that can be approximated as metonymies, synecdoches, epithets, metaphors, synonymies, and appositions, the nahualtocaitl produce the effect of casting a tight web of connectivities that bind together the entities of the world. My readings will also look at many of the strategies by which the nahualtocaitl (attempt to) enact or perform their efficacy. For example, a notable strategy is that superhuman godly characters are presented as the actual speakers in approximately twenty conjurations. In others, the speaker is identified not as a god but as a powerful nahualli-lord, priest, or tlamacazqui. Another important device is addressing superhuman entities by their names of origin in order to oblige their attention.[34] In addition, my readings will explore the instrumental role of primordial or deep mythic time in the nahualtocaitl. In many conjuros the powers of the protagonist gods are drawn to human time and space through references to their mantic roles in creation narratives according to their calendrical names and particular domains.[35]

Another related, major element in the nahualtocaitl is the anthropomorphization or socialization of the environment, a shared feature across different indigenous peoples, nations, and eras in the Americas, and even around the world. Philosopher and ethnographer John Callicott has claimed that for American Indians all entities in the environment have "a consciousness, reason, and volition, no less intense and complete than a human being's. The Earth itself, the sky, the winds, rocks, streams, trees, insects, birds, and all other animals therefore had personalities and were thus as fully persons as other human beings" (Callicott 1982, 305). Contemporary researchers and anthropologists have stated that the modern Cree Indians of Chisasibi, Canada, conceive of the environment as a living community of beings both natural and supernatural (Berkes 2012, 106). The people must know these beings in order to interact with the environment successfully. María Teresa Rodríguez López and Pablo Valderrama Rouy report that in contemporary Nahua communities on the Gulf Coast (mostly in the states of Veracruz and Puebla), all entities in the environment "are animated, including mountains, valleys, lakes, rivers, caves, woods, and narrow canyons" (2005, 181). Alessandro Lupo (2001) reports the same is true for contemporary Nahua communities in the Sierra de Puebla. Many late modern and postmodern anthropologists have also shown that people who interact closely with their local ecosystems in order to gain their subsistence relate to entities in the environment as communicative subjects rather than mere continua of living matter to be exploited, managed, and put to the service of humans (Hornborg 2006, 22). These shared elements of communicability, consciousness, and volition are constitutive of relational epistemologies of being-in-the world, in touch with and embedded in webs of sociality with nonhuman entities. Such modes of relationship situate humans within larger living communities that demand ethical or at least reciprocal engagement with the surrounding world.[36] And, indeed, anthropologists doing work among contemporary indigenous groups in Guerrero have observed kinship and even symbolic sexual relationships that are established with the environment create symbolic matrimonial alliances between hunters and deer, as well as between farmers and their crops (Dehouve 2008).

In the nahualtocaitl, however, not only plants and animals, but also what many westerners would conceive of as inanimate, human-made objects, were addressed in the language of the nanahualtin as communities of entities that could be persuaded to act and respond in specific ways. Tools, mats, kilns, and even sandals were engaged with as intelligent, well-disposed, dignified sentient beings. In light of the pragmatic ends of the nahualtocaitl, respectful communication with all entities in the environment seems to have been part of a strategy for maximizing their functionality.[37] Of course, reverence is always very important, not only in the oral genre of the nahualtocaitl, but in the Nahuatl language as a whole. It appears that the expression of "respect and reverence of the person, agent or patient, and of the person with whom one speaks, or of whom one speaks" (Carochi [1645] 1983, 66; translation is mine) was deemed efficacious in persuading and directing the addressee toward a desired end.[38]

The language of the nahualtocaitl recorded in the *Treatise* treated the heaven(s) and earth as communicative, volitional nonhuman entities saturated with correspondences that men and women of knowledge could mediate, relate to, and utilize for the benefit of the people. As I argue in this book, this view of a living earth was not incompatible, or at least was not viewed by users of the conjuros as incompatible, with the practice of Christianity.

— 4 —

This book contains six chapters. In chapter 1, I examine the Christian construction of the realm of the preternatural that the Spaniards brought with them to the Americas. I review some of the main issues and debates surrounding the wondrous and preternatural in early modern Europe, and how this realm was believed to be where both licit and illicit superhuman and occult agencies operated. I examine some tenets of the demonology expounded by prominent Spanish theoreticians like Pedro Ciruelo and Martín del Río, as well as aspects of the Neoplatonic *magia naturalis* of Marsilio Ficino. I differentiate the realm of the preternatural from that of the supernatural and argue that it was within the former where the godly entities of the Amerindian pantheon were located by the transcontinental, transcultural, transhistorical demonological mindset of Spanish colonizers and ecclesiastics—and by early modern Europe as a whole. In this way, I seek to offer an overview of early modern Christian epistemology as deeply immersed in practices and beliefs in the animated realm of the occult—in some ways not unlike the indigenous cultures it came in contact with. This background enables a more accurate contextualization of why Ruiz de Alarcón and Jacinto de la Serna represented the nahualtocaitl as dangerous, threatening superstitious practices that ought to be uprooted, along with a better assessment of the implications of the inaction by the archbishops to whom the work was dedicated.

Chapter 2 explores the Mesoamerican figure of the nahualli, a sorcerer believed to have the capacity to transform himself or herself into different animals or other entities. The *Treatise* opens by recounting several episodes in which Spanish people "of authority and credibility" had witnessed events involving this form-changing sorcerer. The figure of the nahualli is the inscribed speaker of the oral genre of the nahualtocaitl, the "language or names used by sorcerers" (Coe and Whittaker 1982, 206). I examine this central figure of Mesoamerican epistemology from the early modern Christian point of view of Ruiz de Alarcón and Serna, as well as from the perspective of some of the things believed or known about the nahualli among some indigenous communities in Mexico and Guatemala today.

Each of the next four chapters explores one nahualtocaitl belonging to a different section in Ruiz de Alarcón's *Treatise*. Attentive, close readings of the nahualtocaitl—even in their Spanish and English guises—reveal layers of highly complex references to Postclassic Mesoamerican knowledge and narratives of origin. The nahualtocaitl in chapter 3 is representative of a trade, those in chapters 4 and 5 pertain to sustenance activities involving the environment, and the one in chapter 6 deals with the diagnostic divination of a malady. By choosing a variety of nahualtocaitl I intend to give a sense of how the compact web of knowledge in each is carefully tailored to the specific traditional activity of indigenous life at which the conjuro is directed. In each chapter, I first give specific background on the particular nahualtocaitl. Then I delve into a deep reading of that nahualtocaitl and of many of the connectivities it claims to mobilize.

Not all the nahualtocaitl in the *Treatise* engage the same levels of metaphorical complexity as the four conjuros I analyze. Nevertheless, close readings would show they all evince high levels of internal coherence and coded knowledge. Little is left to chance in the tightly wrought, tropological language of the nahualli. To see how gods, time, space, and entities are actually bound in these names, as well as the effects they are expected to produce, is an important contribution to the understanding of this unique genre.

In the conclusion I review how my close readings of the conjuros show deep webs of communicability deployed for the welfare of the people. From the perspective of the border epistemology of the indigenous declarants, I emphasize how ritual specialists and common users of the nahualtocaitl tried to negotiate an image of this knowledge and practice as not being inimical to Christianity because of their beneficial and time-proven efficacious ends. From the vantage point of the weary archbishops, I read their silence as stoic patience with (what they viewed as) superstitious practices that although admittedly widespread, did not threaten to unseat Christianity. I conclude by suggesting that many environmental ritual practices continued by indigenous groups in Mexico today as part of their cultural legacy and identity can be anticipated in the relational epistemology enacted in the nahualtocaitl Ruiz de Alarcón recorded. For in the names of the nahualli, earth and all its nonhuman inhabitants were addressed with deference and caution, as hypersensitive, intelligent, and volitional beings, in inextricable ligature with humankind. Finally, I propose some further lines of research for this culturally rich genre.

— 5 —

Two valuable edited and extensively annotated translations into English of Ruiz de Alarcón's *Treatise* appeared in 1982 and 1984, respectively. The earlier one was prepared by Michael D. Coe and Gordon Whittaker, and published by the State University of New York in Albany. The authors translated the Nahuatl part into English, and a particular feature of their work—besides a very erudite introduction—is that they present the nahualtocaitl in verse form. The second translation, published by the University of Oklahoma Press, was done by John A. Andrews and Ross Hassig. It is undoubtedly the more accomplished of the two, and the best edition or translation of the *Treatise* to date. Besides an excellent introduction, this annotated translation has an impressive scholarly apparatus, nuanced linguistic analyses, and a three-pronged approach. First, Andrews and Hassig translate both the Nahuatl and Spanish parts of Ruiz de Alarcón's *Treatise* into English. Second, they modernize the Nahuatl; and lastly, they offer an English version of the modernized version in Nahuatl. Their extensive notes, appendixes and paraphrases of the nahualtocaitl are immensely helpful for all scholars working with the *Treatise*. A final useful source is publications by Mexican nahuatlato Alfredo López Austin (1967b, 1970a, 1970b). He has written several important articles on the *Treatise* and has translated several nahualtocaitl into modern Spanish.

The nahualtocaitl I cite in this book come mainly from the Andrews and Hassig edition. I first quote their modernized Nahuatl version, then refer to their translations of Ruiz de Alarcón's Spanish renderings of the conjuros. Lastly, I cite their translation into English of the modernized Nahuatl version of the incantations. I also often interweave Coe and Whittaker's translations. While I do not fully agree with their presentation of the nahualtocaitl as ethnopoetry, I find the more reverential tone of their translations is often closer to the Nahuatl and Spanish originals than Andrews and Hassig's straightforward, more direct style.

— 6 —

Before closing this introduction, a few words about the violence of cultural translation are in order. As I have made clear by now, as a colonial text Ruiz de Alarcón's bilingual *Treatise* is dialogical, impure, and transformational at many levels. The recorded nahualtocaitl were already dialogical at the moment they were uttered to the creole priest, especially because this usually happened under coercion. The conjurations could not be pronounced then as culturally sealed-off reenactments of a mythical, operative moment when they were originally configured as the embodiment of the language of gods, nahualli lords, or priests (tlamacazque). Ruiz de Alarcón then performed further transformations on this mainly oral, discursive Late Postclassic Mesoamerican genre by transcribing the nahualtocaitl into Latin alphabetic writing and collecting them in a book.[39] The work also decentered the conjuros by offering a fairly competent translation of the Nahuatl into Spanish (even though Ruiz de Alarcón missed crucial cultural references). Finally, the cura himself could never have imagined that the collected nahualtocaitl would be circulating among literate, secular, indigenous, and non-indigenous international audiences ever since the end of the nineteenth century, when the *Treatise* was published for the first time. And in the twentieth century, the *Treatise* has been further morphed into two English translations. Given all these complex levels of linguistic and cultural translations, mediations, and transformations, can contemporary readers claim to recover any legitimate understanding of the nahualtocaitl recorded in the *Treatise*? Is there any way to get something right out of a readerly experience that the pieces were never intended for? Will the reception of the nahualtocaitl in this twenty-first-century monograph produced in the U.S. academy reproduce some of the translational violence done first by the *Treatise* and later to the *Treatise* itself? It is not unlikely. But then again, it can be argued that all hermeneutic acts attempting to understand cultural objects, epistemologies, and ontologies of the past entail distortions, if only because their creators could have never fully foreseen their future audiences and readings. Being the unintended, unimagined, uninvited audiences of cultural productions and knowledges of the past may certainly entail a violence of epistemological impertinence and imposition, albeit surely more marked in some cases than in others. But not to continue attempting to approach the alterity of the past and of other cultures respectfully may risk an equal or even more violent result of eventual indifference, segregation, exclusion, or alienation.[40]

It is a fact that the *Treatise* was the repressive work of Hernando Ruiz de Alarcón, who coerced the confessions of the nahualtocaitl, transcribed them into written Nahuatl, then translated them into Spanish in order to condemn them and ultimately have them extirpated from Central Mexico—and perhaps get himself a promotion in the bargain. But this does not invalidate the work's crucial importance as a record of colonial Mesoamerican indigenous knowledge. Nor can the repressive context of its production completely neutralize the power and audacious beauty of some of Ruiz de Alarcón's translations and even Serna's exegeses. The images of the users of the nahualtocaitl in the *Treatise* circulated and still circulate beyond the authorial control of Hernando Ruiz de Alarcón and Jacinto de la Serna. Far from showing ignorance, inferiority, or malevolence, as the authors intended, these images convey an indigenous dialogical competence able to engage the globalizing, modernizing, colonizing language of Christianity without giving up the knowledge of the ancestors from the land. Reading the *Treatise* in this way offsets at least some of the epistemological violence involved in its production, dissemination, and reception across the centuries. It allows us to share some of the preserved wealth of Mesoamerican Late Postclassic colonial indigenous knowledge and coexistence, recognizing its origin, authority, and belonging. We will never have access to any fullness of meaning. But what can be glimpsed, even if only through a glass darkly, is worth all the effort.

CHAPTER ONE

The Christian Preternatural

During the mid-sixteenth and seventeenth centuries in Europe, popular practices dealing with the preternatural, or the realm between the natural and the supernatural, had many features in common with the so-called idolatry and superstitions of the peoples of Central Mexico and adjacent regions. Turning to wise or cunning men and women to cure diseases, find lost objects, divine the future, and dominate the will of others was a widespread activity not only in Central Mexico but in England, Italy, France, Spain (Thomas 1971, 178, 637; Delumeau 1977; Caro Baroja 1967; Clark 1999; Szőnyi 2004; Zambelli 2007; Cameron 2010) and New England (Godbeer 1992). Both Europeans and Mexican Indians believed the world swarmed with good and evil spiritual beings that interfered in the lives of humans. And indeed, as is well known in early modern European scholarship, Protestants and Catholics mutually accused each other of being deluded by the devil, with Protestants associating Catholicism and the pope with the Antichrist, and Catholics retorting that Protestants were blinded by Satan's venom of heresy (Clark 1999, 526–45). Thus, because early modern Christians firmly believed in both good and evil disembodied beings, spirits, and marvelous effects produced by superhuman agencies,[1] missionaries and clerics proselytizing among the indigenous peoples of New Spain took seriously, albeit to different degrees, the efficacy and ontology of the Mesoamerican pantheon of deities. For the ecclesiastical and missionary personnel in Mexico, Nahua belief in the superhuman forces of their gods was not a fancy of barbaric imagination. It was not only a childish error but also something that was part of both groups' respective constructions of the reality—or realities—of the world. Knowledge and inquiry about Nahua pre-Hispanic practices, rituals, and beliefs were not only recorded in innumerable chronicles and histories with more or less acceptable accuracy, but also interpreted and misinterpreted with the affective power of what was deemed to be ontologically and immediately real.

Because of this epistemological horizon, it is important to approach Latin American colonial texts within the context of the Christian supernatural and preternatural; these complex, highly populated, dangerous, and passionately debated realms constituted what was possible and impossible for early modern Europe. Sixteenth-century Mexica, for instance, claimed that their gods had announced to them that Mexico-Tenochtitlan would cease to exist, and the Spaniards believed them. Ominous signs had appeared a decade before the Caxtilteca (Spaniards) actually arrived to trigger Anahuac's awful, painful labor of globalization: "Ten years before the arrival of the Spaniards an omen first appeared in the sky, like a flame or tongue of fire, like the light of dawn. It appeared to be throwing off [sparks] and seemed to pierce the sky" (Lockhart 1993, 50). The flame, appearing every night for a full year, was taken as a sign of impending destruction.[2] Another omen during those years was the appearance of "thistle-people with two heads but one body." After they were taken to Moctezuma and he had seen them, they disappeared (Lockhart 1993, 56). The Franciscan Gerónimo de Mendieta recounts the same "marvelous prodigies and portents" in his *Historia eclesiástica indiana* (circa 1596) without doubting for a moment their ontological and historical possibility (Mendieta 1993, 178–82).

In this chapter, I review briefly some of the main features of the wondrous and the preternatural in early modern Europe, and how it was believed to be the realm where angelic, superhuman, and occult causal agencies operated. Recognizing how pervasive this realm was in early modern Christianity will help us understand better how it mixed with the Mesoamerican Postclassic worldview with which it was to collide in the sixteenth century and beyond, as well as the affinities, sympathies, and repulsions between the two. It will also help us to understand why Mesoamerican ways of relating to the world—although inevitably altered and decentered by contact with a colonial, alien, universalizing ontology—were able to hold ground, as evinced by Ruiz de Alarcón's *Treatise*.

1

Taking their cue from classical and biblical sources, Christians from the religion's very inception believed that demons inhabited the middle air or sublunar space between the moon and the earth, as well as the underworld of hell.[3] According to St. Augustine in his treatise *On the Divination of Demons*, the perception of demons "readily surpass[es] the perception possessed by earthly bodies, and in speed too, because of the superior mobility of the aerial body." Such superior mobility afforded demons superhuman speed, which permitted them to "foretell and declare many things that they have recognized in advance" (quoted in Flint 1991, 147), as well as to travel very quickly from one place to the other, and thus know what was taking place remotely, almost at the moment it was occurring (not unlike our multimedia satellite and high-speed communication technologies!).

Eleven centuries later the influential Spanish theologian and mathematician Pedro Ciruelo, like other demonologists of his time, expounded similar opinions in his extraordinarily succinct, scholastically inspired *Reprouacion de las supersticiones y nechizerias*.[4] In this influential treatise Ciruelo wrote that, although demons had lost their grace and glory when they were expelled from heaven, they did not lose the knowledge and infused virtues proper to their natures: "They are able to have very clear science of all corporeal things that are less perfect than themselves, who are live spirits. Thus, they have knowledge of all the order of the corporeal world, and of all the course of nature" (Ciruelo 1978, 70; translation is mine). Namely, because of their angelic intellectual perception, they could penetrate the deepest and most occult secrets of all the cosmic, physical order and its most recondite causalities.

Although demons' powers and knowledge overwhelmingly surpassed those of human beings, their potencies were not supernatural; that is, above and beyond nature. Demons were well within the natural order in the sense that they functioned strictly according to their conferred angelic species and were always subject to God's will (Flint 1991, 153; Cervantes 1994, 18; Clark 1999, 152, 161–72; Campagne 2003, 42–48; Levack 2006, 36). The devil could not alter the divinely established order unless God expressly permitted him to do so in order to test men and women, to punish them for their sins, or for an inscrutable design of his. This was a central tenet of Christian demonology that would remain current well into the seventeenth century, if not beyond. Therefore, while the devil sometimes merely fooled his human adepts with illusions of wonders, at other times he actually performed marvels because his knowledge of natural causes and correspondences far exceeded human understanding and agency. The devil could put this knowledge to work in order to produce extraordinary effects, or *mirabilia*, but always within the boundaries of the natural world. He, then, made use of preternatural phenomena, or "unusual occurrences that nonetheless depended on secondary causes alone and required no suspension of God's ordinary providence" (Daston and Park 1998, 121). In his *Disquisitiones magicae* Spanish demonologist Martín del Río defined the realm of the preternatural as a site of "many wonderful operations done by good or wicked angels, either by means of localised movements or by a sudden application of natural agencies. Since natural things are not capable of offering resistance to these powerations because their power is not the equal of that of angels, effects obtained thus are, broadly speaking, natural rather than supernatural" (Del Río 2000, 57).

Some decades earlier, the Dominican Bartolomé de Las Casas, protector of Indians, had conjectured in his monumental *Apologética historia sumaria* (1555–59) about "accidental transmutations" that the devil could produce by intervening in humans' perceptual organs in order to produce illusions. Las Casas claimed that this was what St. Augustine had argued in book 18 of his *City of God* regarding Circe's transformation of Ulysses's companions into pigs: "And this was only by appearance and deceit of the eyes, in such a way that that bestial form was extracted from the imaginative memory, where the treasures of the species or images are, and from which an imaginary vision was caused, and consequently, because of its strong impression, it resulted [became perceptible] in the other potencies and organs" (Las Casas 1967, 1:509; translation is mine).

Demons could also produce wonderful effects by moving heavy things from one place to another since "every bodily creature has the natural aptitude of being . . . moved from place to place by the spiritual creature." Las Casas asserts that demons are "just like good angels in natural gifts, because as Saint Dionysius says in chapter 4 of his book *De divinis nominibus*, by sin [the fallen angels] were not divested of their gifts and properties that God in their creation had apportioned them." The Dominican friar attributes to angels the power to move the heavens: "and not only the Holy Scriptures, but gentile philosophers . . . concede [that the heavens] are moved by the intelligences and spiritual substances that we call angels." Further, Las Casas maintains that good or bad angels can move people through the air "with much celerity and promptness and in the moment they went . . . to one or many diverse parts" (Las Casas 1967, 1: 461; translation is mine). Also, by their superior knowledge of the hidden passive and active virtues of natural entities, demons could apply them quickly, easily, and readily ("ligera y fácil y prestamente"; Las Casas 1967, 1:484), and thus produce marvelous cures and other effects. And, of course, because of their superior knowledge and understanding of the natural world, they could predict contingent future events with much more precision than the most accomplished natural philosopher could ever do.

Although angels and demons could never overstep the abilities of their species, the effects they were able to produce (not surprisingly) seemed extraordinary to the ordinary sensory perception of men and women—and supernatural to uninformed or rash human opinion. In sum, the preternatural realm consisted of marvelous or prodigious events perpetrated by disembodied intelligent beings through their superior capacity to manipulate hidden or occult forces in nature. This is why angelic forces—both good and evil—were woven into early modern natural philosophical inquiries into what was possible and impossible at the limits of the realm of nature (Clark 1999, 151–293; Campagne 2003). For only God could produce miracles or supernatural events that disrupted, reversed, or canceled the order that he had created in the natural world. The preternatural, as marvelous as it seemed and even though it involved the supra-cosmic sphere of angels, could never involve the impossible except by divine permission, in which case it was a miracle.

Because *maleficium* (harmful magic) entailed the agency of demons, it clearly fell within the realm of the preternatural. Maleficium had been condemned as a social crime since the time of the Roman Empire and also of early medieval Christianity. However, a significant, dreadful shift in the conception of maleficium commenced in the thirteenth century as it was more virulently linked with heresy, superstition, and idolatry in a very broad range of sources (Levack 2006, 4–12; Peters 2015, 65–68). In an influential article, John Bossy has argued that one of the causes of this change was the gradual displacement of the Seven Deadly Sins by the scriptural Ten Commandments as the Christian moral system. If witchcraft (or Wiccecraefte—the old English word seems to convey more accurately the meaning of wise craft or knowledge) had been defined during the earlier Middle Ages as "the offence of causing by occult means malicious harm to the body or goods of one's neighbour" (Bossy 1988, 230), or even causing the death of one's enemies, the moral code of the Commandments made these acts high crimes against Christendom.

With the advent of the printing press, the late fifteenth century saw increasing production and dissemination of theoretical tracts on sorcery, witchcraft, and demonological activity, written by secular judges, clerical inquisitors, and demonologists.[5] One of the best known and most important treatises contributing to the early modern conception of witchcraft as a religious crime was the terrifying *Malleus Maleficarum* (Peters 2015, 80–81). The two Dominican inquisitors who wrote it in 1486 or 1487, Heinrich Kramer and James Sprenger, declared, "We must especially observe that this heresy, witchcraft, not only differs from all other heresy in this, that not merely by a tacit compact, but by a compact which is exactly defined and expressed it blasphemes the Creator and endeavours to the utmost to profane Him and to harm His creatures, for all other simple heresies have no open compact with the devil" (Kramer and Sprenger (1971, 20). Witchcraft implied not only the social crime of harming or even killing others by malefice. Now it also entailed idolatry, the most serious offense against the First Commandment "because idolatry takes away the honor and obedience due to God and gives them to his capital enemy; that is, the devil" (Ciruelo 1978, 25; translation is mine). The early modern horror of witchcraft was that it involved much more than invoking the help of demons to commit an act of hate against another human; it was an all-corrupting, depraved commerce with the devil that abjured God and his creation. It contributed to a manifestation in the world of all the powers of evil and perversion, creating underground societies with their own rules and rituals. It engaged passionately, bodily, and intellectually, with the powers of the marvelous diabolic. As a consequence, the preternatural role of the devil gained "a grandeur and formidable character" (Bossy 1988, 230), more debased and abject than ever before. This conception resulted in the horrific witch-hunt phenomenon of the early modern period in which Brian Levack (2006, 23) estimates that as many as 45,000 people may have been executed.[6]

Crimes against the First Commandment were not limited to witches accused of worshipping the devil or openly abjuring Christianity. People who resorted to sorcerers for healing or divination, to find lost objects or missing persons, to improve performance, to cure animals, to procure love or its contrary, or even to counter witchcraft were also guilty of commerce with the devil and its minions. For magical, superstitious acts conferred virtues or properties on things, persons, times, and spaces that had no basis in reality (Clark 2015, 229). So, for instance, Ciruelo would argue that if an *ensalmador,* or folk healer, attempted to cure a wound by placing a piece of paper or cloth over it and reciting words, this was a vain observance. For paper, cloth, and words had no natural powers to cure wounds, and God "detests all those who use vanities because they are things empty of natural virtue" (Ciruelo 1978, 81). If the wound were indeed healed by this practice, then superior demonic forces must have intervened. As Martín del Río explained, "Deeds which supersede natural capacity are a product of demoniacal magic. This is the case when it can be positively concluded that the applied object lacks sufficient force to produce the effect without reasonable motive to attribute the effect to God or to the good angels" (Del Río 1991, 204; translation is mine). Thus, when natural causation was insufficient for the witting or unwitting production of an effect, and there was not sufficient reason to attribute the effect to God, there must have been an illicit incursion into the realm of the preternatural, where diabolic, intelligent forces hovered. Because dealing with the enemies of God was forbidden, a vain or superstitious activity would also be considered idolatrous, even if the perpetrators were unaware of it or its intended ends were benevolent.[7] Of course, the boundaries between the natural, preternatural, and superstitious realms are permeable, since they depend on the horizons of what is known and unknown in specific historical and cultural contexts, in this case, early modernity.

All the worries about the wondrous horrors of witchcraft, superstition, and implicit and explicit pacts notwithstanding, the devil and his legion were not the only actors in the realm of the marvelous and preternatural. This realm also entailed the agency of hidden properties—occult because they were irreducible to the powers and qualities of the four elements. Unrecognizable by the senses, occult powers were almost impossible for the human mind to understand or measure with certainty. Among the posited instances of such forces were the imperceptible effects of planet and star alignments on the human body, and on character and inclinations. They also included "non-elementary actions [such as] . . . the dormative effect of opium, the convulsions caused by poisons" (Millen 1985, 207), and the paradigmatic case at the time of the marvelous magnetic powers of lodestone, which could not be accounted for by its specific mix of the four basic elements. Another important classical and medieval source of occult powers was the "body's immaterial substantial form" (186). This elusive substance, immune to accidents and independent from any manifest qualities of the four elements, is what gave being or form to specific entities. Galen (129 to circa 200–216 C.E.) "who was primarily responsible for the lasting effect of the idea of occult qualities in medicine and philosophy" had proposed that the whole form of an object contained "indescribable properties" that could not be accounted for by an Aristotelian theory of matter (Copenhaver 1990, 272). And indeed, fast-forwarding ten centuries, Thomas Aquinas (1225–74 C.E.) would propose that the powers of celestial bodies played an important part in the eduction of these forms and in their impression on earthly bodies (Copenhaver 1984, 536).

A major player in the resurgence of early modern interest in occult powers as part of natural philosophy—rather than only as forces that were manipulated by diabolic agents—was the humanistic, learned recovery of the philosophical texts of Plato, Neoplatonism, and even Hermeticism, and of their theories on hypostases, emanations, and chains of beings. These texts fostered a benign conception of magic insofar as it was effectuated through knowledge of—or at least acquaintance with—the way the cosmos and nature operated as ordered by the power, truth, and beauty of the One God. Renaissance Neoplatonism emerged in full force during the fifteenth century in the Florentine Academy presided over by Marsilio Ficino (1433–99 C.E.). In surely the most influential humanistic feat of the fifteenth century, Ficino translated from Greek into Latin the complete works of Plato (circa 427–347 B.C.E.), which he published in 1484, along with the *Corpus Hermeticum*, a heterogeneous collection of Greek gnostic treatises.[8] Ficino was also important for translating, paraphrasing, or commenting on the work of the great School of Plato: Plotinus (204/5–70 C.E.), Porphyry (234?–305? C.E.), Iamblichus (250?–330? C.E.), and Proclus (412–85 C.E.). Along with some important medieval and Arabic sources, these Neoplatonists provided Ficino with philosophical grounds for a theory of natural magic (Copenhaver 1984, 1986; Kaske and Clark 2002; Szőnyi 2004).

Briefly, this erudite early modern theory of magic was based on the three Plotinian hypostases: the One, the Mind, and the Soul. From the Soul's circular movement, the form-idea of the cosmos came forth, undergirded by the indeterminateness and shapelessness of matter (Mackenna 1916, 154–56; 185–87; Gregory 1999, 24–64). The cosmos had a (Ptolemaic) geocentric orientation, with the stars—quasi-eternal bodies containing individual angelic or soul intelligences (or "reasons")—revolving in the outermost sphere of the cosmos, closest to their non-material soul origin. The World Soul arranged the stars into figures, and these figures cascaded down the heavenly spheres, imprinting their virtues and powers on all related planetary and earthly bodies. Copenhaver (1986, 351) calls book 3 of Ficino's *De triplici vita* (Three Books on Life) "the most important Renaissance treatise on magic." In this influential work Ficino (2002, 245) writes, "There is nothing to be found in this whole living world so deformed that Soul does not attend it, that a gift of the Soul is not in it." Moreover "in the stars—in their figures, parts and properties—are contained all the species of things below and their properties" (Ficino 2002, 245). That is, in the stars eternal, in a much higher and original form of time and being, all earthly substantial forms, bodies, and events had always been contained and were preordained.

Now Ficino conceived of the Magus, or practitioner of natural and spiritual magic, essentially as a philosopher "who knows about natural objects and stars . . . [who] seasonably introduces the celestial into the earthly by particular lures" (Ficino 2002, 387). The Magus possessed knowledge of the hidden properties, virtues, correspondences, sympathies, and antipathies pervading nature and the celestial world. He understood how angelic intelligences governed the stellar spheres, which in turn influenced the lower realms of worldly creatures, entities, and events (Ficino 2002, 387; Copenhaver and Schmitt 1992, 288–89; Clark 1999, 217). The Magus had knowledge of numbers and measures, by which means he could capture the "dark fires of the stars" and the marvelous influence of their figures and motions. He could make the right connections in order to put to use nature's most recondite secrets, which was "crucially important in the grounding notion of the dignity of man by the time of the Renaissance" (Szőnyi 2004, 77). In other words, natural magic as part of natural philosophy underscored the possibility of an inquiry into preternatural, occult causalities—such as the powers of similitude—untinged by dealings with malevolent demonic agencies.[9] Far from being satanic and a product of superstition, the Renaissance magician was deemed respectable and wise: "For what does that Magus, the first adorer of Christ, profess? . . . He is a cultivator of the world . . . just as a farmer for the sake of human sustenance tempers his field to the air, so that wise man, that priest, for the sake of human welfare tempers the lower parts of the world to the upper parts" (Ficino 2002, 397–99). Ficino was referring here to the adoration of the three Persian Magi, who had been able to glimpse the divinity of Christ because of their knowledge of the stars and had thus been first to worship him on earth as "a new philosopher-king-magus, the new Zoroaster" (Allen 2002, xix). More than wise, the Magi were also priestly insofar as they could prepare—for the good of humankind—sublunar bodies and entities to make them more receptive to corresponding imperceptible celestial effluvia (Ficino 2002, 387, 389). Through their deep knowledge of the occult workings of nature and the language of the stars, learned Magi obtained the power to act, and also to come closer to God.[10]

Not surprisingly, this audacious view of the Magus's magical knowledge as a pragmatic, applied art and of natural magic as an exalted way to know nature and even grow closer to the Creator raised many eyebrows, especially among ecclesiastics.[11] Because devils also understood and manipulated occult forces within the realm of the preternatural, natural magic and witchcraft were never far apart: they were "ontologically and epistemologically equivalent" (Clark 1999, 233). Thus, natural magic could as easily be attributed to demonic interference as demonic agency could be deemed to be the effect of natural, occult powers of nature. In any case, many ecclesiastics viewed an assiduous inquiry into the realm of magic with various degrees of suspicion (Walker 1975, 51–53; Caro Baroja 1967, 1:36; Kaske and Clark, 55–70). For even in the case of Ficino, the purely natural power of correspondences and sympathetic analogies may not have been the only agencies lurking in his magical treatise. According to D. P. Walker (1975, 50), "De V.V.C. [*De vita coelitus comparanda*, book 3 of *De triplici vita*] is really about planetary demons" because for the Florentine Magus himself, sympathies and chains of beings would not have been sufficient to produce effects all the time (Kaske and Clark 2002, 49).[12] Hence, the agency of demons was necessary for directing, speeding up, or concentrating astral influences based on correspondences. Ranking lower than souls yet higher than humans, demons would mediate between the souls of stars, planets, and humans with which they had affinity in the long chains of beings.[13] Needless to say, Ficino did not advocate worshipping demons nor communicating with evil beings. But he did recommend singing to the planets at particular times to obtain their favor or capture their benefits (Ficino 2002, 359)! In order to distinguish their practice of natural magic from demonolatry, many Renaissance Magi claimed not to be addressing angelic, intellectual beings inhabiting supra-celestial spheres but only to be tapping into natural forces at the sublunar level (Clark 1999, 219–20).[14] As the proper Christian subject he wanted to show he was, Ficino endorsed a non-demonic form of magic "reaching no higher than the human spirit" or the World Soul (Walker 1975, 53). He admitted, however, that bad demons lurking in the realm of the spirits such magic could always intervene in such magic (Copenhaver and Schmitt 1992, 156). His ideas were sufficiently suspect that Ficino later had to write an apology to defend himself from charges of heresy for book 3 of his *De triplici vita*. However, it should be noted that in Spain the book was never included in the Indices of Prohibited Books, and the work and its ideas actually circulated widely (Byrne 2015, 35, 50–66).[15]

Given the proximity between natural and demonic magic, catechisms after the Council of Trent would enforce a very cautious, conservative line against all sorts of magic, instructing the people that it was a transgression of the First Commandment to believe in dreams, divination, and fortune-telling (Clark 1999, 500). Hard-line clerics and pastors insisted that even good (white) magic practiced by local healers and sorcerers was idolatrous. Even the moderate Erasmus himself had proscribed in 1533 "all curious artes and crafters, of divynyng and sothesayeng, of juglying, of doing cures by charmes or witchcraft" because although they did not imply an explicit compact with the devil "yet nevertheless is ther some secrete dealyng with them, and so therfore a secrete denyeng of god" (Clark 1999, 500).[16] I will return to the thorny issue of divination in chapter 6. In Protestant England, the Elizabethan Injunctions of 1559 explicitly prohibited the use of "'charms, sorcery, enchantments, invocations, circles, witchcrafts, soothsaying, or any such like crafts or imaginations invented by the devil'" (quoted in Thomas 1971, 258). And as late as 1692, New England minister Deodat Lawson was still trying to persuade the congregation at Salem Village that those who fought witchcraft with counter-magic were successful only by intervention of demonic spirits (Godbeer 1992, 62–63).

By now it should be clear that discourses related to the realm of the wondrous and preternatural were quite forceful in early modern Europe. Of course, these discourses were deeply enmeshed in national and international European politics (Clark 2015, 244–50; Cameron 2010, 197–239), and there were fierce debates regarding the boundaries of the preternatural and the possibilities of its actual imprint in the natural world (see Campagne 2003). An illustrative case is the 1610 inquisition in Logroño that led to a controversial auto de fe in which six people were burned at the stake and five burned in effigy. Both inquisitor Alonso de Salazar and royal historian Pedro de Valencia expressed skepticism about whether the witches' preternatural criminal sabbat had actually taken place. Their position would be supported by the Supreme Council of the Inquisition in Madrid (la Suprema), which distributed a questionnaire that local inquisitors were henceforth to use to obtain concrete, juridical evidence about witches' departures to the sabbat.[17] But throughout early modernity even the most skeptical individuals rarely denied the existence of pure spirits and the possibility of their preternatural agency (Henry 1991, 215–16; Campagne 2003, 42). Moreover, recent work by historians has shown that beliefs in magic and the preternatural persisted even after 1700 among both literate and illiterate populations in Europe, raising questions about the so-called Age of Reason (see O. Davies 1999; Handley 2007; and O. Davies and Blécourt 2004a, 2004b).

It is appropriate to close this chapter with a reminder that the intensified concern with the marvelous and the spirit world in the early modern period (and beyond) was compounded by one of the most influential historical events of all times. For good or ill, Columbus came across islands at the very limit of what was imagined to be the *finis terrae* in 1492, and a few years later, in 1498 and 1502, the islands led to a continental landmass unknown to Europeans (Columbus [1493, 1498–1500] 1986; Vespucci [1503] 1916). The preternatural—the realm of the wondrous, the angelic, and the demonic—would be the universalizing epistemological site from which European colonists would account for all the deities and superhuman powers ruling the peoples and civilizations of America.

CHAPTER TWO

The Nahualli

Given the early modern European dread of evil spirits, suspicions about the preternatural, and associations between pagan gods and the devil (established by St. Augustine in the fifth century), colonial pastoral opinion regarding Amerindian involvement with superhuman, non-ordinary entities was more likely to connect it to the demonic preternatural than to *magia naturalis* (that is, to non-illicit dealings with the occult properties of nature). Hernando Ruiz de Alarcón's was no exception. One of the very first figures of Mesoamerican epistemology he addressed in his *Treatise* was the nahualli. This was the name given to powerful, shape-shifting ritual specialists who dealt with occult knowledge and spiritual entities for divinatory, curative, or maleficent ends (Nicholson 1971, 439). Since Ruiz de Alarcón, and Jacinto de la Serna after him, believed in the existence of the nahualli, the authors' testimonies and explanations regarding this figure give us evidence of early modern Christian beliefs about the limits of what was possible in the preternatural. But more importantly, because the nahualtocaitl called out the names of the nahualli, a discussion of this figure will help us grasp the Mesoamerican epistemology undergirding the incantations. For the nahualtocaitl assumed, encouraged, or performed a world in which the boundaries between entities were permeable and fluid. In the first part of this chapter I treat the figure of the nahualli from the viewpoint of the Christian preternatural as evinced in Ruiz de Alarcón's and Serna's reflections. In the second part, I give an overview of this significant figure in the Mesoamerican worldview from its origins in the Olmec civilization up to the twentieth century.

— 1 —

When the "spiritual colonizers"[1] arrived in Mexico and confronted indigenous religious practices, they deemed that by the inscrutable design of God, the lands of Anahuac were ruled by the devil and his acolytes. Thus, the friars gave the Mesoamerican pantheon of superhuman entities significant ontological credit, but with a twist. Whereas Postclassic Mesoamerican conceptions of divinity attributed both beneficial and nefarious aspects to the gods, the orthodox Christian demonological mindset recognized the existence of the indigenous pantheon, but reduced it to essentially negative, proscribed manifestations.[2] The indigenous gods were fallen angels or demons, or at times Lucifer himself.[3] According to the Christian conception of the preternatural, the fallen angels of Mesoamerica would also be presumed to be infused with knowledge about the innermost, nano-cosmic operations of nature, as well as to produce with this knowledge marvelous effects—or appearances—in the world. In chapter 1, I discussed some of the superhuman powers that St. Augustine attributed to demonic nature in his foundational *City of God*. Thus, even if God had allowed the superhuman ethereal spirits, or disembodied intelligences, that the Nahuas called gods to produce some undeniably beneficial effects for the people (which according to European demonology was perfectly possible), especially baptized individuals could no longer be permitted to invoke them or attempt to mobilize their powers.

Hernando Ruiz de Alarcón and Jacinto de la Serna shared with a vengeance this orthodox, colonial, early modern Christian view of Late Postclassic Mesoamerican religious culture and its surviving practices in Central Mexico. Ruiz de Alarcón in the preface to his *Treatise*, and Serna in his *Manual*, impatiently condemned the Nahua subjects for not yet having relinquished their gods and not even being willing to do so in the foreseeable future. Both creole priests deemed the figure of the nahualli as diabolic and as proof of indigenous impious recalcitrance. The term *nahualli* is polysemous because it can refer either to the person or to the nonhuman form he or she took (Nicholson 1971, 439; López Austin 1988, 1:365; Maffie 2014, 39). The most salient aspect of the nahualli—which both Ruiz de Alarcón and Serna acknowledged—was the capacity to transform into different animals or other beings—or to create the illusion of doing so.

In the opening pages of the *Treatise* Ruiz de Alarcón claimed that the nahualli was "extraordinary and outside what is known of other nations and peoples who are accustomed to having a pact with the Devil" (Ruiz de Alarcón 1984, 47). Nonetheless he argued that he could explain its uncommon morphology. He presented three testimonies from "witnesses who are flawless" (namely, Spaniards) in cases involving the "extraordinary" nahualli (45). Perhaps the most dramatic of the three is the account of Father Andrés Girón, a priest residing at the Taxco mines when the treatise was written. Girón narrated how some time earlier when he was heading with some companions toward a settlement near the city of Guatemala to hear Mass, the group had to ford a river. On seeing a caiman approaching, one of the party killed it with two shots. They pulled out the carcass from the water, scorched it with some reeds they found on the bank, and moved on toward the settlement. When they arrived, the travelers encountered a great commotion because an Indian woman had fallen dead. The priests and his companions discovered it had happened at the very moment when the caiman was shot. She showed exactly the same wounds as the beast, and her back was likewise all scorched. Everybody in the settlement agreed that this woman was a nahualli witch (46–47).

Ruiz de Alarcón does not show any skepticism about the wondrous simultaneity of the deaths of the caiman and the Indian woman. Although he and later Serna erroneously believed that the complex of the nahual lacked a correlate in European witchcraft,[4] the plasticity of the Christian universal concept of the devil allowed Ruiz de Alarcón to give this ostensibly unique, marvelous indigenous phenomenon a plausible preternatural explanation:

> I deduce, first, that when a child is born, the Devil, by the express or tacit pact that its parents have with him, dedicates or subjects it to the animal which the child is to have as a *nahual*—which is like saying, as owner of his birth and master of his actions, or what the gentiles used to call fate. And [second] by virtue of this pact the child remains subject to all the dangers and travails that the animal may suffer until its death. And on the other hand the Devil makes the animal always obey the command of the child, or else the Devil himself carries it out, using the animal as instrument. And in this way the impossible, thought-up transformations and other difficulties are not needed [to explain what happens]. (Ruiz de Alarcón 1984, 47)

According to Gonzalo Aguirre Beltrán and Alfredo López Austin, Ruiz de Alarcón confuses the notion of the nahualli with that of tonalism. In the Nahua belief system, everybody had an animal protector, double, and companion. When human babies were born, their *tonalli*, or destiny heat force, was shared with their animal companions, which were born at the same moment. The animal then became the individual's *tona* (Aguirre Beltrán 1963, 105–7; López Austin 1988, 1:374).[5] Sometimes the tona could be the first animal that visited the newborn at night when it was left at the temple. Although the person and the animal lived separately throughout their lives, their fate (*suerte*) was mystically linked. Thus, when the person died, the animal that was his or her tona also perished, usually from the same cause (Aguirre Beltrán 1963, 105). In contrast, the transformation of the nahualli into one or several animals was deemed to be temporary. The individual assumed different forms by sending his or her *ihiyotl* "to take cover in various beings, animals predominantly, or by placing themselves directly inside their victims' bodies" (López Austin 1988, 1:373). The ihiyotl was another soul force believed to reside in the living human body according to the Postclassic Mesoamerican epistemology. It was located in the liver, the site of human passions, desires, and feelings.[6] Much like the tona, the animal into which the sorcerer had sent his or her ihiyetl or under whose cover she or he was, would suffer any harm inflicted on the nahualli, and vice versa (Aguirre Beltrán 1963, 102).

The caiman was one of the animals under which powerful sorcerers cloaked themselves. Because the Indian woman had died simultaneously with the reptile, her portrayed relationship with it as that of a nahualli was perhaps not as fully mistaken as Aguirre Beltrán and López Austin claimed.[7] In any case, what is most interesting for us at the moment is not so much Ruiz de Alarcón's technical errors about Mesoamerican beliefs as his Christian epistemological construction of the fuzzy realm of the preternatural in which both Nahua marvels—the tona and the nahualli—could find a place. A belief in evil angels plus the explanatory power offered by the concept of the devil's superhuman (albeit not supernatural), quasi-perfect knowledge of all things natural allowed the conjecture that the devil was able to manipulate the hidden properties of natural things and lower beings. He did so in order to bring about wondrous effects such as the one Ruiz de Alarcón narrated: namely, to subject an animal completely to his will so that he could use it as an instrument of his deeds, linking its fate with a human being until death. And indeed, as Aguirre Beltrán perceptively suggested, the European concept of the familiar—a demoniacal spirit that the devil puts at the service of his acolyte, usually in the form of a black cat—offered some morphological resemblance to the tonal complex that Ruiz de Alarcón may have mistaken for the nahualli (Aguirre Beltrán 1963, 111–14). This resemblance may have had enough structural parallelisms to facilitate his and Serna's reading of the Mesoamerican nahual as a diabolical exploit.

In his *Treatise* Ruiz de Alarcón points out that children initially command their nahualli because their parents have made a pact with the evil one on their behalf. However, when a child arrives at the age of "the use of reason"—which the Catholic Church stipulated was seven years of age—the child "reiterates the pact or ratifies it tacitly or expressly. Without this condition it is not credible that the Devil has so such power, especially against a baptized person" (Ruiz de Alarcón 1984, 48).[8] It is telling that for the creole cura the major element of impossibility was not the prodigious common fate between animals and humans, but that the devil could force on a baptized human being such a marvelous linkage with a beast. In other words, it was more incredible that the devil could impose such a relationship than that the relationship itself could exist. Therefore, Ruiz de Alarcón judges the nahualli to be satanic, because no person could have such a wondrous connection with an animal without having consented to the agency of the devil.

Jacinto de la Serna, possibly a speaker of Nahuatl and Matlazinca, refers in his *Manual for Ministers* to Ruiz de Alarcón's *Treatise* when writing about the nahualli and its origin in the Nahua cult of the sun. Recall that Serna had a fortuitous if not providential encounter with the manuscript copy of the work during his visita to Atenango del Río in 1640.[9] It is important to consider Serna's revisiting of the topic of the nahualli. His ornate elaboration of Ruiz de Alarcón's work, on which he bases his own treatise, illuminates many other important aspects about this figure, as I will discuss shortly. It also reveals the extent of Catholic orthodox belief in the experience of the preternatural at the highest echelons of the Mexican Church and university in the mid-seventeenth century. It is significant in this respect that Serna describes the nahualli not only based on the literary authority of Ruiz de Alarcón, but also on "many such cases that there are of this kind that have been experienced in the shores of the sea" (Serna 1892, 367). That is, Serna claims both textual authority and empirical proof for the marvelous co-substantiality of the nahualli and its animal companion: he claimed to know of many acknowledged instances of the nahualli beyond the ones Ruiz de Alarcón cited in his *Treatise*.

Serna also interprets the morphology of the nahualli complex as a demonic pact, but in a more theologically elaborate way than Ruiz de Alarcón does. He points out that the nahualli implies a sinful erasure of the likeness to the image of God, since human beings, possessing the most beautiful form of creation, nonetheless preferred to transform themselves into lower creatures (Serna 1892, 367).[10] Basing himself now on the authority of the Jesuit José de Acosta, who in turn alludes to St. Augustine's *City of God* on the question of the deceptive wonders of the Antichrist, Serna explains the ontology of the nahualli complex as an illusory superimposition of the devil on human perception. Along with Acosta and Las Casas (see chapter 1), he affirms that the devil has the preternatural powers to produce the illusion of humans transforming themselves into animals, but not the actual power to override and change their substance. When an action is inflicted on the animal and reflected on the *nanahualtin* (plural of *nahualli*) "to those who see them the Devil puts on this appearance, so that they look like caimans or lions" (Serna 1892, 368).[11] Because human perception is fallible, particularly when compared to the angelical, men and women are often unable to discern appearance from reality. This is a topic in demonological theory that recurs constantly in Spanish and Spanish American baroque art and literature, as is famously exemplified in the interplay of illusion versus reality in Cervantes's masterpiece *Don Quixote*. The devil, always with God's mysterious dispensation, takes advantage of this moral and ontological deficiency to confuse, seduce, and astound humans. Spanish demonologist Martín Castañega had proposed that the devil could tie up visible rays so as to make them represent the figures he wished, or that he could divert them so as to prevent their being looked at straight on (Clark 1999, 166). Martín del Río argued that Satan could swap objects so quickly that he could deceive onlookers, making them believe in a real metamorphosis. He could envelop real bodies in illusory shapes and deceive human imaginative faculties by strategically situating objects with respect to the eye (Del Río 1991, 223–25). In an even more convoluted explanation, Bartolomé de Las Casas (1967, 1:486) stated that whenever good and bad angels wanted figures to appear, they would take a quantity of air, compress it to make it visible, then shape it until it acquired the desired form! Because the devil was unable to actually change the forms of substances, the indigenous complex of the nahualli is explained as an artful optical delusion enabled by him "that absolutely knows all natures of things and powerfully moves them" (Acosta quoted by Serna 1892, 368).[12]

The marvelous geocultural Mesoamerican complex of the nahualli is thus recognized as ontologically and universally possible by a powerful Christian explanation. Serna explicitly invoked a theology of the devil as angelic knower and malevolent trickster and illusionist, which had enough plasticity and ambiguity so as not to be incommensurable with or contrary to many aspects of what was known about the power of Mesoamerican indigenous experiences of the nahualli as a prodigious or non-ordinary wielder of transformational capacities. In fact, the description of the devil as supreme trickster and lord of delusions was similar to that of Tezcatlipoca, who was the patron god of nanahualtin (or sorcerers), master of metamorphosis, prince of darkness and death, seducer, supreme mocker, and deceiver of men (Brundage 1979, 80–89; López Austin 1988, 1:368–69; Burkhart 1989, 92; Cervantes 1994, 41; Olivier 2003). Much like the devil-enabled witches, Tezcatlipoca was believed to confer his power to create metamorphic illusions onto diviners and sorcerers (Olivier 2003, 250). These parallels offered grounds for the globalization of Tezcatlipoca as a manifestation of the Christian devil, and for the non-ordinary figure of the nahualli as one of his deceitful illusions among the indigenous peoples of Mexico. Even the most beneficial aspects of Tezcatlipoca—such as that he could confer great wealth and riches (Sahagún 1989, 1:38) or that the nanahualtin were able to cure—did not contradict the tenets of Christian demonology. It could be that the cosmogonic stories and descriptions of Tezcatlipoca and the nanahualtin recorded in many missionary chronicles and in indigenous informants' testimonies had already been influenced by the newly arrived Christian outlook—hence their resemblances with the preternatural powers of the Christian devil—but this hypothesis is beyond the scope of the present study. For now, the point is that this resemblance would allow the figure to exist both as a geocultural Mesoamerican phenomenon of great non-ordinary powers and as a wondrous Christian, diabolical one. For although Nahuas may have believed that a nahualli could transform into animal form at a very concrete, substantial level in order to command the full array of sensory, bodily perceptions and forces of the animal she or he had transformed into, Christians would hold that such a perceptual register and agency were an illusion.[13] But in the end, whether deemed real or illusory, the special powers derived from these transformations were recognized in both worldviews.

Serna records other indigenous beliefs about the nahualli in Postclassic Mesoamerica that are pertinent for an understanding of the rationale of the nahualtocaitl. Although of course he explains them away as fables and illusions induced by the devil, Serna writes about two very ancient traditions among the Indians. In one there had been "two worlds with two modes or ways of peoples." In one of these worlds "humans had been transmuted into animals, the Sun, the Moon, and the stars." Consequently, people attributed rational souls to all these nonhuman entities, including stones and the four elements. This is why "they invoke and talk with these things as if they talked with humans (hombres)" (1892, 362–63). Thus, for instance, because they believe humans of previous eras or suns were transformed into trees, whenever they go to fell trees "they greet them, and capture their benevolence in order to cut them" (384). The second tradition refers to a time when the gods transformed stones and animals into the humans now living (363). Serna then links up these two traditions with the origin story of the gods Nanahuatzin and Tecciztecatl—already recorded by Sahagún—both of whom jumped into fire in order to metamorphose into the sun and moon of the fifth era. In Serna's version of the myth, he emphasizes that all the gods waited for the appearance of the new sun with offerings, so that it would transform them into creatures of commensurable dignity like "noble animals, celestial and terrestrial, eagles, lions, always with abundant things to eat" (365). With this emphasis, the learned rector of the University of Mexico interpreted how a previous time of metamorphoses was fueled by sacrifice and consummated by the new sun of the current era. This was the (systematic) indigenous cosmogonic explanation for an egalitarian relationship of humans to the world (which Serna considered to be erroneous). Present-day humans communicated with nonhuman beings as if the latter were persons because the Indians believed that all of them—including the gods themselves—had been transformed into other beings in a previous era (362–65). These traditions reported by Serna speak of a transtemporal and interspecies permeability between human and nonhumans that undergirds the figure of the nahualli. Thus, whenever sorcerers took the shape of their nahualli, or animal companion, they were also traveling back in time.[14] Or in the words of Mircea Eliade (1972, 94), "Each time a shaman [or a nahualli, I would add] succeeds in the animal mode of being, he in a manner re-establishes the situation that existed *in illo tempore*, in mythical times, when the divorce between man and the animal world had not yet occurred." More recently, Brazilian anthropologist Viveiros de Castro has also proposed that Amerindian mythical thought expresses a mixture of human and animal attributes "in a common context of intercommunicability, identical to that which defines the present day intrahuman world" (2012, 55). Specifically, mythical time is a very early, primordial time in which animal and human points of view were not fully differentiated, and thus were highly permeable, fluid, and even interchangeable.

Further developing this theme of interspecies mobility and temporality, Serna recounts the myth of Yappan previously recorded in Ruiz de Alarcón's *Treatise*. At a time when present-day animals were people and gods, a man named Yappan was doing penance in order to prepare for the transformations of the new sun. Tempted by the goddess of love Xochiquetzal, Yappan broke his vow, and was transformed into a scorpion as punishment (Serna 1892, 381–82; Ruiz de Alarcón 1984, 204–8). Serna underscores the importance of knowing these "fables" in order to understand the conjuros of the Indians (1892, 381, 382). Indeed, as we will see, a number of nahualtocaitl make reference to stories that took place at an earlier, transformational time when people, gods, and entities were morphed into one another, giving birth to the entities of the present day.[15]

In the first book of his *Treatise*, Ruiz de Alarcón had already observed that there were three possible source verbs for *nahualli* that could apply to its meaning: the first was "'to command'; the second, 'to speak with authority'; the third, 'to hide oneself' or 'to wrap oneself up in a cloak.'" The author chose the third verb as the most suitable etymology, claiming that *nahualli* came from the verb *nahualtia*, "to hide oneself by covering oneself with something" (Ruiz de Alarcón 1984, 48). He thus concluded that *nahualli* most likely meant "a person wrapped up or disguised under the appearance of some animal" (48).[16] Serna (1892, 297–98) agrees with this etymology, linking it to the tradition of the tona (animal companion) attributed to the individual during the birth ceremony. In a couple of instances throughout their respective treatises, both Ruiz de Alarcón and Serna fittingly define the language of the animal-covered nanahualtin as "disguised names," "muffled up names," or very difficult allegories in which metaphors and tropes are continuously used (Ruiz de Alarcón 1984, 40).[17] As linguistic disguises, covers, and substitutions, the nahualtocaitl (that is, names of the nahualli) tapped into the hyper-permeability of a previous temporality when the boundaries between entities were fluid and unfixed.

2

The nahualtocaitl in the *Treatise* and the *Manual* acquire even more significance when we examine—even if only very briefly—some aspects of the long history of the nahualli in Mesoamerica. Scholars have traced evidence of nahualistic experience or constructs back at least to Olmec culture, considered the matrix civilization of Mesoamerica. The Olmecs thrived during the so-called Early and Middle Formative periods (circa 1500–400 B.C.E.) (C. Pool 2007, 6). Sculptures, stellae, axes, and figurines representing composites of humans and animal species; of humans with animal figures on the head, shoulders, or back; and of humans in ritual poses of animals, were produced in La Venta, San Lorenzo, and Tres Zapotes in southeast Veracruz, Mexico (P. Furst 1967, 1995; Coe 1972; Coe and Koontz 2008, 59–78; Duverger 1997, 229–33, 242–60; C. Pool 2007, 106, 112–20). These figures have been interpreted as evidence of a belief in a metamorphic dynamic, or at least in intimately binding relationships between animals and humans, informing the nahualli complex (Coe 1972; P. Furst 1967; Musgrave-Portilla 1982, 7; Duverger

2007, 231–32). In 1946, Miguel Covarrubias coined the term "were-jaguar" for the widespread Olmec stone axes that merged human characteristics with animal features he believed to be mainly jaguars. Covarrubias identified them with the nahualli (Covarrubias quoted in Tate 2012, 19). Although agreeing that the motif of the were-jaguar was widespread in Olmec statuary and that it evinced "a jaguar cult," Peter Furst (1967, 144–45) proposed that the were-jaguar was a shamanic figure. Many other interpretations of Olmec were-images have been proposed since then, but the overall consensus is that they portray powerful interspecies relations.[18]

The nahualli entailed the experience or belief in the transformation of a human being into an animal or other nonhuman form. Because this transformation always involved a lot of non-ordinary power—even if it occurred solely in the realm of dreams—only a very select group of people could undergo it: sorcerers, sages, kings, and other very high-ranking individuals. As L. Marie Musgrave-Portilla has explained, "The exceptional man or woman—the famous leader or the semidivine personages of the origin myths—would logically possess the abilities of the brujo-nahual as further evidence of his or her unusual personal force" (1982, 16). Not surprisingly, the most powerful nanahualtin usually embodied or were transformed into the fiercest and most dangerous animals: jaguars, eagles, snakes, coyotes, and alligators or caimans (López Austin 1988, 1:369; Musgrave-Portilla 1982, 45–46; Martínez González 2011, 90–96). Serna had documented this belief when he singled out tigers, eagles, caimans, and snakes both as animals under which powerful sorcerers usually took cover and as exemplars of animal companions conferred according to the calendar in birth ceremonies (Serna 1892, 297–98).

High-status morphing individuals and powerful nanahualtin were not the only people who were deemed to have relationships with other species, however. Everybody was believed to have a common destiny with an animal companion—as illustrated in the story about the Indian woman who died simultaneously with the caiman. Although some Mesoamericanists claim there is no evidence that a belief in animal companions was present in Central Mexico before the sixteenth century (see especially Foster 1944), others have traced this belief back to Olmec Formative culture. Many pieces of Olmec statuary art depict babies and young children with animal features (Paz 1995, 455; Duverger 2007, 228–29; Coe and Koontz 2008: 62). Josef Paz argues that statues of infants with jaguar attributes may reference not nahualistic godly were-creatures or jaguar shape-shifting shamans, but the alter ego or animal (that is, tona) and the birth of the child with whom it was linked (Paz 1995, 455–56).[19] This in turn would lead to the 260-day divinatory calendar of the tonalpohualli, which underpinned fundamental and unique aspects of Mesoamerican high civilizations. It is worth recalling that in this regard the Olmecs either invented or were already using the tonalpohualli (Caso 1971, 333; Duverger 2007, 54–60). According to the belief structure around the 260 units that composed the cycle of this singular Mesoamerican creation, a series of recurrent powerful generative forces converged in unique forms and degrees of influence on each day, shaping that day and imprinting the creatures born on it with a particular soul force (tonalli). Humans and animals sharing a tonalli established a lifelong relationship even if they never met. Only sorcerers could help ordinary people identify their particular tona, which was always a specific animal not an entire species (Paz 1995, 453–54).

For his part, John Monaghan (1998, 142) has pointed out that it is insufficient to define the tona only as an animal companion since rain, plants, comets, and other natural phenomena may also be linked to humans or to parts of their personhood, and since tonallis are not restricted to humans.[20] Monaghan proposes "co-essence" as the most accurate translation for the tona because the central features of the correspondence between entities are that they were born or emerged in the same calendrical unit and they share a heat energy and even a consciousness, not merely an association (1998, 141–42). If the tonalli can be defined as a particular soul warmth, luminosity, destiny, or inclination (López Austin 1988, 1:204–5; J. Furst 1995, 136), the powers that converge in a day unit of the tonalpohualli can be said to be a common force that establishes shared characters and destinies among the entities born on that day, even if they are unknown to each other and have different life spans. This suggests that a lot of attention was given to metonymic correspondences or links by proximity. Thus, although the tona did not necessarily entail the shape-shifting of the nahualli, it implied that human beings, animals, plants, and even natural phenomena could be "mystically bound" by virtue of sharing the particular configuration of godly-generative forces of the day of their emergence (Monaghan 1998, 142).

More recently Carolyn Tate (2012, 93) has proposed the fascinating hypothesis that Olmecs depicted these close interspecies relations in the form of the human embryo. From her study of Olmec axe figurines, she claims that these objects do not represent were-jaguars or animals, as previously thought, but rather empirically observed miscarried embryos as symbols of "the concept of life or 'soul' force, a seed state, or ontological primordial pluripotentiality" (264). Drawing on contemporary obstetrical statistics on miscarriages and on the physical features of the embryos,

Tate proposes that images in axes and other objects of Olmec statuary culture were based on the empirical observation of actual embryos miscarried between the sixth and twelfth weeks of gestation, a precarious period in pregnancy (39). Tate does not deny that Olmec statuary may depict "the concept of interpenetrating identities between humans, plants, and animals" (33). She believes however that the possibility embryonic images were drawn from empirical observation is an important contribution to the conversation about nahualistic powers in Olmec visual and material culture. In addition, she suggests that axe images may offer support for decoding the 260-day cycle of the divinatory, sacred calendar of the tonalpohualli as corresponding to the human gestation period (47, 59, 273). Dennis Tedlock (1985, 232), Mary Ellen Miller (1986 39), and Elizabeth Boone (2007, 17) had already suggested that the 260-day cycle of the tonalpohualli could have originated with women counting and observing the full temporal course of their pregnancies. Be this as it may, the idea of the embryo as a symbol of natural ontological primordial pluripotentialities, or as a sac or bundle of seeds (or stem cells?) is another perspective from which to address the experience of "interspecies fluidity" that is at the heart of the nahual/tonal complexes (Tate 2012, 93).

After this discussion about the relationships that may be represented by the figures of the nahualli and tonalli, it is pertinent to point out how book 4 of the *Florentine Codex* supports the conflation of the notions of the tonalli, the nahualli, and the tonalpohualli. Like everybody else nanahualtin often received their co-essences according to the day of their birth. Book 4—which focuses on divinatory arts—establishes that form-changing sorcerers were born in the seventh trecena of the tonalpohualli opened by One Rain (Sahagún 1950–82, 4:41); the shape, warmth, and inclinations of the godly forces of this day were especially propitious for nanahualtin and their powerful co-essences.[21] Nanahualtin were also born on the day One Wind, whose presiding deity was Quetzalcoatl "representative of the wind, the whirlwind" (Sahagún 1950–82, 4:101), and One Reed. Other sources, such as the *Codex Telleriano-Remensis* and the *Codex Tudela*, also specify auspicious days for the birth of nanahualtin. These days were usually the first of their trecenas and therefore the most influential. However, in the case of the seventh trecena presided by One Rain (analyzed further in chapter 6), all thirteen days were considered favorable for sorcerers. Thus, although people did not become nanahualtin merely by virtue of the day of their birth,[22] these colonial sources make an important link between the nahualli-as-sorcerer and a specific tonalli, or birthdate. And although the divinatory calendars fell into disuse during the colonial period, the notion that nanahualtin are associated with specific birthdates is still current among indigenous populations in Mexico today (Martínez González 2011, 296).

Martínez González (2011, 145) discusses the argument that the difference between ordinary humans and nanahualtin is not so much—or not only—that the latter have an especially powerful co-essence, but that they know its identity and can manipulate it. The tonalli soul force of all humans departs from the body during sleep, and can even share consciousness with its co-essence as it wanders in the realm of the oneiric, although ordinary people do not usually remember this experience on waking (Musgrave-Portilla 1982, 37; Monaghan 1998, 142).[23] Both Musgrave-Portilla (1982, 37) and Martínez González (2011, 140–45) explain that nanahualtin were able to control their dreams and project their soul force—whether the tonalli or the ihiyotl—into the body of their co-essence and act "hidden" within that form.[24] Although not all transformations involving the nahualli took place during dark, most of them did because "the passage to the world of the night enables a passage to mythical spaces, spaces without time in which past, present, and future encounter each other and converge" (Martínez González 2011, 510; translation is mine). The nahualli-person then was someone who was able to master the realm of dreams, a space-time where the boundaries and identities between entities also dissolve and interpenetrate. Only the nahualli-person would be able to remember and draw power and knowledge from nighttime encounters with his or her co-essence and act upon them in the world. This notion of the night as the space-time where past, present, and future vanished and controlled transformations of the nahualli-person took place will be helpful in interpreting the nahualtocaitl.

Recall that the non-ordinary, preternatural, or prodigious powers of the nanahualtin could be used to help or harm people. According to the *Florentine Codex* there were good and bad nanahualtin. The former were *tlamatine nonotzale,* men and women of knowledge who gave advice and served the community: "someone who can be trusted: he is serious, respectable, not the subject of deceit. . . . The good nahualli is a guardian . . . he is discreet, devoted, useful, he never harms others. The good nahualli is the depositary of tradition, one who leads and "illuminates the world for the people; he knows Mictlan" (Sahagún 1950–82, 10:31). The good nahualli is also associated with the "judicial astrologer"—the tonalpouhqui (day keeper)—who understands well the characters of the tonalpohualli and is able to see the future.[25] Benevolent nanahualtin used their knowledge and transformational powers to heal people, find lost things, divine eventuality, control the weather, and procure good harvests. As the community's moral guardians and protectors from outsiders, however, good nanahualtin could also deploy terrifying aspects (Musgrave-Portilla 1982, 13; Martínez González 2011, 324–32).[26]

Malevolent nanahualtin, on the other hand, were destructive, antisocial individuals who would terrorize and mock the people with their metamorphic powers: "[He is] a hater, a destroyer of people; an implanter of sickness, who bleeds himself over others, who kills them by potions . . . who burns wooden figures of others" (Sahagún 1950–82, 10:31). The bad nanahualtin cast spells on people to confuse and distress them. They drove people mad with their hateful gaze or made them sick by introducing alien objects into their bodies. Evil nanahualtin also invoked preternatural powers to act against people, to breathe onto them words of misfortune (López Austin 1966; Martínez González 2011, 367–68). The *temacpalitotique*, specialized evil nanahualtin who hypnotized people and put them to sleep, were rapists and thieves (López Austin 1966).

Good and bad nanahualtin were both exceptional people who wielded non-ordinary transformational powers to bring about effects in the world. Only the intentions and results of their acts separated evil from good sorcerers. The good nanahualtin—as non-ordinary men and women who healed people, who knew about the powers of the cycles of time and of celestial bodies, who were erudite about the medicinal properties of plants, about rain-making, and about finding lost objects—had commonalities with the learned Renaissance Magi and cunning folk, who also mastered occult astral and medical bodies of knowledge to the people's advantage. And as discussed in the introduction, most of the nahualtocaitl recited to Ruiz de Alarcón and recorded in the *Treatise* could be deemed to be the power words of good nanahualtin because they sought to bring beneficial effects to the people.

— 3 —

The belief, imagination, and experience of the nahualli and tona are still operative today. Nobel Peace Prize winner Rigoberta Menchú confirms the existence of both figures among the K'iche' people in Guatemala. Menchú affirms that every child comes into the world with a nahualli, a double who is "representative of the earth, the animal world, the sun and water" (Menchú 2009, 20). Because they have a double that is a member of another species in this world, humans are in constant communication with nature: "There is not one world for man and one for animals, they are part of the same one and lead parallel lives" (22). Menchú states that nanahualtin tend to be animals, but sometimes they can be trees (21). She points out a very important feature also evident in Ruiz de Alarcón's and

Serna's merged notions of the nahualli and the tona: "Every animal has its human counterpart and if you hurt him, you hurt the animal too" (20). These are some of the very general things about the nahualli Menchú says she can share with her readers. She can never reveal her own nahualli, however, because this is a secret of her people (22).[27] But what she is able to share with her indigenous and non-indigenous audiences says many things about a powerful interspecies connectivity among human and nonhuman beings in the world. Rigoberta Menchú's version of the nahualli fuses with the tona since all indigenous people—not only sorcerers or shamans—are born with an animal guardian. Although Menchú does not identify the nahualli as a shape-shifting figure, we can appreciate in her portrayal an intimate, parallel, protective relation between animals and humans who share a birthdate and hence a destiny that links them throughout their lives.

The Nahuat of the northern Sierra de Puebla have another version of the nahualli and the tona, as expounded in oral narratives recorded by James Taggart in 1983 in Huitzilan de Serdán and Santiago Yaonáhuac. In these *municipios*, the nahualli and tona have been redefined into metaphorically juxtaposed spatiotemporal concepts that clearly incorporate Christian cosmological elements. The periphery is an amoral realm, "which the Nahuat regard as filled with creative and dangerous forces" (Taggart 1983, 55). Peripheral environments include forests (*kwowta*), mountains, canyons, abysses, or inhospitable places (56). The periphery is also anterior in time and undifferentiated. It is in counterpoint with the center—the moral space of the human community, the milpa, and the pueblo—which arose later with the creation of the sun and tonalli. This event is interpreted as identical with the birth of Christ, and by extension, with Christ himself: "the coming of the sun began a division between human (Christians from the earth—*taltikpak cristianos*) and animals" (56). Although they represent different spatiotemporal eras, periphery and center are co-present in the world. Therefore, humans can actually go back in time by stepping into the periphery and encountering the less differentiated creatures that inhabit it, such as talking animals (56, 61). Humans also have animal companion spirits (*tonalme*) that mediate between the center and the periphery. There are also *nagualme*, form-changing individuals who undergo transformations in order to punish their enemies, but also to correct wrongdoers (59, 162). In the Nahuat narratives recorded by Taggart, the nagualme and tonalme are "anomalous" liminal figures that bridge and move between the human/center and the animal/periphery domains. Specifically, they are figures with interspecies mobility.

Similarly, pre-Hispanic and contemporary Maya recognize an opposition between the ordered world of the milpa and town versus the forest wilderness.

The latter is "a dangerous, uncontrollable place of demons and fierce, biting beasts" (Taube 2003, 479) that can be fatal to humans. Much like the Nahuat, the Maya according to Karl Taube cast the forest as a place of ancient beings. A perilous, threatening place of darkness, the forest is however also the realm of dreams, where the animal part of humans (*way*, "animal spirits") manifest themselves (484). Namely, the forest is the overwhelming, liminal realm of interspecies communicability of the nahualli. Dreams and the night are where the identity of one's tonalli, co-essence, or animal soul is revealed (Pitt-Rivers 1970, 190), and where plants communicate their powers to the wandering tonalli of the human dreamer "beneath the earth's surface" (Laughlin 2000, 105).

Pre-Columbian art historian Rebecca Stone also has recently argued that "sensory anomalousness" is a requirement for the shaman (Stone 2011, 54). Animals are one of the recurrent features of "Amerindian and Latin American" visionary experiences rooted in what she calls a shamanistic view of the world. Animals may appear to the entranced person "merely as present, attacking and even killing them, psychically connected, in a friendly guiding relationship, and/or as the animal into which they transform" (Stone 2011, 39). Of course, the last form of interaction between the shaman and the animal has a lot in common with the figure of the nahualli. The experience of the nahualli as simultaneously co-essence, shaman, and transforming sorcerer entails inhabiting interspecies perspectives and bringing this knowledge into the human world.

Many indigenous informants, social scientists, and independent scholars have warned or reported that these visionary, identity-dissolving experiences can be empowering, but also very frightening and dangerous. Indeed, Gordon Wasson (1980, 48–49) reports that for recent initiates, shamanistic experiences and visions can be terrifying. Jeremy Narby (1998, 7) states that the shaman is constantly facing challenges and battles and fighting off fear. Don Andrés and Doña Talín of Guatemala warn about the dangers of shamanistic light power that "it could put out your eyes" (Barbara Tedlock quoted in R. Stone 2011, 62). Engaging with spirit worlds and interspecies transformations can either cure or weaken and even kill. Because people can be destroyed if these forces are misused, they should only be tapped for good ends. According to Stone, in traditional settings, shamanic visions are used with a concrete purpose: "to diagnose an illness, see a given person from far away, find a lost article" (R. Stone 2011, 61). Contacting the ambivalent powers of the spirit worlds is socially acceptable only when undertaken for the beneficial ends of the individual and the community, as the good nanahualtin in the *Florentine Codex* did.

In the introduction and in this chapter I pointed out that the opaque metaphoric language of the form-changing, dream-controlling, knowledge-wielding nanahualtin recorded by Ruiz de Alarcón and then reproduced by Serna was basically benevolent. Although there must have been conjuros to achieve evil ends, no nahualtocaitl recorded in the *Treatise* was intended to destroy people or property, ruin harvests, conjure hailstorms, cause despair, or make somebody ill. And not unlike the notion that everybody had an interspecies relationship with a tona, a co-essence, or a nonhuman companion by virtue of the day they were born, the powers of the metaphor-filled, transformational language of the nahualli was accessible not only to ritual specialists, but also to anyone who could pronounce the right names. The nahualtocaitl recorded by Ruiz de Alarcón embody and perform a Mesoamerican epistemology of cosmological transformism in which the boundaries between godly, human, and nonhuman entities; between past, present, and future, all were dissolvable and unfixed. But the muffled names of the good nanahualtin did not bring confusion, disorientation, or fear to the people, as the creole priests claimed. As I will show in subsequent chapters, the people tapped competently and confidently into the powers of an earlier, liminal space-time plenum in order to provide knowledge for preserving and enhancing the lives of the people in the ordinary realms of an all-too-fragile world.

CHAPTER THREE

Quetzalcoatl Fights Highwaymen

A Nahualtocaitl for Safe Travel on the Roads of the Empire

In this chapter I analyze crucial segments of the first nahualtocaitl recorded in Ruiz de Alarcón's *Treatise*. It opens the second tract of the collection, which contains nearly twenty conjuros for the successful completion of a wide array of activities having to do with different trades. The conjuration analyzed here is to be recited by lone travelers on desert roads to ward off thieves and highwaymen. Following it are others for inducing sleep, cutting wood, rigging limekilns, hunting, finding beehives, keeping pests away from harvests, and fishing. Except for the one to produce sleep, which might have very dubious ends, all the nahualtocaitl in this tract can be considered beneficent. Many of the activities they address require training and protocols, but none were extraordinary or marvelous, at least not from the viewpoint of early modern Christian natural philosophy. Nor were the incantations in this tract strictly magical in the sense of being expected to produce tangible effects without appropriate and necessary paralinguistic actions. Thus, they did not quite meet Martín del Río's definition of superstitions as deeds that attempted to supersede natural causation (Del Río 1991, 204). Neither were the words of the nahualtocaitl arbitrarily or purposelessly applied to the situation at hand; thus, they were not entirely condemnable as irrational, vain observances. On the other hand, because the conjuros undoubtedly engaged in forbidden contact with Mesoamerican preternatural entities, it is not beyond expectation that Ruiz de Alarcón and Serna would have found them threatening. In any case, because the nahualtocaitl facilitated the success of traditional activities that were clearly important for the sustenance and protection of the people, Ruiz de Alarcón's informants unwaveringly resisted revealing them or giving them up.

1

Hernando Ruiz de Alarcón wrote his *Treatise* in Atenango del Río, a village in the province of Chilapa, north of the Balsas River. The pre-Hispanic history of this territory has come down to us as a rather complex series of conquests, invasions, and coexistences of small independent or semi-independent communities in an area of significant agricultural wealth (Gerhard 1972, 111). When the Spaniards arrived, the province was at the very center of Coixcatlalpan, the land of the Coixca people. The latter had conquered the Chontals, who themselves had invaded the area, most likely then populated by speakers of Matlatzinca and other tongues. At the time of the Spanish Conquest, however, the region was firmly controlled by the Aztec Triple Alliance (Toussaint 1931, 9–12; Coe and Whittaker 1982, 7).[1] Contact with the Spaniards initiated a gradual but dramatic indigenous population decrease in the province due to epidemics, conscription in the silver mines (Toussaint 1931, 34, 221), and out-migration to escape harsh conditions. Silver would become "the vital fluid of the body economic of colonial Mexico" (Bakewell 1997, 171) and Taxco, not too far northwest of Atenango, would rank as the fourth- or fifth-largest producer of this metal in the whole of New Spain (Haskett 1991, 447). It is not known if the towns of Chilapa had to render forced labor (*repartimiento*) service to the mines, but there is evidence that Atenango sent maize tribute to Taxco in the mid-sixteenth century, possibly to support the workers (Coe and Whittaker 1982, 10). This indicates that the town was involved with the silver economy and its attendant social and cultural mixes and upheavals resulting from the harsh colonial forms of labor. Be this as it may, the estimated population of the province in 1600 was only 4,390 tributaries. Thirty years later, the number had plummeted by almost 66 percent, to 1,480 (Gerhard 1972, 113).

In terms of the Church presence in Chilapa, the Augustinians had entered the southern region of the province in 1533 and founded a doctrina in Asunción. The Atenango area north of the river was within the jurisdiction of the Archbishopric of Mexico and was first visited by secular priests from the town of Huizuco. Following the congregations of 1600, a secular curate started living at San Juan Atenango del Río (Gerhard 1972, 113). The pueblo had a church, and Ruiz de

Alarcón had received the town as beneficio by 1613.[2] It could have been Archbishop Juan Pérez de la Serna who installed him in his beneficio, since all beneficiados had to be approved by the bishop or archbishop, and Pérez de la Serna took office in 1613.[3] Ruiz de Alarcón's duties as beneficiado—for which he would have received guaranteed remuneration—involved celebrating Mass and taking care of souls. He had to reside in his parish town, which he did until his death. Because of his later additional appointment as *juez comisionado*, Ruiz de Alarcón also had some external jurisdiction to investigate idolatrous practices in adjacent towns.

The native texts he recorded in the *Treatise* as a result of his commission are in the Coixca and Tlalhuica varieties of the Nahuatl language (Harvey 1972, 300; Coe and Whittaker 1982, 8–9; 319–21). Although these varieties did not differ greatly from the Classical Nahuatl of Tenochtitlan, they showed particular distinguishing features that set their speakers apart as different peoples from the Mexica. The informants and confessants of the sixty-plus nahualtocaitl Ruiz de Alarcón collected came from communities in the northern Coixca region, such as Tepequaquilco, Iguala, Atenango, the Taxco mines, and Tasmalaca; from the Chilapa area south the Balsas River in present-day Guerrero; and from Tlalhuica speakers from towns such as Cuauhnahuac, Yauhtepec, and Xiuhtepec in present-day Morelos. It is significant that Huitzilopochtli does not appear among the deities invoked in the conjuros reported to Ruiz de Alarcón. Andrews and Hassig (1984, 20) observe that this absence may have been due to the relatively late introduction of Huitzilopochtli into the Guerrero region during the Aztec Triple Alliance conquests. But although the mighty Mexica god is not addressed in them, the conjuros do deploy many Postclassic cosmogonic traditions recorded in prominent colonial sources produced in Central Mexico during the sixteenth century, such as the *Historia de los mexicanos por sus pinturas*, the *Florentine Codex*, *Anales de Cuauhtitlan*, the *Leyenda de los soles*, and the *Histoyre du Mexique*.[4]

Some observations suggest the Postclassic city of Culhuacan as a possible place of origin for a few traditions of the nahualtocaitl. Lying on an isthmus between Lakes Texcoco and Xochimilco, Culhuacan had been partner and then successor of the great imperial city of Tula or Tollan which fell in the mid-twelfth century. As the standing bulwark of Toltec civilization, Culhuacan had enormous prestige and legitimacy in the Valley of Mexico. Because of its relative geographic proximity to the warm-climate, cotton-producing area around Morelos, the cultured city had had a long-standing relationship with that region since the tenth century C.E., in the early Postclassic period (N. Davies 1980, 28, 158). It is not unlikely that as a prominent city Culhuacan continued to exert significant cultural influence on the

Valley of Morelos after the Tlalhuica arrived there circa 1220, in the second wave of Chichimec migrations to Central Mexico (Maldonado Jiménez 2000, 33–37; Smith 2012, 38). The wealth of sophisticated Mesoamerican cultural traditions woven into the nahualtocaitl from the Tlalhuica region may attest to this influence. As a case in point it is pertinent to note that Cihuacoatl appears in at least two nahualtocaitl and Xochiquetzal in nine. Cihuacoatl was a Toltec deity of the earth and patroness of Culhuacan (N. Davies 1980, 27; 1987, 22; Nicholson 1988; Maldonado Jiménez 2000, 66). She was worshipped in Xochimilco and, significantly, was also patron goddess of Huaxtepec, one of the largest cities in Tlalhuicatlalpan (Maldonado Jiménez 2000, 68–69). Cihuacoatl is invoked in these two nahualtocaitl as a ritual name for the rope. However, it was in her manifestation as, or association with, Xochiquetzal, the voluptuous young earth mother and patroness of weavers, that the goddess was most revered by the Tlalhuica (83–86).[5] Finally, the cult to both Cihuacoatl and Xochiquetzal was introduced late in Tenochtitlan (68, 83).

The preceding observations suggest that the conjurations reported to Ruiz de Alarcón represented an oral ritual genre that was current in the region at least after the arrival of the Tlalhuica and Coixca in the early thirteenth century, and before the fearful conquests of the Triple Alliance circa 1430. Many nahualtocaitl could have been drawn from the cultured Culhua and Xochimilca Mesoamerican traditions circulating in the Valley of Morelos, some of which traditions were later adopted by the Aztec conquerors themselves. And although the Nahuatl dialect in which the conjuros were recorded is basically Coixca, Coe and Whittaker (1982, 9) point out that among the informants Ruiz de Alarcón questioned were many Tlalhuica and even Xochimilca. More importantly, the creole cura also states that on several occasions he visited towns in the region of Cuernavaca (Cuauhnahuac) in order to make his inquiries (Ruiz de Alarcón 1984, 51, 169, 184).

This does not mean, of course, that other nahualtocaitl not registered in the *Treatise* could not have been generated after the Aztec conquests, some of them even invoking Huitzilopochtli. Diego Durán—who resided in Hueyapan in the region of present-day Morelos in 1581—points out that the people from the colonial province of Cuernavaca "were the most superstitious and the greatest fortune-tellers, sorcerers that ever existed in the entire land" (Durán 1971, 459). And it was from Yauhtepec, Huaxtepec, Malinalco, and Tepoztlan where Motecuhzoma Xocoyotzin drew "enchanters, sorcerers, sleep-makers, and those who know how to command snakes, scorpions, and spiders" to bewitch the newly arrived strangers (Durán 1994, 512–13). In any case, Durán's comments suggest that the Tlalhuica from Morelos continued to use nahualtocaitl under Aztec rule. And judging by Ruiz de Alarcón's *Treatise*, they did also under the Spaniards up to the beginning of the seventeenth century and most likely beyond.

As the reader knows by now, one meaning of *nahualtocaitl* is "disguised or metaphorical names" (Andrews and Hassig 1984, 349 n. 1), and what Ruiz de Alarcón was able to extract from its users were testimonies of a linguistic practice specific, although not exclusive, to the nanahualtin. Because the nahualtocaitl, or names of the nahualli, were believed to establish interspecies communication with godly and nonhuman entities, they had a specific form and structure distinct from that of ordinary speech. Even though, or perhaps precisely because, he was fluent in Nahuatl, Ruiz de Alarcón often complained in his *Treatise* about the difficulty of understanding this specialized language. Indeed, the nahualtocaitl represents a tightly wrought, highly condensed metaphorical language carrying illocutionary force.[6]

2

In 1618 Juan Vernal declared to Ruiz de Alarcón that he vouched for the efficaciousness of a conjuro for fighting thieves, after having used it successfully to defend himself while carrying tribute for the king of Spain, no less. Vernal was a resident of the Indian town of Iguala, which due to its proximity to Taxco el Nuevo, had to offer repartimiento labor to the silver mines.[7] Ruiz de Alarcón gives very little information about Juan Vernal other than his town of origin and that he was carrying tribute for the Crown when he was assaulted. Unfortunately, we do not know either what kind of tribute Vernal was transporting or where he was instructed to deposit it. We only know that according to his account he had to take seemingly dangerous roads to move his load, and that he claimed he had been delivered from highwaymen by using this conjuration on this as well as on previous occasions. Since Spaniards rarely collected tributes directly from local Indian taxpayers (Gibson 1964, 219), and since Taxco is around thirty-five kilometers from Iguala, it is clear that Vernal was not a low-level tributary Indian from a remote, isolated village where interaction with Spaniards was limited to the occasional visita of a clergyman or some Spanish functionary from a nearby town.[8] Vernal must have been at least a minor official from an indigenous community in regular contact with one of the busiest mining centers in the viceroyalty of New Spain.[9]

From his hardline criollo, clerical position Ruiz de Alarcón represented his native flock as stubborn idolaters who, after one hundred years of intensive evangelization labor, still adhered to ancestral practices taught to their forefathers by the devil. And indeed, the fact that in 1618 somebody like Juan Vernal repeatedly invoked the aid of native deities did substantiate some of the priest's colonialist anxieties that a hardy pantheon of Postclassic Mesoamerican deities was very much alive in indigenous life. For if Vernal was an Indian official who carried His Majesty's tribute, it is not unreasonable to posit that he would have had enough administrative awareness to function effectively in the burgeoning, nontraditional environment of the colonial mining town. But this indigenous subject from Iguala showed little discomfort or epistemological distress over using an incantation of clearly pre-Hispanic provenance to defend himself when carrying tribute for the great and zealous defender lord of the Christian faith, the king of Spain. Vernal was a plural-worlds dweller.[10]

Juan Vernal testified that after voicing a certain nahualtocaitl, he had been able to kill two highwaymen who had tried to rob him on his journey. Vernal was initially imprisoned for the deaths of his attackers, but the authorities had later released him (Ruiz de Alarcón 1984, 73–75). However, the tribute carrier from Iguala was now being charged not for the civil crime of homicide, but for the ecclesiastical transgression of having engaged in proscribed communication with Mesoamerican Postclassic supernatural entities by using the nahualtocaitl.

Andrews and Hassig (1984, 25) have pointed out that Ruiz de Alarcón usually gives little ritual context for the recitation of the conjuros. Indeed, in Vernal's case, the cura does not offer many details other that in preparing for the conjuration Vernal provided himself with "a good club that served him as staff" (Ruiz de Alarcón 1984, 75). When he arrived at his destination, or rather on his way toward it, he addressed the club as follows:

> [1] Nohmatca nehhuātl. NiQuetzalcōātl. NiMātl. Ca nehhuātl ni Yāotl; niMoquehqueloatzin. Ahtleh īpan nitlamati.[11]
>
> [2] I myself, the god *Quetzalcoatl* or the crested snake; I am the god called *Matl*, I who am the very war, and I make fun of everything, for neither do I fear nor do I owe.
>
> [3] It is I in Person. I am Quetzalcoatl. I am Matl. I indeed am Yaotl. I am Moquehqueloatzin. I consider things as nothing [i.e., I am afraid of nothing *or* I respect nothing]. (Ruiz de Alarcón 1984, 75).

In approximately fifteen nahualtocaitl collected by Alarcón, the user voices an inscribed illocutionary speech pertaining to a Mesoamerican deity from the Classic or Postclassic period. Like many other users of the conjuros, Juan Vernal is not represented in the text as a ticitl (doctor), *matlapouhqui* or *pahini* (diviner), or any other ritual specialist, but only as an ordinary person who often traveled on solitary roads and at times had been a tribute carrier.[12] This has some consequence for the systems of knowledge of time and space enacted or performed in the nahualtocaitl. First, it would seemingly entail the notion that users of at least certain nahualtocaitl could be any people who could properly utter the words, not only specialists in dealing with the spirit world. Such a notion would not conflict with the interspecies fluidity and relaxed boundaries between entities that were inherent to the nahualli and the belief or experience of the tonalli as co-essence(s). One of the operational assumptions of the conjuration enunciated by Vernal is that it would allow the user to access or don the powerful speech of Quetzalcoatl, the Feathered Serpent and Wind God. Quetzalcoatl was one of the major creator deities in Mesoamerican cosmogony, and his multifaceted figure was further layered through merging with the historical, deified Toltec priest-ruler Topiltzin Quetzalcoatl (Nicholson 1971, 398, 428–30; Carrasco 1982, 30–32; Florescano 1999). As Diego Durán documented in the sixth chapter of his *Book of the Gods and Rites,* Quetzalcoatl (figure 1) was also worshipped as the patron of Cholula, one of the greatest cities of the Postclassic period, renowned for its rich merchants (Nicholson 2001, 107).[13] Much like the colonial tribute carrier Vernal, the merchants (*pochteca*) from Cholula were known to take long and lonely roads, carrying their goods as far as Guatemala even in colonial times.[14] Moreover, the Dominican chronicler describes that the Quetzalcoatl image that had been kept in the Cholulan great temple carried in his right hand a wooden ax in the form of a sickle (Durán 1971, 130-31). We will see later in the nahualtocaitl that the speaker inscribed as Quetzalcoatl says that he carries a wooden staff or club as a weapon.

The (licit) boundaries between human and superhuman beings deployed in this nahualtocaitl are different from those of orthodox Christianity in Spain. For no regular Spanish Christian subject—other than priests (in the highly restricted sacramental contexts of the Mass) or very select, blessed individuals—would claim entitlement to the voice of Jesus Christ, the Virgin, an angel, or even a saint in order to access their superhuman powers and employ them for immediate well-being or self-protection. We can certainly find poetic impersonations of Christian supernaturals—with more or less decorum—in many codified medieval and early modern dramatic genres such as morality plays and *autos sacramentales,* religious poetry, hagiographies, fictional narratives, or the more restricted context of the "literary prophetic" (Solaguren 1970).[15] But the speaking subjects in this array of genres do not posit their speech act as actually claiming a specific power through co-identity with a divinity. Perhaps the closest parallel could be mystic discourse,

FIGURE 1. Queztalcoatl, god of Cholula, with his *chicoacolli* or curved baton, his feathered shield, and pointed hat. *Codex Tovar* 132.
Courtesy of the John Carter Brown Library at Brown University.

where there is what Nelson Pike (1992, 165) labels a "God-soul identity." In this subject position, the mystic experiences a lack of distinction between self and God, usually after a long period of spiritual preparation. In her great work *El castillo interior* (Interior Castle) Spanish mystic Santa Teresa de Jesús (1515–82) writes that in a state of full union, the soul "can neither see nor hear nor understand" (quoted in Pike 1992, 7); namely, it does not know who or what it is. Deprived of his or her senses, the mystic subject cannot act.[16]

Yet without the mystic's "super sense-perceptual or sub-sense perceptual unitive experience . . . not accessible by way of sense-perception" (Gellman 2014), Juan Vernal "affirm[ed] the presence of a temporary power" (Gruzinski 1993, 161) by investing himself with a godly identity through the words of the nahualtocaitl. Thus, any and every lone traveler traversing dangerous roads could become the great Quetzalcoatl-as-speaking-subject by pronouncing this nahualtocaitl—and would consequently be able to access at least some of the god's powers. This would indicate fairly unrestricted passage between the human and superhuman realms. The latter realm was seemingly available to regular people without their needing to engage in non-ordinary sense experiences such as "sought-out drunkenness and hallucination, sleep and dream, or the ecstasy attained in exhaustion and penance" as Gruzinski (1993, 162) writes of the performativity entailed by the nahualtocaitl. Indeed, recall that when Juan Vernal was interrogated about his use of the incantation, he had openly and fearlessly declared that "he had proof [*experiencia*] of the truth and effect of the words" (Ruiz de Alarcón 1984, 73); that is, the conjuration enabled his accession to godly powers. Of course, we must take this statement with some skepticism, because the creole priest was anxious to demonstrate to his superiors that it was imperative to eradicate the discursive practice of the nahualtocaitl, which he considered—or pretended to consider—highly idolatrous and demoniacal.

Granted that we will never know how much Vernal really believed in the workings of the nahualtocaitl, we can nonetheless attempt to approximate the complex webs of relations posited by its boundary-erasing language. In addition to being Quetzalcoatl, the speaker of the incantation identifies himself as other related gods and powers: Yaotl, Matl, and Moquehqueloatzin. Serna writes that Matl "is the same as the God of the Hands, the God of the works" (Serna 1892, 392; translation is mine).[17] Andrews and Hassig tell us that Matl "is a variant of . . . 'hand.' In the *Treatise* this is considered a god and appears to be equated with Quetzalcoatl" (1984, 230). Coe and Whittaker (1982, 105) translate *nimatl* as "I am the Hand," Since Quetzalcoatl was the creator god of the Toltecs as well as their deified high priest and king—whose artistic accomplishments and craftsmanship had been foundational in the memory of Mesoamerican civilization since the Postclassic period[18]—the metonymical, synecdochic relationship of the hand as a stand-in for this deity and priestly king is not unexpected. Thus, it can be posited that the expert, accurate hand of the creator god or that of the deified priest-king master of all arts is the hand carrying the wooden club in this nahualtocaitl, as we shall shortly see.

Ruiz de Alarcón and Serna translate *niYaotl* as "I am war itself" (Ruiz de Alarcón 1892, 152; Serna 1892, 392). Andrews and Hassig (1984, 244) and Olivier (2003, 28–31) translate *Yaotl* as "Enemy." *Moquehqueloatzin* literally means "He who tickles himself, or He who mocks himself" (Andrews and Hassig 1984, 231). It is usually translated, however, as "The Mocking One" (Olivier 2003, 17, 20); he who jeers at everything and does not fear or owe (Serna 1892, 392); or he who is the Mocker (Coe and Whittaker 1982, 105; Andrews and Hassig 1984, 75). Both names, Yaotl and Moquehqueloatzin, were attributed to Tezcatlipoca, the all-powerful, bellicose, highly ambivalent and disruptive God of the Smoking Mirror, who constantly tricked humans and led opposing parties to battle among themselves, and who "also bestowed wealth, courage, nobility, and honor" (Sahagún 1950–82, 1:5). Because of his capacity to trick humans by appearing in different shapes and forms, Tezcatlipoca was also the tutelary god of the nanahualtin (shape-shifting sorcerers). It is pertinent in this respect to point out that in their introduction to the *Codex Vaticanus B*, Ferdinand Anders, Maarten Jansen, and Luis Reyes García (1993, 137) state that a hand, an eagle claw, or a jaguar claw sometimes appears on vessels as a visual expression of the power of seizing, proper to warriors and nanahualtin. Besides signifying artifice, then, the skillful hand may also be marked as a metonymy, or synecdochic stand-in, for the powers of great warriors and sorcerers in Postclassic ceramic iconography. After summoning the specific powers of these gods, whose hands had links to artifice, war, and nahualism, the user of the conjuro was ready to confront his enemies.

Later in the nahualtocaitl, the inscribed voice of Quetzalcoatl speaks as follows:

> [1] Auh in nehhuātl ahmō nezzoh, ahmō nitlapalloh. Ca ōnichuālhuīcac in tlamacazqui, Cē-Ātl Ītōnal, in tlamacazqui, Cē-Miquiztli, Cē-Tecpatl. Achtotipa ezzōhuaz, achtotipa tlapallōhuaz. Tetl īhuintiz, cuahuitl īhuintiz, tlālli īhuintiz [in] nonehuiyān.

> [2] But I am as if without blood or flesh (i.e., insensible), and I bring the priest . . . with me, and the time or heat of the summer . . . I bring the priest, unique death, one flint, who before anyone else, is to be stained with blood,

> because unexpectedly the stone is to be stained . . . , the stick is to become drunk, the land is to become drunk [that is, with blood] at the same time with me and with my arms.
>
> [3] But as for me, I do not have any blood, I do not have any color [i.e., I am not vulnerable]. I have brought the priest, His-*tonal* is One Water [i.e., the staff], [or] the priest, One Death [i.e., rocks], [or] One Flint [i.e., the knife]. First, he will become covered with blood; first, he will become covered with color. The stones will become drunk; the trees will become drunk; the land will become drunk at my will. (Ruiz de Alarcón 1984, 75, 77; emphasis is mine)[19]

In this segment, and throughout the incantation, the inscribed, illocutionary voice posits itself as attaining godly mastery over the assailants by virtue of lacking sensible, physical attributes that make human (and animal) life possible: blood, color, and flesh (Sáenz de Santa María 1969, 561). Roberto Martínez González (2011, 268) has pointed out that "non-humanity" is registered in the *Florentine Codex* as a quality of Mesoamerican gods and of (dangerous) superhuman entities able to produce extraordinary events. And indeed, although Mesoamerican gods were responsive to human communication (Anders, Jansen, and Reyes García 1993, 134), they were considered to be almost indiscernible to human perception, except in dreams, hallucinogenic trances, or dangerous, sacred places under their influence (Nicholson 1971, 408; López Austin 1993, 112–13).[20] In addition, "a gust of wind, a flash, a voice, a shadow, a creaking, or a slight touch can betray their presence" (López Austin 1993, 112). By virtue of the interspecies mobility experienced in dreams or in the realities of the Mesoamerican world(s), some deities also took cover under shape-shifting nanahualtin (López Austin 1993, 142–43; Martínez González 2011, 270). Among these deities were none other than Tezcatlipoca and Quetzalcoatl, both of whom were linked to patronage and invention of sorcery (see especially book 3 of the *Florentine Codex*).

The speech act of the nahualtocaitl is thus supposedly pronounced by intelligent, non-vulnerable non-corporeal godly powers, without flesh or blood, that could call forth other discerning operative entities like the *tlamacazque* (plural of *tlamacazqui*) A tlamacazqui is "'one who will give something,' i.e., a priest'" (Andrews and Hassig 1984, 238). The German Mesoamericanist Walter Krickeberg describes priests as "those who offer sacrifices to the gods" (1985, 172). He reports that Sahagún lists at least thirty-eight categories of priests and their functions in Tenochtitlan. Andrews and Hassig (1984, 247) specify that in the

Treatise tlamacazqui is used to name any power entity. Serge Gruzinski (1993, 162) points out that anything called tlamacazqui in the nahualtocaitl, from conjurers to objects, plants, and animals, formed "a sacerdotal collectivity" that allowed "accession to the gods and enrollment in a network of exchange and vital gifts." Namely, in the nahualtocaitl, many entities other than humans or gods could be mediators, conduits, and even mobilizers of superhuman powers roaming the earth. Thus, Quetzalcoatl, as creator god and master high priest-king who knew how to make things happen, brought with him the following tlamacazque: Ce Atl, or One Water; Ce Miquiztli, or One Death; and Ce Tecpatl, or One Flint. These are calendrical names, each one referring to one of the 260 days in the sacred calendar of the tonalpohualli. Believed to have been born very early in the creation process, the tonalpohualli marked and established the cycles of superhuman and preternatural divine forces as they appeared on the face of the earth, generating or destroying entities, and morphing certain entities into others (Caso 1971; López Austin 1993; Read 1998; Krickeberg 1985, 176–97; Boone 2007; Duverger 2007, 54–62). The tonalpohualli was therefore essential for understanding the ways the world moves, changes, and behaves; and in this sense it can be considered a fundamental structure of Mesoamerican knowledge. Many cultural practices in Central Mexico were linked to the cycles of the tonalpohualli, because superhuman forces were deemed to follow its order. Thus, knowledge of favorable or unfavorable godly powers present on each day of the calendar would aid people in calculating propitious times for specific activities like naming a child, contracting marriage, setting out on long-distance travel, or launching military action.

Quetzalcoatl calls out the name One Water, addressing the wooden staff or baton that merchants carried while marching long distances in order to trade their goods. Water (Atl) is always the ninth day in the strictly ordered Mesoamerican twenty-day sign count.[21] The patron god of the day Water was Xiuhteuctli, a name for the god of fire that also "means Lord of the years, and of time" (Serna 1892, 281). In the aspect of time, Xiuhteuctli was conceived of as the eldest of the gods and was called Huehuetzin (Old Man). This prestigious deity was also associated with the renewal of time and the domestic hearth (Nicholson 1971, 413; Brundage 1979, 22–27; Anders, Jansen, and Reyes García 1993, 83; González Torres 1995, 201–2; Carrasco 1999, 103–5). As a god of regeneration, he was linked with a tree, rain, and water in the calendrical feast of Huey Tozotli on the fourth month of the solar calendar (Limón Olvera 2001, 61–65).[22] As lord of the renewal of time, Xiuhteuctli also reigned over the New Fire Ceremony, celebrated every fifty-two years (*xiuhmolpilli*), a supremely important unit of time in Central Mexico.[23] Because wooden sticks were used to create fire in this ceremony, the xiuhmolpilli may have provided a particularly significant metonymic connection between fire and wood.

"One" refers to the first position (or first Lord of the Day) in every thirteen-unit count (trecena), whose patron god is Xiuhteuctli.[24] "One Water," then, is a compound name that signifies that the ninth day-sign (Water) occupies the first position in one of the twenty trecenas of the divinatory calendar. This conjunction happens only in the seventeenth trecena, whose patron deity is Chalchiutotolin (Jade Turkey), a zoological deity that usually appeared in Mexican codices with distinctive traits of Tezcatlipoca (Spranz 1973, 463). Domesticated like the dog, the turkey was considered a natural victim for sacrifice (Olivier 2003, 33–34, 115–16). The Lord of the Night corresponding to One Water is Tecpatl, the power of the flint knife used in sacrifices. The power of this Lord of the Night, then, is seemingly in close correspondence with Chalchiutotolin as the presiding deity of the trecena, and to the wooden sticks used to spark the new fire, which also involved human sacrifice in the ceremony of the New Fire.

Notably, Ruiz de Alarcón (1984, 75) translates "Ce Atl" (One Water) as "the time of the heat, or summer," rendering the calendrical name in terms of the attributes of the regent god of both the day-sign Water and the first day of the trecena (that is, the old god of fire and time, Xiuhteuctli). Although his translation is not incorrect, the criollo priest misses the allusions to Chalchiutotolin and Tecpatl. Throughout the *Treatise*, Ruiz de Alarcón fails to recognize repeated invocations of the calendrical days of the tonalpohualli. Such invocations would have made the nahualtocaitl more rather than less transgressive in the cura's mind (see the introduction), so the mistranslation suggests that he did not significantly intervene in or rewrite the conjuros declared to him in Nahuatl. The fact that he erroneously interprets the calendrical names as difficult metaphors, and translates them accordingly, means that Ruiz de Alarcón had less mastery of the oral texts he transcribed than he stated in his dedication letter to Archbishop Francisco Manso y Zúñiga.[25] Furthermore, the cura's misconception also suggests that the indigenous informants did not greatly alter the nahualtocaitl they disclosed to him.[26] At the very least, they did not conceal from him the widespread invocation of the calendrical names of the divinatory tonalpohualli. It is difficult to determine however whether they were fully cognizant of the significance of these names, and whether they believed the cura comisionado would understand them.

Also brought forth by the disembodied, commanding voices of Quetzalcoatl as Matl, and Tezcatlipoca as Yaotl and Moquehqueloatzin, is One Death (Ce Miquiztli). Death is the sixth day-sign, and the moon god Tecciztecatl its patron deity. Tecciztecatl was the lord-priest who offered many implements and much attire made of gold, precious stones, and feathers to become the Fifth Sun, but threw himself second rather than first into the transforming fire (of Xiuhteuctli) and therefore became the moon.[27] Michel Graulich (1997, 126–27) writes that "the moon, Tecciztecatl-4 Flint, then, corresponds to the civilized, the native, the farmer. He still has power but no longer has valor." Given the rich yet somewhat cowardly figure of Tecciztecatl, Graulich posits that the moon is associated with the splendid, sedentary culture of the Toltecs, whose legendary priest-king was the deified hero Topiltzin Quetzalcoatl.

The sixth trecena, opened by One Death, also has as regent Tecciztecatl, along with the godly forces of Tezcatlipoca or of Tonatiuh. Tonatiuh, who was the sun god and patron of warriors, was the "theoretical recipient of all blood sacrifice" (Nicholson 1971, 424–25), and emerged when Nanahuatzin threw himself into the transformational fire. As gods of war and of sacrifice as well as possible patrons of the sixth trecena, Tezcatlipoca and Tonatiuh have correspondences with the self-proclaimed identities of the speaker of the nahualtocaitl as Yaotl, Moquehqueloatzin, and Quetzalcoatl. The Lord of the Night of One Death is Piltzinteuctli, a youthful, solar fertility deity presiding over flowers, feasting, painting, and gaming (Nicholson 1971, 417), all very civilized activities belonging to sedentary cultures. The invoked deities thus resonate with Toltec culture. The moon god Tecciztecatl, patron deity of the day-sign Death and the sixth trecena, presents offerings associated with the sedentary, rich, and civilized Toltec culture; Topiltzin Quetzalcoatl is priest-king of the Toltecs; and Piltzinteuctli is the youthful god of feasting and gaming pleasures. Finally, Quetzalcoatl is creator god of the Toltecs and patron of the pochtecas of wealthy Cholula, whose prime location in the center of the Mexican Highlands made it the predominant economic and trading hub of the region during Postclassic times (Carrasco 1982, 133–40).[28]

Summoned as well is One Flint (Ce Tecpatl). Flint is always the eighteenth day-sign in the twenty-day count, and it is presided over by the aforementioned Chalchiutotolin, or Jade Turkey. One Flint is in the first position of the tenth trecena. The patrons of this trecena are Mictlanteuctli, the Lord of the Underworld, and Tonatiuh, the warrior sun god. Xiuhteuctli is both the Lord of the Night and the Lord of the Day for One Flint. As Lord of the Night Xiuhteuctli dwelled in Mictlan, and thus was present on the journey to the underworld as part of the cycle of death and rebirth (Carrasco 1999, 104). One of the feasts held in his honor—Xocotl Huetzi—commemorated his descent to Mictlan in order to revive or transform dead vegetation (Limón Olvera 2001, 62, 68).

Given that the flint was used in human sacrifice (Olivier 2003, 109–11), it may be fitting that Xiuhteuctli appears as Lord of the Day and Lord of the Night in One Tecpatl, as if to emphasize the dimension of death and darkness preceding life involved in sacrifices using the flint stone. Motolinía (1951, 114–15) observed that fires were started using flint, which was also the material used for sacrificial knives; this connection establishes a metonymical correspondence among flint, fire, and sacrifice. Although Ruiz de Alarcón, Serna, and Coe and Whittaker merely mention the wooden staff or club as a weapon in their respective translations, Andrews and Hassig (1984, 75–76) posit that One Flint is the calendrical or birth name for the knife, and One Death, the birth name for the rocks to be hurled against enemies, referencing two more types of weapons. Whichever interpretation is correct, there are close correspondences among the three calendrical names. The inscribed voice of Quetzalcoatl predicts that, like the powerful, priestly club, rocks, and knife he has brought forth, stones, trees, and the earth itself will become drunk, intoxicated with spilled red blood. Being covered and colored in spilled human blood is portrayed as an exhilarating event, craved by the deities and enabled by the tlamacazque, the priestly power entities that made things happen by giving something or offering sacrifices.

After reiterating the godly powers of insensibility, the illocutionary voice speaks about the oncoming human enemy as follows:[29]

> [1] Ca ye nō iz huītzeh nohuēltīhuān, notlācaxīlōhuān. Ye quihuālhuīcah in nohuēltīuh, in Xōchiquetzal. Quihuālhuīcah in iihīyo yez, in īchcatlahuītec, in īcpateuh, in īc nēchahāhuiltīzqueh.
>
> [2] Come on, for already my sisters come, humans like me. One of them has already brought a bouquet or a bunch of roses, let it be her breath; she brings her duster of cotton and her ball of yarn in order to offend me.
>
> [3] Already also here come my older sisters, my human kinsmen. Already they are accompanying hither my older sister, Xochiquetzal [i.e., a person who is ineffectual in battle]. They are bringing that which will be her breath [i.e., gentle, loving attack], her cotton fluff [i.e., ineffectual clubs], and her ball of thread [i.e., ineffectual rocks], with which they will give me pleasure. (Ruiz de Alarcón 1984, 77)

In order to diminish the power of the enemies, the illocutionary godly voice in the nahualtocaitl construes them as older sisters who are ineffectual in battle. The opponent's weapons are denigrated: the rocks become balls of yarn; the clubs, cotton balls and dusters. Scholars have pointed out that Aztec gender and kinship nomenclature is used in the conjuros to categorize entities (Andrews and Hassig 1984, 10; Gruzinski 1993, 166–67; Raby 2006). This helped the user to establish hierarchical, deferent relationships with invoked beings even when they were antagonistic, enabling the user to seek their cooperation or more effectively neutralize their negative force. The feminine and masculine realms could be beneficial, malicious, or both, depending on the gender of the user. Dominique Raby (2006, 302) points out that an entity identified as "my mother" or "my sons" would most likely have a favorable relationship with all users. However, when men are the conjurers, "older sister" has an adversarial connotation, perhaps derived from Huitzilopochtli's antagonistic relationship to his sister, Coyolxauhqui, in Aztec myth (309). Moreover, Raby argues that when male sorcerers proclaim nahualtocaitl, they weaken their enemies by representing them as feeble feminine entities or kin, armed with weapons made of cotton. Although not uttered by a sorcerer, the nahualtocaitl against highwaymen exactly follows the pattern Raby describes. The antagonists are human, are older sisters, and accompany Xochiquetzal, the goddess of love and patroness of weavers. Their weapons are cotton balls and they carry balls of yarn instead of rocks. Weapons like these cause pleasure not harm, and merely amuse the speaking gods.[30] One could argue that flesh-and-blood humans are as impotent and harmless to the disembodied Quetzalcoatl-Yaotl-Moquehqueloatzin as cotton weapons are to a warrior.

The last segment of the nahualtocaitl reads as follows:

[1] Tlā xihuāllauh Cē- Tōchtli Ahquetztimani. Tlā ximīxtlahpachtlāza. Tlā xihuāllauh, Cē-Ātl Ītōnal. Tezzōhuaz, titlapallōhuaz. Tlā īmītzcalco; ahmō zan cān in tīyāz, huel īītzcalco. Tlā xihuāllauh, Cē Tecpatl. Tezzōhuaz, titlapallōhuaz. Tlā xihuāllauh, Tlāltecuīn.

[2] Come, one rabbit (metaphor, the land), you who are standing or face up. Throw yourself face downward. Come you, heat, one time of one summer, be warned that you are to stain yourself and bloody yourself. Aim at the shins. Watch out that you do not miss the target. Strike the very shins. Come on, flint or rock, for you are to bloody yourself. Come on, let the turmoil of people now sound in my favor.

[3] Come, One Rabbit, She-is-supine [i.e., the land]. Throw yourself face down [i.e., remove any obstacles]. Come, His-*tonal* Is One Water [i.e., the club]. You will be covered with blood; you will be covered with color.

> Let it be at their sides [i.e., strike my enemies in the side]; it is not just anywhere that you will go, but right at his side. Come, One Flint [i.e., the knife]. You will be covered with blood; you will be covered with color. Come, Tlaltecuin [i.e., the path]. (Ruiz de Alarcón 1984, 78)

The last segment of the nahualtocaitl calls forth a new calendrical name: One Rabbit (Ce Tochtli). Serna, Coe and Whittaker, and Andrews and Hassig all follow Ruiz de Alarcón in considering this name a metaphor for the land or the surface of the earth. If they are right, One Rabbit may be not only a metaphor but also a metonymy, whereby an entity's time of origin substitutes for the entity itself. Specifically, I propose that One Rabbit would refer not to one of the 260 days of the tonalpohualli, but rather to one of the four day-signs in which a solar year could commence, and to its place within the fifty-two-year xiuhmolpilli.[31] Indeed, Henry Nicholson has pointed that in most indigenous accounts, the "final terrestrial creation occurred in the year 1 Tochtli" (1971, 400).

Louise Burkhart disagrees with Ruiz de Alarcón's translation of *aquetztimani* as "standing" and with Andrews and Hassig's translation as "she-is-supine." She believes "*mani* suggests extension, not standing" and points out that Molina (1992) translates *aquetza* as "levantar or alçar la cabeza," so supine is inappropriate. Burkhart proposes—and I agree—that the best translation is "lying face-up." As she did in a 1986 article, Burkhart emphasizes that an upward tilt is also essential to the meaning of the word (Burkhart, e-mail communication, August 18, 2015; Burkhart 1986, 115). Thus, if One Rabbit refers to the first year of the Fifth Sun after the deluge, the rendering of "earth lying face-up" could be approximated as signifying that the waters have finally receded and the face of the earth is able to look up or to some extent rise above the water. Additionally, One Rabbit is the beginning of the Toltec era and their calendar (Nicholson 2001, 40). The *Annals of Cuauhtitlan* record, "1 Rabbit is when the Toltecs began. Their year count started in 1 Rabbit," and later, "They said that the one they called their god made them, created them, out of ashes. This they attributed to Quetzalcoatl" (Bierhorst 1992, 25). Thus, One Rabbit brings together "the establishment of earth and sky" (1992, 25) in the Fifth Sun, Quetzalcoatl as the creator god of the Toltec people, and the calendrical start of Toltec civilization on earth. And indeed, Postclassic and Late Postclassic Mesoamericans considered the Toltecs and their founding city of Tollan to be the epitome of sedentary urban life, social order, and legitimate kingly authority in their era (Carrasco 1982; Feldman 1974; N. Davies 1977; Coggins 2002).

The illocutionary voice demands that One Rabbit, or earth lying face-up, "throw yourself face down." Andrews and Hassig (1984, 78) interpret this as commanding the land to remove any obstacles. Coe and Whittaker's (1982, 107) more deferential translation of "Tlā ximīxtlahpachtlāza" as "please stretch out" seemingly supports the same interpretation—if stretching out the upraised head is a metaphor for removing obstacles impeding the deadly strikes of One Water (the staff) and One Flint (the knife).[32] Both tlamacazque are informed of the anticipated outcome that they will be profusely reddened with the coveted blood of the enemy. Finally, the conjurer calls forth Tlaltecuin, "a ritual name for a pathway on the land" (Andrews and Hassig 1984, 237), as an ally, for it too will be drenched in the blood and redness of the impotent attackers. In the *Historia de los mexicanos por sus pinturas*, both Tezcatlipoca and Quetzalcoatl open up four roads through the center of the earth in order to disperse the floodwaters that had destroyed the universe, thereby opening up the way for the Fifth Sun. This also happened in the year One Rabbit (Garibay 1965, 32).

I propose then that the year One Rabbit situates Quetzalcoatl's speech act in the nahualtocaitl as having been uttered after the Fifth Sun was established and the time count of Toltecs had begun according to the *Annals of Cuauhtitlan*. Note that the opening speaker in the incantation is Quetzalcoatl, whom the annals identify as the creator god of the Toltec people. They, in turn, were ruled by the great priest-king Topiltzin Quetzalcoatl—first lord of Tollan and later patron of the pochteca in Cholula—who introduced the arts of making jewelry with precious stones, feather adornments, glazed pottery, and multicolored cotton fabrics, products that merchants would transport over long distances, rendering them vulnerable to assailants.[33] Before becoming king-priest of Tollan, Topiltzin Quetzalcoatl had been a warrior.[34] Indeed, recall that the illocutionary voice in the nahualtocaitl identified itself as a priest, and as Yaotl and Moquehqueloatzin, avatars of the adversarial Tezcatlipoca. Moquehqueloatzin appears in three nahualtocaitl in the *Treatise*, always accompanied by the name of Yaotl, suggesting that one of the ways Yaotl neutralized his enemies was by making fun of them. And indeed, Tezcatlipoca was known for being "the enemy on both sides" as well as the trickster who would play jokes on people to force them to confront their destiny (Olivier 2003, 17, 28–32, 43). Yaotl thus resonates with Topiltzin Quetzalcoatl's earlier career as a warrior (29) and with the warlike attributes of the Plumed Serpent.[35] The portrayal of Moquehqueloatzin as the disembodied mocker who feels nothing is closely related to the way the enemy in the nahualtocaitl is feminized and laughed at as helpless "older sisters." Although Topiltzin Quetzalcoatl is hardly a mocker—on the contrary, he is the victim of Tezcatlipoca's mockeries in Tula—the war waged on the perilous road is not against valiant warriors but cowardly thieves. Thus, it is not entirely out of character that Quetzalcoatl ridicules them.

I believe that any close reading of this—or any—nahualtocaitl, can only be partial and always already limited epistemically. However, the reading can nonetheless show that the godly and priestly identities, as well as the calendrical dates and names, that appear in the nahualtocaitl were not woven together in an inscrutable epistemic idiom from a forever radically inaccessible Mesoamerican elsewhere. For if nothing else, this nahualtocaitl can be mapped as going back to and carrying forward knowledge of Mesoamerican cosmogonic, generative space-times. It speaks commandingly about when the voiced godly forces generated primordial, foundational elements that constituted the culturally significant, iterative time of walking along the lonely roads that Juan Vernal would be taking centuries later. Davíd Carrasco has argued that such temporal weaving is characteristic of Toltec and Aztec sacred history:

> Through the songs, poems, ethics, calendars and histories, a world view was pointed in which present situations were understood as having been set in motion in a remembered mythic past. . . . All significant contemporary conditions originated in a primordial series of actions that would continue through the present and . . . [be] recreated in some future, but measurable time. (Carrasco 1982, 77)

I agree with Carrasco and propose that the genre of the nahualtocaitl also follows this temporality in which past, present, and future are condensed and their borders dissolved or at least made permeable. Indeed, this nahualtocaitl is a meticulously compact, scripted speech that inscribed Postclassic voices of Mesoamerican gods and priests who—after One Rabbit—had protected Toltec fleet-footed travelers carrying their precious civilizing loads along lonely roads. For when any pochteca took cover under the right names of Quetzalcoatl and called out the birth sign of the club he carried, the tlamacazque forces that coalesced in the calculated day of One Water were supposed to manifest themselves in immediate human time. The aim of the call was to engage their primordial executive powers so that the club would strike the approaching enemy accurately, with the utmost precision of a priest: "do not miss the target"; "it is not just anywhere that you will go, but right at his side" (Ruiz de Alarcón 1984, 78). In this way, the future possibility of being drenched in the coveted blood and color of the enemy was predicted to be successful and attributed to the club. And the forces of One Flint and One Death were also closely linked by helping the greedy knife and hungry stones to bring the fight to completion. These webs of primordial time could be performed or made present again by pronouncing the boundary-dissolving names of the nahualli. They had now been brought to bear once more by the tribute carrier from Iguala, and could and would be called forth by many other future couriers whenever they recited the nahualtocaitl, until the time of the current era ran out.

3

After fully transcribing the names of the nahualli Juan Vernal recited, Ruiz de Alarcón closes his chapter by stating that when "he [had] ended his false incantation, . . . he remained very satisfied, considering the good outcome as very certain" (Ruiz de Alarcón 1984, 78). Many Christian ministers and missionaries tending to the Indians mocked and discredited the old gods of Anahuac as Ruiz de Alarcón did in his conclusion. They believed their Christian explanations were intellectually superior and much more solidly grounded than indigenous ones in human and divine argument, letter, and authority. However, Ruiz de Alarcón did not deny that Vernal had actually killed his two assailants after pronouncing the incantation. He merely insinuates that Vernal's assumption of causality between the two events was in error. Specifically, the royal tax bearer was not deluded about having overpowered the two highwaymen, but only about assuming their deaths occurred in an unfailing causal relationship with the recitation of the nahualtocaitl. This does not however mean that Ruiz de Alarcón believed there was no causality whatsoever. The cura comisionado derided the Indians of his parish for believing that the "words of their invocations, incantations, curses, and protestations . . . have an infallible effect according to their meaning" (Ruiz de Alarcón 1984, 73). In line with the general Christian theological consensus of his time discussed in chapter 2, Ruiz de Alarcón believed that Satan, the universal—transhistorical, transnational, transcultural, transoceanic, transcontinental, and transtemporal—Adversary of Humanity had angelic, superhuman understanding of all operations of nature: "there was nothing in nature of which Satan did not know perfectly all the properties" (André Valladier, quoted in Clark 1999, 163). To the weak human intellect the devil's formidably superior knowledge of all natural properties of things could easily seem divine, but of course he was not omniscient in comparison with God Almighty. This was why the nahualtocaitl—or anything fabricated by the devil for that matter—could never be infallible: the demonic agent always risked missing something. Other times the devil—not unlike Tezcatlipoca—deceived and laughed at the people by making them believe things he knew very well were untrue or impossible.

Someone could sympathize with Ruiz de Alarcón's pastoral frustration that Juan Vernal continued calling on his ancient deities even after he was baptized and had been more or less informed that they were only names for the Prince of Darkness and his legion of demons. And he was right to despair, for there was truly little chance that Vernal would give up the language that had always protected travelers from bandits on the road. As long as it kept him unharmed while traveling, Vernal would go on voicing the old nahualtocaitl that even had the power to safely deliver tribute for the king of Spain.

CHAPTER FOUR

Requesting White Blood Tears of Sacrifice

A Nahualtocaitl for Harvesting Pulque Maguey

In an article about features of contemporary Mesoamerican practices of ensoulment, anthropologist Brian Stross writes, "Many peoples in the Western world believe that only humans have souls, while all other things, animate and inanimate, lack them. Spaniards arriving in Mesoamerica even questioned for a time whether the indigenous Mesoamerican peoples had souls. Native Mesoamericans, however, attributed a soul to all living things and considered all of nature to be alive" (Stross 1998, 31). This statement needs some qualification. The reasons why will inch us closer to the Mesoamerican epistemology informing the conjuros examined in this book. First and foremost, Spanish theologians, missionaries, clergy, and jurists did not question the humanity of the native peoples of the Americas (Adorno 2007, 106). What was lamentably in dispute, due to the greed or sheer ignorance of some Spaniards, was the level of rationality of the indigenous peoples.[1] Throughout the colonial period, the rational capacity of the natives was frequently compared with that of an uncouth Spanish peasant or of a child (González Novalín 1963, 324–26; Pagden 1982, 161; Kamen 1985, 200–201; Campagne 2009, 37–44). Thus, hardly any relatively educated Spaniard in the early modern period would have really believed that indigenous peoples did not have souls, just as they did not believe coarse, rude Spanish peasants or children lacked them. Moreover, the medieval and early modern Christian worldview posited that *all living things* had souls. The distinction resided in that the soul had manifold powers and operations that were not equally distributed among all beings because of their different species. Taking his cue from Aristotle, Thomas Aquinas attributed to all plants, animals, and humans a vegetative soul, and to all animals and humans a sensitive soul. But he believed only humans had a rational, subsistent soul, whose operations were independent from the immediate, corporeal senses and which could therefore support higher, more complex cognitive functions (for good or ill, as history has always shown us). Some of these functions are understanding of nonvisible things, the self-reflexive consciousness of the knower that he or she knows something, and the ability to comprehend or abstract universals. The sensitive and vegetative souls are nonetheless components of the rational soul unique to the human species, just like the sensitive soul of animals, capable of perception, memory, and emotion, also encompasses but exceeds the vegetative soul's powers of growth and reproduction. In sum, all living beings have a soul, but the powers that operate in them differ.[2]

By contrast, the Postclassic Mesoamerican epistemology deployed in the nahualtocaitl addressed not only plants and animals as sentient and intelligent social beings but also inanimate entities such as places, objects, cardinal directions, time-spaces and even colors.[3] Each entity has a soul, a *ch'ulel,* a tonalli, a force of awareness animating or breathing within their form, that makes them relational and intentional. They thus interact as "communicative subjects rather than as inert objects," which the ecologist Alf Hornborg (2006, 22) explains is a basic tenet of animism. We saw an example in chapter 2 when the calendrical names of the wooden club, the hurling stones, and the knife were called forth to strike with competent precision.

Entities such as forests, mountains, clouds, hilltops, rivers, springs, streams, rocks, and caves were and still today are conceived as either being alive themselves or being especially suitable dwelling places for deities, spirits, animal and plant guardian spirits, ancestors, or other preternatural, intelligent, invisible forces (Sandstrom 1991; Stresser-Peán 2011; Broda, Iwaniszewski, and Montero García 2001; Brown and Emery, 2008; Staller and Stross 2013). Hence, particular powers manifest themselves in these special sites, where humans can propitiate, communicate with, and relate to them in order to obtain benefits or fend off their destructiveness. Indigenous communities in Mexico, for instance, still believe nearby hills are full of water dispensed by the rain god (*tlatoque*), to whom they make offerings (Sandstrom 1991; Stresser-Peán 2011, 135–41; Staller and Stross 2013). Ceremonies petitioning for rain were still being held in 2001 on hilltops in the Sierra Madre del Sur of Guerrero, and in Alto Balsas, the Valleys of Mexico, Morelos, and Toluca (Broda, Iwaniszewski, and Montero García 2001, 321–29; Villela 2001). Caves believed to be inhabited by spirits can also become topographic shrines; that is, places of devotion because of the spirits that dwell in them. Figures of stone, wood, clay, and paper; houses; and a wide array of other entities may also be inhabited by spirits after specific ritual ceremonies are performed to attract them (Stross 1998; Laughlin 2000; Stresser-Peán 2011). All this evinces a world in which human, nonhuman, and even inorganic entities may wield (or contain) powers of awareness, intentionality, and volition. In the Mesoamerican relational worldview(s) nonhuman entities possess not only the vegetative and sensitive souls expounded by Thomas Aquinas, but also many (albeit perhaps not all) of the communicative competence of the rational soul and its concomitant perspectives, subjectivities, awareness, and understanding Aquinas deemed exclusive to humans.

In this respect, Eduardo Viveiros de Castro has pertinent observations regarding a transspecies human consciousness in Amerindian relational cosmologies:

> In sum, animals are people, or see themselves as persons. Such a notion is virtually always associated with the idea that the manifest form of each species is a mere envelope (a 'clothing') which conceals an internal human form, usually only visible to the eyes of the particular species or to certain trans-specific beings such as shamans. This internal form is the soul or spirit of the animal: an intentionality of subjectivity formally identical to human consciousness, materializable, let us say, in a human bodily schema concealed behind an animal mask. (Viveiros de Castro 2012, 48)

This consciousness can also be attributed to "gods, animals, spirits, the dead, meteorological phenomena, plants, occasionally even objects and artefacts" (47). Such transspecies egalitarian consciousness contrasts with the human superiority decidedly and resolutely posited by Christianity. Recall from chapter 2 that Jacinto de la Serna deemed as sinful the belief in the permeability of boundaries between humans and animals. For him, the (illusion of the) interspecies figure of the nahualli entailed a diabolic erasure of the "most beautiful creature," of the "image and likeness" of God, which is (wo)man (Serna 1892, 367). Although he articulated the superiority of humans in a patronizing way, Serna certainly expressed a central tenet of Christianity. For the Christian creed states that Christ was incarnated in human form and by "grace, i.e., the free gift of God of being united to the Divine Person belongs to the whole human nature, which is composed of soul and body. And hence it is said that the fulness [*sic*] of the Godhead dwelt corporeally in Christ" (Aquinas, *Summa Theologiae*, part 3, question 2, article 10).[4] For Christians then, human nature and its rational soul cannot but tower high above any other species or material form created by God. But it does not follow that it is incompatible with Christianity to recognize that other nonhuman species are sentient and intelligent, and that humans—although supposedly superior by divine design—have a duty and responsibility to take proper care of them.

1

In this chapter I examine a nahualtocaitl that addresses the pulque maguey plant, exhorting her to grow well and yield plenty of sap when she reaches maturity. It appears in the third treatise, entitled "Superstitions of Farmers and Their Incantations," which deals with various nahualtocaitl involving Mesoamerican staples: maize, squash, beans, and sweet potato. All these conjurations were aimed at enhancing the success of the crop and harvest by commanding the plants and seeds to be productive. They could have been used by regular farmers, not necessarily by ritual specialists. Ruiz de Alarcón decries in his introduction to this treatise that the "Enemy" meddles in and perverts even good human occupations. He explicitly refers to agriculture and activities essential for human sustenance. "It is thus that he [the Enemy] established among the farmers the superstition of the incantation and the idolatry of asking him for, and availing themselves of, his favor for good success in the sowing of, and good profit in the harvest of, any kind of seed" (Ruiz de Alarcón 1984, 121). In this statement the cura comisionado censured the relational stances of his indigenous flock's animistic outlook as superstitious. Since for him plants and seeds were not intelligent, rational, or volitional, attempting to persuade them to grow and reproduce was a vain observance. And vain observances, we will recall, were usually believed to be inspired by the devil in order to deceive, confound, and mislead.[5] In this sense, because the incantation addressed nonhuman entities as if they were rational and volitional, it entailed for Ruiz de Alarcón a diabolic mediation that needed to be uprooted. I will come back to the issue of sinful communication with nonhuman entities later in this chapter with regard to Archbishop Manso y Zúñiga's silence about Alarcón's extirpating exhortations.

The creole priest particularly denounces diabolical intervention in the conjuration for pulque maguey since "the astute Enemy has introduced and set ever so firmly in place among these Indians the vice of drunkenness" (Ruiz de Alarcón 1984, 121). He blames inebriation as "the principal cause" of the population reduction suffered by the Indians. However, Ruiz de Alarcón acknowledges that "at the time of Conquest" drunkenness was punishable by death because there were many restrictions on the ingestion of pulque, which was considered a powerful, sacred beverage. He does not dwell too much on these constraints since to do so would put him in the quandary of acknowledging that, at least regarding pulque maguey, the devil had been less successful in perverting the people during pre-Hispanic times than after the arrival of Christianity, when many restrictions on pulque were lifted. By the same token, it is only fair to point out that Ruiz de Alarcón was not alone in decrying the dangers of excessive consumption of pulque, albeit he did so in an overblown manner.[6] For even if the cura didn't know the story, the fall of the splendid city of Tollan because Topiltzin Quetzalcoatl imbibed an extra cup of the sacred drink was deeply ingrained in Mesoamerican Postclassic memory and cultural imagination.

— 2 —

The mescal plant, a type of agave, was and still is an extremely comprehensive source of sustenance in Mexico. Its use harks back to pre-agricultural times in Mexico and Central America (Bruman 2000, 12). When the agricultural crops of maize, beans, and amaranth were introduced and the use of agave for obtaining pulque, or *octli*, reached its apogee in Postclassic Tula (Tollan) the food value of the plant decreased (Mastache, Cobean, and Healan 2002, 264). For the edible part of the maguey is the *quiote* (a budding stalk in the center of the plant), and it never matures if the plant is used to produce *aguamiel*, or sap (261, 263). Other varieties of maguey were used as fuel, and its leaves "as roofing materials, as plates or platters, to make paper, to make cord with which they make shoes, cloth and all kinds of clothes. . . . This plant, by itself, could easily furnish all that is needed for a simple, frugal life. . . . There is nothing which gives a higher return" (Francisco Hernández, quoted in Mastache, Cobean, and Healan 2002, 261). These laudatory remarks about the wondrous, versatile maguey were written by Francisco Hernández, who had been Philip II's personal physician. The king sent him to Mexico in 1570 on a botanic expedition to gather information about medicinal plants.

As if all these highly expedient uses for the maguey were not enough—Hernández continued admiringly—the plant required low maintenance and was strong, sturdy, and highly resistant to stormy weather and harsh droughts. Indeed, as Parsons and Parsons (1990) and Parsons and Darling (1993) document, the plant is highly adaptable to many ecological niches, can be cultivated in many types of soil, and is productive year-round.

There are many species of maguey, but only those from which pulque could be produced were venerated by the Nahua people (Gonçalves de Lima 1956, 26).[7] The deified status of the pulque maguey in the Postclassic Mesoamerican culture of Mexico is consonant with the specialized knowledge required to obtain perhaps its most valued product, aguamiel. Because Ruiz de Alarcón complains about the excesses of drunkenness that may come about through the successful cultivation of this crop, he forewarns his readers that the species addressed by the incantation in the *Treatise* is that of pulque maguey. And sure enough, the nahualtocaitl for planting maguey deploys knowledge of the long process of cultivating the domesticated plant for the production of the sap. The incantation is divided into five sections, each corresponding to a critical part of this process.

Initially, the young maguey is transplanted from its original location to a cultivated plot, where it will remain until it is fully grown. Depending on climate and soil conditions, the average life span of the pulque maguey is anywhere from six to twelve years. The plant is harvested on the verge of reaching maturity, indicated by the incipient growth of a quiote (Bruman 2000, 67–68). Once this stalk starts to develop, the aguamiel is no longer available for human consumption because it is directed toward feeding the quiote, which may reach heights ranging from four to eight meters, with diameters of eight to fourteen centimeters (Parsons and Parsons 1990, 29). In order to secure the rich reservoir of aguamiel, the quiote must be pruned by trained eyes and hands before it starts protruding from the center of the maguey. The tight cluster of leaves protecting the bud tip of the quiote is removed, and then the floral peduncle is cut off with a sharp, pointed pole. This procedure is called the *capazón* (Bruman 2000, 68). From a few months to a full year later, the entire swollen surface of the cut quiote bud is punctured a couple of inches deep, and a cavity is opened at the *meyollotl*, or center of the plant. A week or so later, the *tlachiquero*, or sap collector, will begin visiting the maguey plant twice a day for between two and six months to scrape the soft interior membrane of the cavity so that the maguey will yield her aguamiel to heal the irritation. After six months to a year, the plant will be exhausted and its succulent leaves reduced to dry, fibrous strips (Bruman 2000, 69).

The first section of the nahualtocaitl opens with the delicate process of transplanting the young plant to the field. The digging stick used to remove the young maguey is the first entity addressed:

[1] Tlā cuēl eh! Tlā xihuālmohuīca, tlamacazqui, Cē-Ātl Ītōnal.
Tictecopīntēhuazqueh, ticquetztēhuazqueh in Chicuētecpacihuātzin.

Nictlālītīuh. Nictlālītīuh in cāmpa cualcān, yēccān, nictlachpānih. Oncān noconnotlālilīz; oncān mēhuītihtiyez.

[2] Come on, for already it is time, possessed one whose happiness is in the waters, let us go, for we are to dig up and lift out the worthy woman, the one of eight in order, for I am to go to plant her. I have put her in a very fitting and very fertile place that I have cleared for her. There I have to put her where she will be very much at her pleasure—as if he enticed her with the improvement of the new site.

[3] Let it be soon! Come (H),[8] priest, His-tonal is One Water [the digging stick]. We will begin rooting out Eight-flint-Woman (H) [the maguey] we will begin to set her upright. I am going in order to set her down. I am going in order to set her down in a place which is good, which is fine, which I have swept for her. There I will set her down; there she will be sitting. (Ruiz de Alarcón 1984, 121–22)

Unlike in the other nahualtocaitl analyzed in this book, the inscribed illocutionary speaker in this nahualtocaitl does not self-identify as a god, a nahualli lord, or a tlamacazqui. The speaker is however an authoritative voice that addresses the maguey with full certainty, knowledge, and a keen sense of timeliness. The urgency is clearly evinced in the translation of *tlā cuēl eh* as an exhortative interjection, "Come on, for already it is time!" (Ruiz de Alarcón 1984, 121); and "Let it be soon!" (Andrews and Hassig 1984, 122). Because the moment has arrived for something difficult or critical to happen—the tlamacazque or priestly powers residing in the calendrical name of the digging stick One Water—are called on to show themselves and perform the task: "Xihuālmohuīca!" Because this exhortation is in formal or reverential form, Coe and Whittaker's translation as "please bring yourself forth" (1982, 171) is closer to the original Nahuatl than Andrews and Hassig's "come" (1984, 122). "Please bring yourself forth" better expresses the desire for consent proper to the reverential voice than a direct imperative does. As I pointed out in the introduction, reverence is always very important, not only in this nahualtocaitl, but in both the genre and the Nahuatl language as a whole.

Coe and Whittaker (1982) and Andrews and Hassig (1984) both correct Ruiz de Alarcón's mistranslation "whose joy is in the waters" as "whose sign or His-*tonal* is One Water." The particular superhuman forces present on the calendrical day of One Water were already discussed in chapter 3. It is pertinent to point out, however, that One Water is used throughout the nahualtocaitl as the ritual name for a variety of objects: club, tree, wood, stakes, bow, and digging stick. Thus, calendrical or ritual names stand not for a single entity, but for several with shared attributes. Alfredo López Austin (1967b, 4) has already made this important point in his article on the rules of construction of this rich oral genre. As Andrews and Hassig (1984, 220) point out, all objects addressed or referred to by the ritual name One Water throughout the *Treatise* are made of wood. To these two observations I would add that they also share the quality or positionality of being instrumental in carrying out a specific end aimed at in the conjuro. In the current nahualtocaitl, the ritual name One Water attempts to mobilize the executive powers present in the wooden tool—digging stick, club, or arrow—that can carry out the delicate, sensitive task of rooting out or pulling out (*arrancar*; Ruiz de Alarcón 1892, 175) the maguey shoot.

The speaker attempts to influence the maguey by letting her overhear positive descriptions of her new abode. Speaking still to the digging stick as a tlamacazqui, or "one who gives something," the illocutionary voice states that the plant will be taken to a good, fine place where she will be sitting much to her pleasure ("mui a su gusto"), a fine place that has been swept for her.[9] Brian Stross (1998, 32) states that sweeping is still part of animation rituals in Mesoamerica today. In the next chapter I will discuss at more length the cosmological importance of sweeping in preparation for a hunt. The hunter's wife cleans and purifies the house for receiving the game her husband will bring home. Indeed, Ruiz de Alarcón intervenes in his Spanish translation to comment on what he understands to be the speaker's intent, saying, "as if he entices her with the improvement of the new site" (1984, 122).[10] Because it has been swept, the new location will be orderly, luminous, and purified: a place where the maguey will surely want to be. The swept place where she will be seated in honor serves as bait to lure the plant to install herself in her new environment, enhancing the probability that she will thrive in it.[11]

The enticement of the maguey assumes a relational epistemology in which the environment is made up of hypersensitive, intelligent entities that can be cooperative and friendly or turn dangerous if they are not recompensed properly. The mobilization of desire among the entities of the world has commonalities with early modern natural magic in Europe, which held that the world was a living entity crisscrossed by forces of love, attraction, and repulsion. The task of the philosopher-magician was to understand how these forces operated: "That the Philosophers, considering this affinity and bond of Nature, wherewith all natural things are linked to each other, did thence frame the Art of Magick, saith, and acknowledged both that the superiors might be seen in these inferiors, and these inferiors in the superiors; earthly things in heavenly, though not properly, but in their causes" (Porta [1658] 1957, 14). Natural magic consisted of the intervention by the savant-philosopher-magician in the key forces of attraction that bound beings together, both vertically and horizontally, in order to enhance their powers, slow them down, or neutralize them altogether. Of course, the shape of the Mesoamerican cosmos was very different than the Greco-Roman, Christian-Ptolemaic, or even Copernican concentric circles with earth or sun at the center, and thus it did not separate heaven and earth into the same categories of superior and inferior.[12] Still, Mesoamerican and Christian views of the cosmos shared concepts of influential celestial spheres inhabited by superhuman forces that constantly made imprints on the surface of the earth and that linked beings together. Knowledge of the operative force of consent and desire in nonhuman entities was recognized in the nahualtocaitl as playing an important role in producing the sought-after responses from them.

After the little plant was pulled out and taken to the field, the illocutionary voice continued in its seductive mode:

> [1] Tla cuel eh! Xihuālmohuīca, Chicuetecpacihuatzin. Ca nicān cualcān yēccan ōnimitztlachpānih. Nicān timēhuītihtiyez.
>
> [2] Be welcome now, noble woman of eight in a row, for here it is very fitting and a very good place. Here I have tilled and cultivated in order for you to be very much at your pleasure.
>
> [3] Let it be soon! Come (H), Eight-flint-woman (H) [i.e., the maguey]. Indeed here is the good place, the fine place that I have swept for you. Here you will be sitting. (Ruiz de Alarcón 1984, 122)

In transcribing the incantation into Spanish, Ruiz de Alarcón interprets *Chicuetecpacihuatzin* as "eight in order," because the pulque maguey were planted in aligned rows.[13] Andrews and Hassig (1984, 349n6) again disavow this meaning, stating that "eight in order" is the calendrical name Eight Flint, and *cihuatzin*, venerable woman, and that these names refer to the maguey.[14] There was a constellation of pulque deities collectively known as the Centzontotochtin, or 400 Rabbits, a few of which were known by their individual names, especially when they were patrons of a community (Brundage 1979, 159; Nicholson 1971, 419; 1991, 165–72). But because Mayahuel was "the primary goddess of maguey . . . the plant itself deified" (Benítez 2000, 83) the gendered calendrical name Eight-Flint-Woman in the nahualtocaitl reminds every specific pulque maguey plant it addresses of her highborn kinship to the goddess.

Mayahuel is depicted in several colonial pictorials and narratives as a fertility deity always closely related to the plant and its origin. Thelma Sullivan (1982, 24) translates her name as "powerful flow." Among the most emblematic pictorials is the *Vaticanus A*, in which Mayahuel is painted coming out of a maguey. The Italian annotator of the *Vaticanus* states that because of the extraordinary fertility of her four hundred breasts, Mayahuel was transformed by the gods into the maguey plant. Quiñones Keber (1989, 75, 78) rightly questions this comment, saying that the annotator may have confused the four hundred pulque rabbit deities with the breasts of the goddess, since nothing in the actual image suggests this exorbitance. But she acknowledges that in this pictorial Mayahuel dons the triple-pronged headband proper to fertility deities, and more importantly, has a bowl of pulque, whose precious content is indexed by a flower.[15]

The longest and most detailed narrative about Mayahuel and the origin of the pulque maguey appears in the *Histoyre du Mexique*. It takes place after the creation of the first humans, which occurred in a newly created cave in Tamoanchan. Significantly, the source locates the cave, and thus Tamoanchan, "in the province of Cuernavaca, which is Cuauhnahuac" (Thévet 1905, 27–28; translation is mine). Cuauhnahuac/Cuernavaca, the capital of present-day Morelos, was very close to the settlements of Xiuhtepec and Yauhtepec whence Ruiz de Alarcón drew some of his Tlalhuica informants. Furthermore, the very community of Yauhtepec had had an octli (pulque) god as patron in pre-Hispanic times (Nicholson 1991, 167, 171). Not too far away was Tepoztlan, where there was a pyramid dedicated to that community's patron pulque god, Tepoztecatl. The pyramid in his honor demonstrates the importance of this pulque god and its cult in the region. This supports the thesis that the area south of the Valley of Mexico was one of the centers of the octli cult during mid- and late Postclassic times (Jiménez Moreno 1942, 132–36; Quiñones Keber 1989, 74; Nicholson 1991, 171). It is fitting, then, that Ruiz de Alarcón would have recorded at least one nahualtocaitl for planting pulque maguey in this area.

According to the *Histoyre*, after shaping the humans of the new sun with bones retrieved from Mictlan by Ehecatl Quetzalcoatl, the gods became concerned about providing them with something that would make them cheerful and willing to dance and sing for their creators (Thévet 1905, 27). Ehecatl flew to the heavenly abode where Mayahuel was zealously guarded by her grandmother. The virgin consented to flee with him, and he brought her down to earth. When she was discovered missing, the infuriated grandmother and her ferocious star guardians, the Tzitzimimeh, pursued Mayahuel. To hide from them, Ehecatl transformed himself and Mayahuel into two branches of a tree: Quetzalhuexotl for him and Xochicuahuitl for her. This was to no avail: the Tzitzimimeh tore down Mayahuel's branch, ate it, and returned to the heavens. Ehecatl Quetzalcoatl then buried the remaining bones of the dismembered, devoured Mayahuel, from which the first maguey plant would be born (Thévet 1905, 27–28).

One of the many things to be noted in this origin story is that the mirth of intoxication was conceived as a venue for celebrating the gods, and thus as something sacred. The gift of the sacred liquor came at an excruciatingly high cost, however. It entailed a transgression and a terrible sacrifice as retribution or payment of this debt. Quiñones Keber (1989, 79) highlights the violence of this story and how it stands as a reminder of a god's sacrifice for the sustenance of humans, who were obliged to reciprocate. There are other origin stories for the maguey dealing with Mayahuel's prodigious fertility or her discovery in Tamoanchan of the plant's aguamiel (Sahagún 1989, 2:673). It is however the sacrificial element in the narrative from the *Histoyre* that resonates most forcefully in this nahualtocaitl and in the ritual calendrical name Eight Flint used to address the pulque maguey in the conjuro, as we shall now see.[16]

Flint, or Tecpatl, is the eighteenth day of the basic twenty-day count. As mentioned, the anonymous author of the *Historia de los mexicanos por sus pinturas* explains that tecpatl was "a stone or a flint with which bodies were opened up to pull out the hearts" (Garibay 1965, 29; translation is mine). Thus, tecpatl is the indispensable instrument in the *tlacamictiliztli*, or heart extraction rituals. As one of the twenty day-signs and one of the four year carriers, it is a fundamental, time-constituent image in the Mesoamerican worldview. The patron god-power of the flint knife day is Chalchiutotolin, Jade Turkey, a deity which was a domesticated animal like the dog and thus considered a natural victim for sacrifice. The turkey was also associated with the sin of sexual transgression in Tamoanchan—and hence with Tezcatlipoca—since it was imagined to die when it came into contact with adulterers (Olivier 2003, 115). Tecpatl as the calendrical name of the maguey plant in the nahualtocaitl underscores then the sacrificial element linked to the maguey plant sprouting from the mangled body of Mayahuel. Perhaps the Jade Turkey as Tecpatl's regent deity also alludes to a sexual transgression when the virgin goddess consented to be stolen away by Ehecatl and rode on his back.

Flint appears as the eighth day in the eleventh trecena of the tonalpohualli. The god-power of the eighth day in every trecena is Tlaloc, the rain god, one of the oldest deities in the Mesoamerican pantheon. Rain is essential for all plants

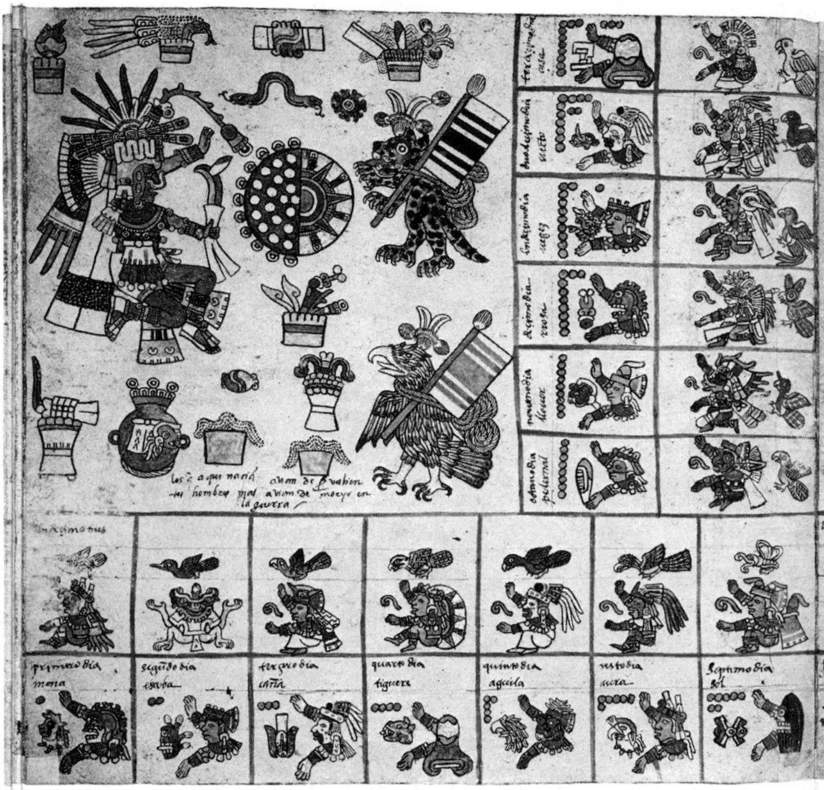

FIGURE 2. Trecena 11 of the tonalpohualli. Pahtecatl is the regent god, with a warrior eagle and jaguar wrapped in sacrificial cords and carrying sacrificial flags. A pulque jar is shown below the god. Eight Flint Woman appears in the lowest left cell of the vertical columns. Eight disks indicate the coefficient; the day-sign Flint is in the middle, and the Night Lord [Piltzinteuctli] is to the right. The adjacent cell features the Day Lord [Tlaloc] and the Volatile [Eagle]. *Codex Borbonicus* 11.
Courtesy of Special Collections, University of Miami Libraries, Coral Gables, Florida.

to grow, but maguey has a unique relationship with it because its aguamiel was a replacement for water in the dry regions of the Mexican Highlands. This substitution is registered in some codices where Mayahuel, the goddess of pulque and fertility, appears in place of the goddess of water, Chalchiuitlicue, Tlaloc's wife (Gonçalves de Lima 1956, 111, 158–59). The special relationship between rain and pulque as powerful fertility entities was also manifested in the *veintena* ceremony of the Tepeilhuitl (Mountain Feast) dedicated to the rain gods Tepeticton, in which victims with the insignia of the pulque gods, or Totochtin, were sacrificed to the mountain/rain gods (Nicholson 1991, 163–64). Many of the 400 Rabbits also belonged to the consort group of the tlatoque, or rain gods (Brundage 1979, 159).

The regent god-power who presided over the eleventh trecena was Pahtecatl, whose day-sign was Monkey. According to Sahagún (1989, 2:673), the Codex *Telleriano-Remensis* (folio 15v; Quiñones Keber 1995), and the *Vaticanus A* (folio 24v), Pahtecatl was reputed to have discovered the root *ocpactli,* which when added to the maguey sap, catalyzed its fermentation and yielded the highly valued pulque. In the *Codex Aubin,* the *Borbonicus,* and the *Telleriano-Remensis,* an eagle and jaguar appear with sacrificial flags facing Pahtecatl (see figure 2). Eagles and jaguars were fierce animals of the sky and earth, and consequently they represented warriors. In her comment on the eleventh trecena in the *Telleriano-Remensis* Quiñones Keber (1995, 178) posits that this trecena was probably consulted by warriors soon to face death on the battlefield or as sacrifices. The annotators of the *Telleriano-Remensis* do not make the explicit connection among octli or pulque, warriors, and sacrifice in the eleventh trecena but Sahagún's informants do in book 4 of the *Florentine Codex.* In the discussion of the day Two Rabbit, the informants declare that after drinking pulque warriors went to war mocking death (*Florentine Codex* 4:17, quoted in Quiñones Keber 1995, 178); that is, feeling strong and fearing nothing. Oswaldo Gonçalves de Lima (1956, 112–13) also writes that pulque was drunk before going to war and at the sacrificial stone, both by the sacrifices and by the tlamacazque who performed the heart extraction.

Besides its invigorating effects, pulque also had various medicinal uses. Motolinía (1951, 332) states that all indigenous medicines were administered with this beverage, and that when drunk in moderation "it is wholesome and very nutritious." Consequently, Pahtecatl was also known as the medicine god. However, octli had the ambivalent role of the *phārmakos.* Frances Kartunnen (1983, 185) translates *pah-tli* as "medicine, potion" adding that "this often has the sense of 'poison' as well as beneficial medicine." Indeed, if drunk in excess octli or pulque was dangerous because the root produces a very strong, intoxicating beverage. Finally, note that in the *Vaticanus A* and in the annotations to Pahtecatl's trecena in the *Codex Telleriano-Remensis* Pahtecatl is twice called the husband of Mayahuel. In the *Telleriano-Remensis* the god even exhibits certain costume elements belonging to Ehecatl-Quetzalcoatl, thus establishing a connection (Brundage 1979, 159; Quiñones Keber 1995, 177). Although Quiñones Keber points out that no other ethnohistorical source relates these two deities, the facts that Ehecatl stole Mayahuel from her seclusion and that Pahtecatl was deemed to be her husband may represent a subtle convergence of traditions expressed in the latter's donning of Quetzalcoatl's insignia. James Maffie thickens the connection between Ehecatl Quetzalcoatl and Pahtecatl, pointing out that the first day-sign of the eleventh trecena is Monkey, and that after the destruction of the second sun, presided over by Ehecatl Quetzalcoatl, the people were transformed into monkeys. He also mentions an intriguing statue of Ehecatl wearing a monkey buccal mask, and points out the connections between Ehecatl Quetzalcoatl and Pahtecatl as sexual partners of Mayahuel (Maffie 2014, 307–12).

Last but not least, another relevant godly power present in Eight Flint was the Lord of the Night, who for this day-sign is Piltzinteuctli, Our Noble Lord. I will analyze him more in depth in chapter 5 as the sensual god of solar night associated with fertility and the goddess of love, Xochiquetzal, as well as with feasting, dancing, and gaming. The last three activities were signature courtly events of sedentary Mesoamerican Classic and Postclassic culture, occasions when pulque was likely to be consumed. In still another associative tie, other patron deities of these sophisticated, feasting activities presided over by Piltzinteuctli were the five Macuiltonaleque (Nicholson 1991, 168). These gods were palace deities who, together with the terrible Cihuateteo, were equated with the disruptive and punitive Tzitzimimeh (Pohl 1998, 195). The Cihuateteo were the souls or spirits of women who had died in their first childbirth and came down to earth on their feast days to cause sickness to children (González Torres 1995, 38–39). One of their five feast days was One Monkey, the opening day of the eleventh trecena overseen by Pahtecatl. The Tzitzimimeh were thought to incite murder, lasciviousness, and drunkenness, especially at royal feasts, and also to punish the overindulgent (Pohl 1998, 202). This resonates with our nahualtocaitl because the *Histoyre* records that the Tzitzimimeh castigated Mayahuel for having escaped with Ehecatl Quetzalcoatl, and the intoxicating beverage of pulque was produced from her dismembered body.

Thus, the calendrical name Eight-Flint-Woman coalesces the powers of Tlaloc, the fertility-giving rain god; of Pahtecatl, god of medicine and intoxication; of Jade Turkey, the bird god of sacrifice; and of Piltzinteuctli, the sophisticated, transgressing god of the solar feast. They were all linked with the pulque maguey plant in the network of cosmogonic figural correspondences and origin narratives circulating in Central Mexico and to its south since at least the Postclassic Period. The gendering of the pulque maguey plant as *cihuatl* in Eight-Flint-Woman emphasizes the sacrifice of the plant, because in order to produce aguamiel, the quiote (stalk) had to be cut.

Finally, it is pertinent to recall that it was during the apogee of Tula (Tollan) that the cultivation of maguey to produce pulque became widespread (Mastache,

Cobean, and Healan 2002, 264)—perhaps along with awareness of its inebriating dangers. Indeed, in the *Anales de Cuauhtitlan* Topiltzin Quetzalcoatl was deceived into drinking a fifth cup of pulque, which led him to neglect his priestly duties, and even worse, to commit incest with his sister Quetzalpetlatl. He then abandoned the city in shame (Bierhorst 1992, 34–36). The *Florentine Codex* also contains an incident where Topiltzin Quetzalcoatl is tricked into drinking the powerful beverage. Intoxicated, he starts to weep as he discovers he has been deceived (Sahagún 1989, 3:209–10). The episodes that follow narrate the catastrophic fall of Tollan, although Quetzalcoatl does not feature in any of them. It may not be a coincidence that in the Postclassic Mesoamerican imagination, Topiltzin Quetzalcoatl—priest of Ehecatl Quetzalcoatl who had transgressed by stealing Mayahuel—was tricked, punished, and humiliated by drinking in excess the beverage from the pulque maguey that was produced from her punished, dismembered body.

The next part of the nahualtocaitl—or perhaps a different nahualtocaitl altogether—was recited when the maguey was fully grown. Depending on specific environmental conditions, this could take anywhere from seven to ten years (Mastache, Cobean, and Healan 2002, 262). This was the critical moment when the budding quiote had to be slashed so that the plant would provide its gift of aguamiel. In the incantation, the illocutionary voice addresses both the wooden stick that is to effectuate the decisive cut and the maguey plant that will undergo the artful, yet violent operation:

[1] Tlā xihuālmohuīca, tlamacazqui, Cē-Ātl Ītōnal. Ca ye āxcān. Ca ōtihuēiyac Chicuētecpacihuātzin. Zā moyōlcaltzinco no conoaquīz tlamacazqui, Cē-Ātl Ītōnal.

[2] Come here, possessed one whose happiness is in the waters {stick}. Now is the time, for you are already ripe, woman of eight in order {maguey}. Be informed that the possessed one, whose happiness the rains are {stick}, is to enter to the hollow of your heart.

[3] Come (H), priest, His-*tonal* is One Water [i.e., the pruning stick]. Indeed already it is now [i.e. the time has come]. Indeed you have become big, Eight-flint-woman (H) [i.e., the maguey]. I will just insert the priest, His-*tonal* Is One Water into your heart chamber (H). (Ruiz de Alarcón 1984, 122)

The illocutionary voice of the nahualtocaitl addresses both the digging stick and the maguey plant as intelligent, sentient, competent entities. It is time for the precise, executive power of the tlamacazqui One Water to enter into the heart chamber of the fully grown Eight-Flint-Woman to perform its duty. The language of the illocutionary voice models functionality by calling on the wished-for, accurate effects to take place promptly. It is a language that images the readiness and willingness of entities to accomplish what needs to be done according to who or what they are. It is a language that uses the powers of tropology, or linguistic substitution, to bind the entities of the world, and it does so knowingly, sure of itself, with full certainty of its capacity to obtain results. It is also a language of authority that speaks firmly but with the delicacy of deference, congruently with Nahuatl's notable investment in honorific forms. And just by communicating what is going to happen to the plant with reverence and respect, already some power, some attraction is supposed to be mobilized in order to entice the maguey to consent to the sensitive, painful operation.

The metaphorical analogy to human sacrifice in which the heart was also drawn out is surely an element in the production of meaning and in the expected (or hoped for) mobilization of powers. Although not represented in the fabric of the nahualtocaitl itself, Ruiz de Alarcón describes the actual capazón process of the efficient and expert removal of the quiote bud that was previously announced to the maguey. He articulates it clearly and openly as an act of heart extraction, except the maguey plant will not die immediately, as the human victim does: "Speaking and acting, he pushes the sharp stick to the center of the maguey and removes the heart" (Ruiz de Alarcón 1984, 123). She is left alone after the extraction for from two weeks to a full year, until the right time for the production of aguamiel comes around (Parsons and Parsons 1990, 31). The fourth and last section of the nahualtocaitl is then recited:

> Tlā cuēl eh! Tlā xihuālmohuīca, Tlātlāuhqui Chīchīmēcatl. Tlā āxcān. Tlā xicpohpōhua Chicuētecpacihuātzin īyōllōcalco tinemiz, tiquīxcualtilīz. Ca ye āxcān tiquīxāyōtīz, ticchōctīz, tictlaōcoltīz, tiquītōnaltīz, tiquīxmehmēyallōtīz in Chicuētecpcacihuātzin.

> Well then, come on for it is already time, do your duty [to the spoon], red Chichimec. Come on, already now scrape and clean your work, which is to be within the seat of the heart of the woman one of eight in a row, you are to leave her visage very clean, and you are to make her then cry and be sad and shed many tears and sweat so that a stream flows from the female, the one of eight in a row.
>
> Let it be soon! Come (H), Red Chichimec [i.e., the spoon]. Let it be now.[17] Clean Eight-flint-woman (H) [i.e., the maguey] in her heart chamber where you will live, where you will clean off her face. Indeed already it is

> now that you will make Eight-flint-woman (H) shed tears, you will make her weep, you will make her sad, you will make her sweat, you will make her flow at the eyes [i.e., exude aguamiel]. (Ruiz de Alarcón 1984, 123)

In this section the illocutionary voice of knowledge exhorts the copper scraper (or spoon) to proper action. The spoon is addressed tropologically as Red Chichimec.[18] The Chichimecs were nomadic hunter-gatherer groups from the northern frontiers of Mesoamerica. Red was often associated with the north in Postclassic Central Mexico, and it is the color associated with Chichimec entities in the *Treatise* (Raby 2006, 304–5). The Chichimecs were considered wild and barbaric by the urban, sedentary peoples of Central Mexico, but they were also thought to be warlike, courageous, and austere. They were identified with the valiant Nanahuatzin, the unrefined, humble, pimply god who unhesitatingly jumped into the fire to become the sun. In fact, many ruling dynasties in Postclassic Central Mexico claimed to have Chichimec ancestors (Graulich 1997, 126–28; Coe and Koontz 2008, 153).

Andrews and Hassig point out that throughout the nahualtocaitl "the word Chichimec is a metaphor for any of several dangerous or harmful things" (1984, 222). And indeed, in the context of this conjuro the Red Chichimec is a fitting substitute for the scraping copper tool. It is called on to perform a task that, although not deadly, is dangerous and requires the courage and unflinching resolve of a warrior. For after the stick (tlamacazqui One Water) has extracted the budding quiote (heart) of the maguey, the spoon (Red Chichimec) is exhorted to move into the eviscerated meyollotl (heart chamber) and carefully scrape the interior cavity smooth and clean. This process will irritate the surface skin, making the maguey plant shed the coveted, white-blood aguamiel to ease her pain (Parsons and Parsons 1990, 36). The tlachiquero will then come twice a day with the Red Chichimec to scrape the cavity, so that the maguey will keep yielding her stream of tears and sweat. Within a matter of months, she will have cried herself to death. The goddess Mayahuel is memorialized by and in the grieving pulque maguey that emerged from her broken bones.

The horticultural process of obtaining aguamiel is thus constructed, figured, animated, and talked about in the nahualtocaitl in terms of expenditures expected from an entity so that another may come forth. No hidden pleasure exudes from this sacrificial economy. An enjoyment of the dark powers of violence and domination or of inflicting pain on the maguey victim is not what moves the Red Chichimec to perform the scraping. Neither does the illocutionary voice of the conjuro conspire with the spoon to exploit the maguey plant or take advantage of her. Rather, the sacrificial imagery of this nahualtocaitl seems to draw its efficacy from commanding that a requisite service be performed by each entity at the right time, which is at once: "Come on, for now it is time, do your duty red Chichimec!" (Ruiz de Alarcón 1984, 123; "Let it be soon! Come, Red Chichimec"). The call to duty to all the communicative and sentient forces involved in the long process of obtaining sap from the maguey, as well as the expectation of their masterful performance, involves violence because these acts must be carried out regardless of the pain and destruction they may entail. This is the violence of the unflinching resolve of the Red Chichimec warrior. This is the will to timeliness, order, and expert performance that is modeled by the resolute priestly voices of the nahualtocaitl.

The sacrificial imagery in the conjuro for harvesting maguey exemplifies the tightly wrought universe assumed, unveiled, and performed by the ritual genre of the nahualtocaitl. It inserts the plant into a complex cosmogonic web of pleasure, transgression and sacrifice. For it is not by mere chance that the process of producing and collecting aguamiel is constructed with metonymical and metaphorical images that resonate with the heart-extraction sacrifice that it enabled, and with the mutilation of the transgressing patron deity from whom it derived. The sweet, much-desired gift of white blood came from the sacrificed maguey plant, which originally emerged from the dismembered Mayahuel. And pulque was also the inebriating, sacred beverage given to warriors whose bodies were to be opened with the flint, and whose coveted, precious blood would be shed at the *techcatl*, or sacrificial stone (Gonçalves de Lima 1956, 42, 112–13; Clendinnen 1991, 91–93; Quiñones Keber 1995, 178; Maffie 2014, 312). All these correspondences, links, and connections were condensed in the birth name of the venerable Eight-Flint-Woman and in the cosmogonic narratives of the gods that converged in that day-sign.

Everything then was closely tied and related in the prescriptive, hyper-intelligent language of the nahualtocaitl. This connectivity was not unlike the Neoplatonic orders of being that bound the world vertically and horizontally by virtue of proximities, analogies, and resemblances among entities (Foucault 1973, 17–30).[19] Perhaps it is also similar to Ficino's natural magic, in which specific words and songs were believed to be powerful imitators of the meaning of things and as such could produce effects (Ficino 2002, 357–61). Indeed, calling forth calendrical names and their web of connectivities in the nahualtocaitl was designed to make things happen, because doing so showed entities how to behave and replicate themselves in the world according to the knowledge, power, and remembrance of their godly origins.

— 3 —

In the *Treatise* Ruiz de Alarcón is not unaware of the nahualtocaitl's assumption that its tropological language has efficaciousness or executive powers. He concludes his report by remarking disdainfully that the user of the conjuro "asks—speaking metaphorically—that those lamentations and sweatings and streams be made, signifying that a large quantity of aguamiel should occur there, so that his harvest will be more abundant and the harvest of the Devil no less, since all of it comes to end up in their excessive and pernicious drunken sprees" (Ruiz de Alarcón 1984, 123). The creole priest's metonymical linkage of this nahualtocaitl to the devil's activity because the harvest of aguamiel eventually leads to inebriation is tendentious and prejudiced. For, given that Alarcón did not comprehend the meaning of the calendrical name Eight-Flint-Woman, and despite the sacrificial analogy that he did comment on, not much in the conjuro to the pulque maguey could be deemed to be outright offensive to Catholic doctrine. No Mesoamerican god or even priest was inscribed as the speaker of the incantation. Although addressing the spoon as Red Chichimec could have been suspect, its use as a tool for scraping was appropriate to its function. The plant was not expected to grow well unless it was carefully replanted, nor would its coveted sap be available if the budding quiote were not cut at the right time nor the interior of the cavity scraped on a regular basis for several months. Thus, Ruiz de Alarcón could not argue that the nahualtocaitl was invoking demons to do the horticultural work or accelerate preternaturally the harvest process by virtue of their superhuman knowledge of the operations of nature. Nor could he claim that the maguey, pruning stick, or spoon were being worshipped, since they were only being urged and commanded to fulfill their proper functions as crops and agricultural tools. True, the desired effect (the bountiful production of aguamiel) was spelled out to these bodies so as to give them a linguistic image of what they were supposed to repeat or copy extralinguistically. This could have sounded pointless or superstitious to an eager extirpator like Ruiz de Alarcón. Yet none of the conjurations for farming that he collected was expected to succeed without humans performing the material acts necessary to bring the events to completion. In this sense, the nahualtocaitl for harvesting the precious aguamiel that would later produce the (admittedly intoxicating) drink of pulque could not be said to meet in full the threshold for vain observance as defined by sixteenth-century demonologists. And perhaps more significantly, neither did the Spanish Crown in Mexico City prohibit the (supposedly demonic) drink of pulque.[20]

Still, in an area that had been a center of the octli cult in pre-Hispanic times (Nicholson 1991, 171), there could have many been other nahualtocaitl for enhancing the fermentation of the drink used in sacrifice, or for maximizing its ambivalent, intoxicating effects. Did Ruiz de Alarcón's informants slyly hold back conjurations for the pulque maguey they felt the Catholic priest would consider more scandalous than this one, which called out her calendrical name to obtain her white tears of blood?[21] We may never know. But what we do know is that the nahualtocaitl for the cultivation of the pulque maguey, whose fermented aguamiel had brought the people closer to the gods in pre-Hispanic times, did not cross the line of intolerable, idolatrous, superstitious beliefs and practices for Archbishop Francisco Manso y Zúñiga, to whom the *Treatise* was dedicated. Perhaps in the relatively peaceful years that followed the catastrophic flood of 1629 when he took office and the subsequent pestilence that desolated Mexico City, the archbishop finally sat down to read Ruiz de Alarcón's work. If so, he may not have seen in this nahualtocaitl preposterous, disconnected, or barbarically deluded ways of thinking about and talking to the world. After all, the archbishop could have considered, the late Emperor Charles V's own chronicler, Pedro Mexía, had written in his acclaimed and well-known *Silva de varia lección* (1550–51) about much more outlandish things.[22] For in a world believed to be influenced by the occult influences of planetary rays and celestial movements (Mexía 2003, 505–7, 515), marvelous, preternatural things were bound to happen. For example, Mexía relates that the first-century Roman-Jewish scholar Josephus had written in his *Judaic Wars* about a wondrous root called *baaras*, found near a place called Mecherante. The root glowed at night like fire and cured people who were possessed by demons. This mysterious root could not be pulled out of the ground except by spraying it with the urine of a menstruating woman. The downside of this very bizarre, very sexist remedy was that whosoever snatched out the root in this way perished unless he was already carrying a piece of it on his person (Mexía 2003, 515–16). In another chapter Mexía talks about contemporary testimonies to the existence of nereids and tritons, marvelous things "so much written about, and that [so many] people take as certain, that there is no reason not to believe" (Mexía 2003, 174; translation is mine).[23] And in still another chapter about occult antipathies among entities he relates that "mice are contrary to scorpions . . . so much so that the scorpion bite can be cured by placing a mouse on top of it" (Mexía 2003, 559).

The chronicler of the Holy Roman Emperor did not reject these instances of the marvelous in the worlds of Christianity and Classical Antiquity as outright impossible or superstitious. In comparison, the power words of the nahualli who merely tried to persuade the maguey to give more aguamiel by addressing her reverently but with authority were hardly incredible. True, the nahualtocaitl attributed to the maguey a rationality and volition Christians thought it incapable of having. But perhaps, after considering the matter for a while, His Illustrious Lordship Archbishop Manso y Zúñiga may have concluded that the conjuro's sensitive imagination of a plant's suffering, caused by the copious flow of tears that would drain her to death, was perhaps something Christians should ponder over more deeply.

CHAPTER FIVE

Fatal Attraction

Transgression, Love, and Death in a Nahualtocaitl for Hunting Deer with Bow and Arrows

Hunting wildlife is a predatory activity that involves taking animals' lives for the benefit of humans. In the Postclassic Mesoamerican worldview, the environment brimmed with intentional, volitional beings, and hunting entailed a conspicuous debt contracted by the hunter toward animals and their spirit keepers. Eduardo Viveiros de Castro (2012, 59) has argued that in Amerindian relational cosmologies hunting has been valorized "as the archetypal mode of practical interaction with the non-human world" even among horticulturalist societies.[1] Closer to the Mesoamerican cultural area, Danièle Dehouve (2008) and H. E. M. Braakhuis (2001, 2009) also propose that hunting has offered an animistic symbolic model for agricultural practices up to the present time. Hunters and agriculturalists engage in marriage relationships with the game or crops they will consume. They establish pacts with the plants' or animals' spiritual keepers as fathers-in-law and carry out rituals of renaissance so that the supply of food sources continues being generated for humans. Indeed, even today among indigenous communities in Guerrero, Yucatán, Panama, Oaxaca, Puebla, and Guatemala that self-identify as Christian, ritual ceremonies intended to negotiate permission from keeper spirits have been observed in hunting and agricultural practices (Laughlin 2000; Braakhuis 2001, 2009; Brown and Emery 2008; Dehouve 2008, 2010; Sandstrom 1991; Sandstrom and García Valencia 2005;

Taube 2003; Olivier 2014). Brown and Emery (2008, 311) explain that negligent hunters who do not observe ceremonial and ritual protocols risk angering animal guardian spirits who can then cause them serious illness or even death. Horticulturalists who do not perform proper homage rituals after harvest may lose their tonalli soul, which can then be captured by a wrathful earth (Dehouve 2008, 13). Because nonhuman entities have emotions, awareness, and intentionality—or are inhabited by spirits who have them—they are capable of retaliating against or harming humans who do not properly address, serve, or take care of them (Laughlin 2000; Taube 2003; Viveiros de Castro 2004, 2012; Brown and Emery 2008, 302).

In this chapter I discuss a nahualtocaitl for hunting deer with bow and arrows that enacts this animistic, relational Mesoamerican epistemology in a powerful way. It appears in the second tract of the *Treatise*, the same location as the conjuro for traveling safely on lonely roads (see chapter 3). As mentioned, the second tract contains nahualtocaitl which have to do—more or less tenuously—with enhancing the success of activities in different trades. I say tenuously because farming, much like hunting, cutting wood, and rigging limekilns, should certainly be considered a sustenance activity. Yet Ruiz de Alarcón groups the conjurations for agricultural activities in a separate tract. The satisfactoriness of the general structure of the *Treatise* aside, in this book I have chosen to discuss the nahualtocaitl for hunting—which belongs to the second tract—after the one for harvesting pulque maguey, which opens the third. This order facilitates the flow of my discussion about the sensitive, highly socialized environment enacted in them.

The nahualtocaitl for hunting deer with bow and arrows follows the longest conjuro in the *Treatise*, also for hunting deer, but using snares. These two nahualtocaitl mobilize traditions of progenitor relations between deer and maize, hunting, and the birth of the god of agriculture that have deep roots in Postclassic Mesoamerica. Although I will engage both conjuros to some extent, I have chosen to focus on the one for hunting with arrows because its brevity allows me to explore it in greater detail. I am also interested in this conjuro because Ruiz de Alarcón offers significant information about the claims of its efficaciousness by its user, Agustín Jacobo. Moreover, the conjuro to hunt deer with snares has been recently analyzed by Danièle Dehouve (2010).[2] Rather than revisiting her reading, I highlight her main insights to see how they bring me closer to the cosmogonic narratives enacted in the nahualtocaitl for archers.

Recall that the Nahuatl used in the *Treatise* is a Coixca-Tlalhuica variety, which was very close to Mexicano, the Nahuatl spoken by the Mexicans, but was considered "less refined" (Harvey 1972, 12:300). As previously noted, the Coixca and Tlalhuica peoples were part of the second wave of Nahuatl-speaking immigrant groups that established themselves in valleys surrounding the Basin of Mexico during the thirteenth century (Harvey 1972, 311; Hémond 1996, 271; Dehouve 1994, 31; Maldonado Jiménez 2000; Smith 2012, 38). The Coixca migrated to the present state of Guerrero and captured territory from the Chontals who were previously established there. The Tlalhuica settled in the area of Morelos. Both the Tlalhuica and Coixca coexisted in more or less tense relations with their non-Nahua-speaking neighbors until the Tlalhuica defeated the Coixca between 1418 and 1428 with the help of the Mexica. The feared Triple Alliance then started intervening more in the area from 1430 on, and both the Tlalhuica and Coixca were conquered by the Mexica in 1460. Thereafter, they would be tributaries to Tenochtitlan, Texcoco, and Tlacopan (Harvey 1971, 606–7; Coe and Whittaker 1982, 6–9; Dehouve 1994, 33–48).

According to Sanders, Parsons, and Santley (1979) and Hémond (1996), the Coixca region of the Balsas River was a habitat for the white-tailed deer.[3] This environmental factor could explain the presence of two different incantations for hunting deer in the *Treatise*, one of them being the longest conjuro in the collection.[4] However, deer were a major food source only for the Yope people farther south.[5] Sanders, Parsons, and Santley (1979, 286–87) estimate that by the Middle and Late Postclassic periods the consumption of white-tailed deer meat constituted only between 0.4% and 0.1% of the average diet in Mesoamerica. The warm-climate areas of the present-day states of Guerrero and Morelos to which the Coixca and Tlalhuica migrated were less urbanized and wealthy than the altepetl of Central Mexico. However, those warm regions had already been influenced by the sedentary Toltec and Culhua cultures. Thus, although venison was not a major component of the diet, the recording of two nahualtocaitl for hunting deer suggests that the presence of the animal may have made its hunting a significant activity among the Coixca-Tlalhuica, even if only for ceremonial consumption. Indeed, the fact that hunting deer has always been one of the most ritualized hunting activities leads Aline Hémond to affirm that it was "an expression of a relationship with the wilds more than a source of food" (1996, 269; translation is mine). In her publication about present-day hunting activities, maize cultivation, and sacrifice in the municipality of Acatepec in Guerrero, Dehouve (2008) argues that hunting deer provides the paradigm for careful ritual protocol in any activity involving resource extraction from the environment, especially farming maize.

Indeed, a close relationship between deer and maize as enabling agents and allies of humans in Postclassic Mesoamerica is still operative in several other indigenous communities in Mexico and Guatemala today (Myerhoff 1974; Benítez,

1975; Eger Valadez 1996; Braakhuis 2001; Dehouve 2008; Olivier 2014). Barbara Myerhoff stated in her beautiful ethnography about Huichol deer hunting culture that "the deer is the animal to which one is grateful. He gives the Huichol his blood as well as the peyote. . . . The deer blood makes the maize grow, and more important, makes the maize nourishing" (1974, 199). She points out that a deep connection between deer and maize runs through the Huichol cultural imaginary. And indeed, Carl Lumholtz had already reported in 1902 that according to Huichol myths "corn was once a deer" (quoted in Myerhoff 1974, 200). He believed that this association most likely arose from the fact that deer had been a main food source for Huichols, just as maize was in the twentieth century. Similarly, Fernando Benítez points out that deer and corn have many parallels among the Huichols. Both are believed to date from the beginning of time, "both engage in their own ritual death; and from their bloody sacrifice, their acts of creation, derive 'that which exists'" (Benítez 1975, 92). Susana Eger Valadez has documented a creation myth among wolf shamans from Nayarit in which "the magic of deer blood" is revealed to them. This deer blood had the power to "nourish the Rain Mothers and the Sun God, who would then permit the maize to grow" (Eger Valadez 1996, 269). For his part, H. E. M. Braakhuis (2001, 2009) has observed that love magic rituals in Mayan towns in Guatemala link hunting and maize cultures. The nahualtocaitl for hunting deer with bow and arrows shares a basis with these twentieth-century beliefs and practices. As we will see, it also mobilizes the forces of love and desire, summoning the deer as the transgressing sire of maize civilization whose progenitor's debts can be paid off only with its sacrifice.

1

In his introduction to the nahualtocaitl for hunting deer with snares Ruiz de Alarcón notes that anybody who set out to hunt in this manner had to undergo ritual preparation. These preparations involved ceremonies of sweeping the house, preparing the fire, and laying down three hearthstones (Ruiz de Alarcón 1984, 94–95; Serna 1892, 434). As mentioned in chapter 2, sweeping was a ritual act of purification. According to Louise Burkhart (1997, 33–34), temples were always well swept and the resulting cleanliness was considered an offering to the gods, along with bloodletting and other material sacrifices. Burkhart discusses how when husbands left for war women swept their houses more thoroughly and frequently (37). She also indicates that when merchants departed for long trips they exhorted their wives to sweep, suggesting that emphasis on maintaining an orderly environment at home—or failure to do so—could have a corresponding influence on the male household members' activities outside the house (35–38).

Three hearthstones were always placed at the center of the abode. They were the guardians of Xiuhteuctli, the old fire god who resided in the center of the universe.[6] In the *Annals of Cuauhtitlan*, the goddess Itzpapalotl instructs the Chichimecs to lay their game from the prescribed hunt on the fire, guarded by the three hearthstones named Mixcoatl, Tozpan, and Ihuitl.[7] Serna (1892, 438) states that archers conjured similar imagery. As they went off into the forest with their bows and arrows, they recited the following nahualtocaitl:

> [1] Ye nonēhua nehhuātl, nicnōpiltzintli, niCenteōtl. Ye nichuīca Cē-Ātl Ītōnal. Yehhuātl īhuān īācayo in ōquichihchīuh in nonān, Tōnacācihuatl, Xōchiquetzal, cihuātl. Ōmpa ihcatiuh Ītzpāpālōtl.

> [2] Already I am leaving, I, the orphan, the one god, and I carry the bow, the bow and its arrows, which my mother, the goddess *Tōnacācihuatl* {Ceres} and the one called *Xochiquetzal* {Venus} made and devised. And on the arrow there goes inserted and adapted a point of wide flint, which I am also to carry.

> [3] Already I am departing, I who am Icnopiltzintli, Centeotl. Already I am carrying His-*tonal* Is One Water [i.e., the bow]. It is he [i.e., the bow] and his reed [i.e., the arrow shaft] that my mother Tonacacihuatl, Xochiquetzal [i.e., my wife], who is a woman, made. Itzpapalotl [i.e., the arrowhead] goes standing there [i.e., I have Itzpapalotl with me]. (Ruiz de Alarcón 1984, 105)

Centeotl, the god of maize, is the speaker of the conjuro. As scholars who have studied the nahualtocaitl have observed, and I have pointed out in previous chapters, in many conjuros the inscribed speakers are the particular Mesoamerican gods who participate in the traditions referred to in the incantation. The image of the speaking deity invests the words of the conjuro with overwhelming executive authority. It is the most powerful depiction of illocutionary force possible. Entities in the conjuro are consequently addressed or referred to with the certainty that they will carry out the commands or wishes of the mighty, superhuman voice. The specific ongoing human activity for whose success the nahualtocaitl is being recited is thereby inserted in a powerful cosmic frame where it becomes an iteration of a previous primordial event.

"Icnopiltzintli" is in apposition to Centeotl and is one of his names. In an appositive construction, a noun or clause is juxtaposed to a name to explain, clarify, or amplify its meaning (Andrews and Hassig, 1984, 306). And, indeed, Icnopiltzintli refers to Centeotl's origin in the tradition enacted by this nahualtocaitl. Coe and Whittaker (1982, 145) translate the name as "the Little Orphan."[8] He is the son of Xochiquetzal, the erotic earth-moon goddess of fertility and sexual desire whose relations with deities show her to have been "very free with her favors" in the prudish words of the English Mesoamericanist Sydney Thompson (1939, 135). Xochiquetzal was patroness of love and prostitutes (Graulich 1997, 55). Because of her beauty and sexual power she had many lovers, both licit and illicit. Perhaps the most notorious offspring of her amorous affairs in the Mesoamerican Postclassic cosmogonic imagination was Centeotl, the god, spirit, or soul force of maize. But the downside of that felicitous love encounter was that her child, Centeotl, had no father at home. He was thus an orphan: "Icnopiltzintli," little, poor, and abandoned. Indeed, the theme of Centeotl's orphanhood is very extended. In some contemporary traditions, he is an orphan hero suffering persecution from his grandmother, who hates him because she has to raise him and sees him singing and dancing all day long—revealing his noble origins.[9] The resentful grandmother tries to kill her grandson or sends him to face deadly challenges against creatures—some quite ferocious—that Centeotl is nonetheless able to outsmart and defeat (Hernández Bautista et al., 2004; Sandstrom and Gómez Martínez 2004). Although the child-god always triumphs over his evil grandmother, she can abuse him because he is not well protected (García de León 1969; Braakhuis 2001; Hernández Bautista et al. 2004; Dehouve 2008).[10]

In the nahualtocaitl, shortly after declaring who he is, Centeotl enunciates the actions he is performing and voices the calendrical name of the bow, One Water. As explained in previous chapters, calendrical names belong to the tonalpohualli, the divinatory 260-day calendar. Calling the bow by its name of origin brings forth or mobilizes the tonalli, or specific heat life soul force pertaining to that calendar day, unique among the 260. Recall from the discussion in chapter 3 that One Water is the first day of the seventeenth trecena. Important powers that converge on this day-sign are those of Xiuhteuctli, the old god of fire, who is center of the universe and of the hearth and home. Xiuhteuctli is always the reigning patron of both the first place of the trecena and the day-sign Atl, "water." Interacting with these powers are those of the patron god of the seventeenth trecena, Chalchiutotolin, who is a sacrificial creature, and those of Tecpatl, the obsidian knife god who is the corresponding power Lord of the Night. All these forces, with some carrying more influence than others, converge on One Water and give it its special form, character, or energy-heat. And to call out the calendrical name is, at least to some extent, to mobilize the conjunction of these powers in the bow so as to optimize its performance and capacity to hit its mark—much like the club in the conjuro recited by Juan Vernal.[11]

In order to further enhance the targeting intelligence of the bow, the inscribed illocutionary voice of Centeotl informs and reminds it and the arrow shaft that they have been made by "in nonān Tonacācihuātl, Xōchiquetzal cihuātl" ("my mother Tonacacihuatl, Xochiquetzal [i.e., my wife], who is a woman"). Andrews and Hassig (1984, 341 n. 2) posit that Tonacacihuatl and Xochiquetzal are in an appositive relationship. Thus, Tonacacihuatl Xochiquetzal could be said to be the mother woman (goddess) of the speaker, Centeotl. Tonacacihuatl was the female counterpart of Tonacateuctli (Our Flesh [Corn] Lord), the principal creator deity (Spranz 1973, 285–86; Boone 2007, 40). She was therefore a primordial, generative power, the female half of "the primeval parents of both gods and man" (Nicholson 1971, 411). All things sprang from Tonacateuctli and Tonacacihuatl. They were invoked in prayers, but no major cult was dedicated to them (Spranz 1973, 286; Graulich 1997, 51).

A pertinent observation for the analysis of this conjuro is that according to Eduard Seler (quoted in Spranz 1973, 286) some informants interpreted one of the names of Tonacateuctli as a god of the old Chichimec hunting peoples of the north. As his wife or female counterpart, Tonacacihuatl would have helped him to prepare for the hunt, as indeed she does in this nahualtocaitl by making the arrows and the shaft. Tonacacihuatl merged with Citlacue or Xochiquetzal (González Torres 1995, 180), the latter of whom "personified the more youthful side of the earth mother . . . a goddess especially concerned with pregnancy and childbirth" (Nicholson 1971, 421). Eloise Quiñones Keber (1995, 162) observes that in the *Codex Telleriano-Remensis* Tonacacihuatl is depicted with a blue nose ornament in the shape of a butterfly and a headdress of green feathers, items which are also insignia of Xochiquetzal. The appositive Tonacacihuatl Xochiquetzal thus reenacts the blending of these goddesses because of their strong connection as fertility women or wife-mothers. Therefore, the powers of sex and regeneration were involved in the preparation of the arrows and shaft for the hunter-husband, maize-son, and inscribed speaker of the conjuro, Centeotl.

The flint arrowhead is called Itzpapalotl, or "Flint Butterfly": "Itzpapalotl [i.e., the arrowhead] goes standing there [i.e., I have Itzpapalotl with me]" (Ruiz de Alarcón 1984, 105). This goddess had commonalities with Xochiquetzal in that both had been expelled from Tamoanchan, the axis place of the universe where the gods had been created and where each had sinned (López Austin 1997, 98–120).

There, Xochiquetzal had illicit sex and became pregnant with Centeotl himself (Graulich 1997, 56). For her part, Itzpapalotl broke the branches of the sacred tree, making it shed its jeweled blood. Consequently, both goddesses, along with many other gods, were cast down because of their transgressions (Graulich 1997, 53). The gods then engaged in an ongoing, agonistic round of creations and transformations, during which time the calendars, and eventually earth and humans, would emerge (López Austin 1997, 84–120).[12] But the relevance of Itzpapalotl for this nahualtocaitl goes further. In another cosmogonic tradition of the transformational, generative times of the gods, Itzpapalotl was associated with Mixcoatl, god of the hunting Chichimecs (Spranz 1973, 85–86; González Torres 1995, 95). In the episode recorded in the *Annals of Cuauhtitlan* mentioned earlier, she ordered the Chichimecs (guided by four hundred Mixcoa) to shoot arrows in four directions to hunt the eagle, the jaguar, the serpent, and the deer, then to offer the game to the old god Xiuhteuctli (Bierhorst 1992, 23; Graulich 1997, 172; Davies 1977, 430–32). Furthermore, in a gruesome episode recorded in the *Legend of the Suns*, Itzpapalotl fell down from the heavens as a bicephalic deer. She then transformed herself into a woman, trying to kill Mimich, a Mixcoa who had chased her. Mimich shot Itzpapalotl with arrows and led the fire lords to her. After she was burned, she burst into colored flints (Bierhorst 1992, 151–52). Mimich's brother Mixcoatl chose a white flint from the exploded goddess, wrapped it in a bundle, and carried it on his back (Bierhorst 1992, 152). This made him a powerful hunter (Graulich 1997, 170). I propose that these origin stories involving Iztpapalotl's metonymic association with Xochiquetzal as transgressor,[13] her transformation into a bicephalic deer, and the bundle of her white flint giving power to the deer hunter are woven together and brought to bear in the nahualtocaitl when she is said to be standing at the arrowhead.[14]

The inscribed illocutionary voice of the hunting Centeotl then reveals the prey he is setting out to seek:

> Yēquen eh nichuīcaz notah, Chicōme-Xōchitl, Piltzintēuctli. Nicānaco. Nichuīcaz. Ye quichixcācah nonān, Xōchiquetzal.

> "I am also to carry and with this I come to catch and I am to carry my father, the one of the seven roses, a noble and a lord, for my mother, the goddess Xochiquetzal {Venus}, is awaiting him."
>
> At last I will carry my father, Seven Flower, Piltzinteuctli, [i.e., the male deer]. I have come to seize him. I will carry him. Already my mother, Xochiquetzal [i.e., my wife], is waiting for him. (Ruiz de Alarcón 1984, 105)

Centeotl is thus heading out with his empowered bow and arrow and the special shaft made by his mother, Xochiquetzal, to seize and carry back to her none other than his father. As the orphan child obeying his forsaken mother, he is uniquely and propitiously positioned to find him. For her part, it can be said that Xochiquetzal is trying to bring back her lover, using her son's obedience, the misery he has undergone as an orphan, and the enhanced hunting weapons she has provided him with.[15] The conjuration for hunting deer with bow and arrows feeds then on the passions of erotic and filial love, desire, and perhaps also hatred.

And who was this great, departed lover and father whom the very goddess and "epitome of voluptuosity and sexual desire, flowers, feasting and pleasure" (Nicholson 1971, 421), as well as her child, were longing to see again? None other than Chicomexochitl Piltzinteuctli, whom Ruiz de Alarcón (1892, 166) describes as "the one of the Seven Roses, noble and lord" ("el de las siete rosas, noble y señor"). Although not entirely accurate, the cura's translation into Spanish is delicate, sensitive, and poetic, noticeably rendered with care. The polished misnomer seems to be taken from an episode of a chivalric romance. "The One of the Seven Roses" evokes the nobility, mystery, and magic of Lancelot of the Lake, or of the Youth of the Sea, the Knight of the Green Sword, the Knight of the Lions, or Lisuarte of Greece. The latter were famous heroes, of aristocratic origins, appearing in the *Amadis of Gaula*. This novel was so beloved that Miguel de Cervantes made a point of saving it from the flames of the famous book burning performed by the priest of La Mancha as an auto de fe to destroy all the chivalric novels that had made Don Quixote lose his mind.[16] Indeed, as Rolena Adorno (2007, 214–19) has reminded us, writings about the New World contained frequent, ambivalent references to books of chivalry because of their engagement with magic, sorcery, and the wondrous. Of course, Ruiz de Alarcón may simply have wanted to denigrate the nahualtocaitl further by associating the name Chicomexochitl Piltzinteuctli with a literary genre denounced as pernicious and deceitful by many moralists in Spain (217–18). But if this was his intent, the creole priest ironically enhanced the fascination of the name through the lyrical, chivalric resonances of his translation.

In the Postclassic Mesoamerican world, however, "The One of the Seven Roses" was much more than a powerful, gallant nobleman of ancient and illustrious lineage. Piltzinteuctli was a solar deity who was the source of generative power and sexual lust. He presided over highly refined, sedentary leisure activities involving feasting, flowers, painting, dancing, and gaming (hunting for sport) (Nicholson 1971, 417). Cecelia Klein (1976, 6) represents Piltzinteuctli as a sun god, but one of the night and hence of the underworld. Piltzinteuctli was sometimes associated with Tezcatlipoca because in several sources it was Tezcatlipoca who seduced Xochiquetzal, stealing her from her husband, Tlaloc (Muñoz Camargo 1979, 203; Brundage 1979, 161–62; Graulich 1997, 56; Olivier 2003, 32, 214; Seler 2014, 329–34).[17] Tezcatlipoca also shared many attributes with Xochipilli, Lord of Flowers, "who was . . . a solar deity of music, arts and play" (Olivier 2003, 214; Klein 1976, 4). In some sources, Xochipilli was deemed to be Xochiquetzal's male counterpart (Klein 1976, 4; Seler 2014, 330) and, like Piltzinteuctli, the deity of nobles or palace people (Olivier 2003, 214). Here, then, is a merging of Tezcatlipoca with Piltzinteuctli and Xochipilli as seducers of Xochiquetzal, and as sophisticated princes and courtly lovers of music and flowers.[18] In a Tezcocan creation myth recorded in the *Histoyre du Mexique*, Xochipilli was even identified as the offspring of Piltzinteuctli and Xochiquetzal (Thévet [1548] 1905, 30).

Chicomexochitl is a calendar name: Seven Flower. Andrews and Hassig (1984, 222) explain that in the *Treatise* it is the ritual name for deer and that it appears in appositive structures with Teotlalhuah (Desert Owner) or with Piltzinteuctli. In this nahualtocaitl for archers, Chicomexochitl is used in apposition not with Teotlalhuah but with Piltzinteuctli—structured as a general, compound-noun metaphor. I argue that Chicomexochitl Piltzinteuctli condenses cosmogonic traditions more accurately than Chicomexochitl Teotlalhuah would. The former name establishes a metonymical, temporal relationship among the deer, the god, and the day-sign Seven Flower. Indeed, Seven Flower was the feast day of Xochiquetzal, a celebration in which weavers and painters were prominent participants (Serna 1892, 350; Thompson 1939, 132; Nicholson 1971, 435). Sahagún's informants said that scribes honored that day, as did "women embroiderers and cotton thread workers." They added that most "embroiderers lived in great vice and became terrible whores" and that Xochiquetzal was their goddess (Sahagún 1950–82, 4:7). Serna (1892, 350) explains that the patron god of this feast was Chicomexochitl, "inventor of the paintbrush," and that women celebrated Xochiquetzal, inventor of weaving. Later on, Serna (1892, 423) also states that Chicomexochitl was a manifestation of Piltzinteuctli.[19]

Especially significant however is that in the Codices *Vaticanus B 96* and *Borgia 53*, Piltzinteuctli disguised himself as a deer on "the day of the annual festival held in honor of his beloved, the moon goddess Xochiquetzal" (Klein 1976, 6), in order to woo, seduce, and make love to her.[20] Although he does not mention the day Seven Flower, André Thévet (1905, 31) records in the *Histoyre du Mexique* an origin narrative from Chalco in which Piltzinteuctli sleeps with Xochiquetzal in a cavern and conceives Centeotl. Some fragments of this event are also represented in the ninth of twenty sacred hymns collected by Sahagún.[21] Relevant to the present nahualtocaitl, Piltzinteuctli, Prince Lord God of the Early Dark Sun, palace patron deity of flowers, painting, dancing, and gaming, went down in secret to a cave moon lake of pleasure on the festival day of the lovely, lustful patron goddess of weaving and embroidery.[22] All the activities they presided over pertained to the high cultures of Mesoamerica represented by the archetypical Toltec city of Tollan (Carrasco 1982), whose emergence both gods enabled through the conception of the deity of maize.

Now, it should be noted that the deer, the gift animal of Mesoamerica, whose lovely hide proved irresistible to Xochiquetzal when Piltzinteuctli appeared perhaps disguised in that form, was linked to sexual excess and desire (Burkhart 1986, 119). Book 10 of the *Florentine Codex*—which deals with vices and virtues—points out that prostitutes "follow the wide road, the road of the rabbit and the deer" (quoted in Burkhart 1986, 122). This observation is relevant to our nahualtocaitl because, as mentioned earlier, Xochiquetzal was patroness of prostitutes. And clearly, in many versions of the origin narrative that resonates in this conjuro, the love encounter between Xochiquetzal and Piltzinteuctli constituted a transgression. Michel Graulich sums up the encounter as follows: "a prohibition is broken; Xochiquetzal-Tlazolteotl-Itzpapalotl picks a flower (in other words, engages in an illicit relationship with Tezcatlipoca-Piltzinteuctli); the tree breaks; Cinteotl, loved by the complacent gods is born; expulsion from Tamoanchan; Cinteotl appears as cultivated plants and the Morning Star, the first light of the world; and the earth appears" (Graulich 1997, 57). In short, the refined love encounter that engendered the beloved god of maize entailed an infraction, an excess.

Examining some calendrical elements of Seven Flower (Chicomexochitl) may help us grasp even better its deep relational logic as the ritual name for the male deer and how it is deftly woven into the nahualtocaitl. First, the patron deity of the sign Flower is, not surprisingly, Xochiquetzal herself. Flower appears in the seventh place only in the second trecena of the tonalpohualli. The patron deity of this second trecena is the great cultural god Quetzalcoatl, and the first day-sign of the trecena is Jaguar. The lord of the seventh day of the trecena is always Centeotl, and the volatile is Butterfly, the bird sign of Itzpapalotl. Finally, the Lord of the Night of Seven Flower is Tecpatl, or Flint—the sacrificial knife.

As the patron god of the second trecena, Quetzalcoatl exerted a strong influence throughout this thirteen-day cycle. In his priestly and kingly manifestation as the (archetypical) spiritual mediator between heaven and earth, Quetzalcoatl is associated with the jaguar as an animal that performs self-sacrifice (Olivier 2003,

102). In his aspect of Ehecatl, god of the wind, Quetzalcoatl wore black body paint and a pointed hat—an object associated with cultured elite—made of jaguar skin (Krickeberg 1985, 137–38). Another tradition relevant to this nahualtocaitl is found in the *Leyenda de los soles*, in which Quetzalcoatl is accompanied by a jaguar, a wolf, and an eagle to fight his uncles, the murderers of his father, Mixcoatl, whose nahual was precisely a deer (Bierhorst 1992, 154). In the *Historia de los mexicanos por sus pinturas*, the Chichimecs steal from Camaxtle-Mixcoatl the godly bicephalic deer that had been giving him victory in war and thereby providing him with blood to feed the sun. The Chichimecs' chance came when Mixcoatl slept with Chimalman, a relative of Tezcatlipoca. Ce Acatl Quetzalcoatl, first king of Tula, was the felicitous offspring of the sexual encounter that enabled the theft (Garibay 1965, 36–38). All these fragments and layers of tradition stories—whose temporalities are not always certain, especially regarding relations of precedence—converge in a particularly powerful, propitious way with Quetzalcoatl as regent god of the second trecena. But perhaps most importantly, in the *Leyenda de los soles* the great god of Mesoamerican civilization is associated with the discovery of maize. Looking for food to feed the newly created humans of the Fifth Sun, Quetzalcoatl transformed himself into a black ant to enter the Food Mountain where maize kernels lay (Bierhorst 1992, 146–47). Quetzalcoatl is thereby closely linked to Centeotl. Centeotl, in turn, as lord of the seventh day of the trecena, has as his corresponding volatile the Butterfly, the nahual of Itzpapalotl. Recall that Itzpapalotl burst into flints of many colors, and that Mixcoatl, the divine hunter-warrior of deer, took a white one as his power object. In addition, Itzpapalotl was connected to Xochiquetzal because both were transgressors who fell from Tamoanchan, and in this nahualtocaitl Itzpapalotl is the arrowhead Centeotl takes with him to bring back his father.

Jaguar as the first day of the second trecena also points to the presence of Tezcatlipoca, whose nahual is a jaguar (Krickeberg 1985, 134; Olivier 2003, 8). In addition to self-sacrifice, the jaguar was associated with war, transformations, and sorcery, as well as with the night, caves, fountains, fertility, strength, and darkness (González Torres 1995, 99; Olivier 2003, 95–98). Some sources relate the jaguar with the rain god Tlaloc. Olivier even proposes that "the jaguar, the caves and Tlaloc call up images of rain and fruitfulness whose mythical model is Tlalocan Tamoanchan" (2003, 98). As mentioned, we also have the remembrance of Tezcatlipoca stealing Xochiquetzal from her husband, Tlaloc (Muñoz Camargo 1979, 203). In addition, Klein (1976, 6) writes that "both Piltzinteuctli and his Mayan counterpart, the Jaguar God, were associated with the number 7." Based on the origin story enacted in the nahualtocaitl, and in the specific context of the feast day Seven Flower, the most pertinent aspect of the jaguar would likely have been his fertility. This, in turn, was also associated with darkness and fountains, since it was in a cave, at night, in Tlalocan Tamoanchan, that Piltzinteuctli made love to the fertile moon goddess Xochiquetzal.[23] Last, but not least, Flint as Lord of the Night of Seven Flower suggests that a sacrificial aspect is very much present in the ritual name of the male deer.

Regarding the transformation of Piltzinteuctli into the stately deer Chicomexochitl, some remarks by Ruiz de Alarcón about the nahualtocaitl for curing scorpion bites (sixth treatise, chapter 32) are illuminating. He says that "a certain Don Martin Sebastian y Ceron from Chillapan, very respected among the natives as a sage" reported "according to his heathen tradition" that during the first age "the one that is now a deer was called Piltzinteuctli . . . and he had some superiority over the one called Yappan, who is the one changed into a scorpion. . . . They now call the deer chicomexochitl" (Ruiz de Alarcón 1984, 206). In this transformational story of origins circulating in Ruiz de Alarcón's home province of Chilapa, Yappan was a penitent who was turned into a scorpion after being seduced from his penance by Xochiquetzal. The reported tradition focuses on Yappan and therefore does not specifically describe Piltzinteuctli's affair with the goddess or how he actually became a deer. However, the tradition clearly registers the god's transformation into Chicomexochitl and the fact that a sexual transgression had been committed with Xochiquetzal that resulted into a metamorphosis.

The Chalcan tradition recorded in the *Histoyre du Mexique* has it that after being born of Xochiquetzal and Piltzinteuctli Centeotl crawled under the earth; cotton then emerged from his hair, nutritious and delicious seeds from his ears and nose, fruits from his fingers and "from his nails came a kind of large maize, which is the cereal they eat now" (Thévet 1905, 32; translation is mine). From all parts of Centeotl's body came the most important crops that nourished the sedentary culture of Tollan. The *Histoyre* concludes that because of all he gave, Centeotl was loved by everybody: by the gods because he provided sustenance for the humans who would serve them, and by the humans of the Fifth Sun because Centeotl took away the deadly pangs of hunger. Fittingly, another of Centeotl's names was Tlazohpilli: the beloved child.

There is another origin tradition that resonates in the nahualtocaitl. In this version, after giving birth to the maize child his mother (namely, Xochiquetzal) drowned him in a spring (near the cave?) because she could not feed him (or perhaps show him in public?). But Centeotl was reborn from the water, and once grown up, he went back to Xochiquetzal and schemed with her to bring back his father (Braakhuis 2001, 393). Although the present conjuro does not make any explicit allusion to infanticide, rebirth, or return to the abandoned single mother, it does enact a concerted plan for a resolute and determined search for the sire. Hence, the inscribed voice of the maize god calls out in the nahualtocaitl:

> [1] Nictēmōco cān in comōlihuic tepēyacatl, cāmpa teliuhqui quitocatinemi. Piltzintēuctli, Chicōme-Xōchitl, nictēmōco cān mani. Mixcōācihuātl, in Ācaxōchtzin. Nichuīcaz.
>
> [2] I come to look for him wherever he may be, whether it be in the ravines or on the slopes, or whether he walks on the hillocks. I have come to look for the noble and the *principal* of the seven roses, and no less the one who is delicious or enchanted meat. I am to carry it to the goddess Snake.
>
> [3] I have come to seek him in the place where the mountain spur is ravine-filled, in the place where he goes following the rough terrain. It is Piltzinteuctli, Seven Flower, whom I have come to seek wherever he may be. And with it I have come to seek Mixcoacihuatl [i.e., the female deer], Acaxoch [H] [i.e., the deer]. I will carry him. (Ruiz de Alarcón 1984, 105)

Anxious to satisfy his mother's longing to have her lover back, or perhaps to retaliate for his absence, Centeotl acts as her indefatigable proxy. As I have suggested earlier, however, it is not too much of a stretch to posit that the orphaned child-hunter seeks his father not only for his mother, but also for himself. He expresses an unbending resolve to find and take his father in the mountain spurs full of narrow ravines; in rough, hostile lands no matter how dangerous, far, or steep; "in any place whatsoever" (Coe and Whittaker 1982, 145) where his father-turned-deer may be. Ruiz de Alarcón's translation into Spanish suggests an explicit parricidal dimension to the nahualtocaitl that is merely insinuated in Andrews and Hassig's and Coe and Whittaker's modernized English versions. In the criollo priest's version Centeotl says that he will carry the delicious and enchanted venison—his father—to the Snake goddess who, according to the context of the nahualtocaitl, should be Xochiquetzal. The criollo cleric mistakenly translates Mizcoaciuatl [Mizcoacihuatl] as "goddess Snake" rather than literally as "Cloud Serpent Woman."[24] Ruiz de Alarcón's belief that the nahualtocaitl were decidedly idolatrous may have led him to favor a translation that emphasized parricide and the associations of Xochiquetzal with lust and sex, and hence with a snake goddess as sinful temptress.

Andrews and Hassig (1984, 231) correct Ruiz de Alarcón's misreading. They interpret Mixcoacihuatl as a compound name. *Cihuatl* means "woman," and *Mixcoa* is a syncopated form of *Mixcoatl*, meaning "woman of Mixcoatl," or the female deer. Recall that Mixcoatl was the Chichimec hunter-god and astral divinity who carried Itzpapalotl in a bundle and whose nahualli was a deer. He had also fathered Ce Acatl Quetzalcoatl with Chimalman (Bierhorst 1992, 153). In other words, Centeotl is saying that he is seeking not only the father-deer, but also its woman: a doe. A number of traditions converge here, with Quetzalcoatl as offspring of Mixcoatl standing in complex metonymical relations with the god-child Centeotl.[25] In light of this origin story, I propose that Mixcoatl resonates here with Chicomexochitl Piltzinteuctli as a manifestation of Tezcatlipoca (Xochiquetzal's seducer), since the latter transformed himself into Mixcoatl after having created the earth (Garibay 1965, 33). The doe as the woman of Mixcoatl is a clear allusion to the erotic relationship between the hunter and his game that informs the activity of hunting, especially of deer (Braakhuis 2001; Dehouve 2008; Brown and Emery 2008; Olivier 2014). Centeotl comes to look not only for the father, but perhaps also for the doe after which or with which he may have run away, perhaps after Piltzinteuctli's transformation into the lofty Chicomexochitl?

According to Andrews and Hassig (1984, 220), *Acaxoch* is a name-form for deer.[26] It syncopates "reed" and "flower," and substitutes for "deer" (*mazatl*). In its four occurrences in the two nahualtocaitl for hunting deer, Andrews and Hassig interpret Acaxoch as adjoined to Mixcoacihuatl.[27] Coe and Whittaker (1982, 137, 140) follow Ruiz de Alarcón, translating *Acaxoch* as "nacaxoch" (*ynacaxoch* Mixcoacihuatl): "Flesh-Flower of Cloud-Serpent Woman." Alfredo López Austin and Danièle Dehouve each translate *Acaxoch* as "nacaxoch," in their respective translations as "the flower of the flesh of Mixcoacihuatl" (López Austin 1967b, 18) or "the florid [delicious] flesh of my older sister Mixcoacihuatl" (Dehouve 2010: 316, 327).[28] Specifically, their translations both place Mixcoacihuatl in an inalienable possessive state of delicious, florid (*xochitl*) flesh (*nacatl*). Although they sound somewhat strange, Ruiz de Alarcón's, López Austin's, Coe and Whittaker's, and Dehouve's translations nonetheless make sense because in the nahualtocaitl Acaxoch or nacaxoch always appears associated with Mixcoacihuatl rather than with Chicomexochitl. Thus, *ynacaxoch Mixcoacihuatl* could very well mean "the delicious flesh of the (doe) woman of Mixcoatl."

On the other hand, Andrews and Hassig's proposed etymology of *Acaxoch* as "reed-flower" is also plausible.[29] Although *Acaxoch* is less specific as a name-form than as a calendrical name, it may not be entirely coincidental that the patron deity of *acatl* (reed) as a day-sign in the *Codex Borbonicus* is Tezcatlipoca and the patron deity of *xochitl* (flower) is Xochiquetzal herself. As I have shown in this chapter, these two deities constantly circulate in multiple origin stories related to hunting deer, variously figuring as the seduced and abandoned Xochiquetzal, as Mixcoatl-Tezcatlipoca (the hunter with a deer power nahualli), or as Piltzinteuctli-Tezcatlipoca (who transgressed in Tamoanchan by having sex with Xochiquetzal). The erotic link to the deer may resonate in the name-form *Acaxoch* even if its etymology is literally translated as "reed-flower."[30]

Finally, to wind up this last section of the nahualtocaitl, Centeotl also goes in search of Mixcoacihuatl Acaxochtzin, esteemed deer woman of Mixcoatl, whose high regard is marked by the reverential suffix –*tzin*. The nahualtocaitl fragment concludes with the maize god's statement that he will carry him, namely, the male deer. Although there is no direct mention that Centeotl will be taking back his father in the form of venison, it is not unlikely that he will, since the child-god is carrying deadly conjured weapons.

And what of the father; husband; noble lord-deer; prince; and patron of feasting, dancing and gaming? What happens when he hears his archer son calling for him in the ravine-filled mountains, on the slopes, in the hilltops, or in the deserts, wherever he might be, in order to shoot him and take him back to his lover? If no deer are seen after voicing the conjuro, hunters "should bellow a lot and say *tahui* or Mixcoacihuatl" (Ruiz de Alarcón 1984, 106). Ruiz de Alarcón then represents the "dizen que," or popularly ratified knowledge, regarding the operative powers of the incantation. According to him, bowman Agustín Jacobo reported that "they [the people] state that the deer obey this incantation without any objection and that they not only show themselves but wait for the shot, which is also on target, and it does not miss by virtue of the incantation made to the bow and arrow" (Ruiz de Alarcón 1984, 106).[31] Jacobo further stated that whenever he used the incantation "he infallibly found game and killed it" (106).

Agustín Jacobo's words, as recorded by Ruiz de Alarcón, express a belief in the irresistible power of this nahualtocaitl. Perhaps the imagined or actually experienced efficaciousness of the conjuration lay in its reminder to every deer hunted of the pivotal role the deer once played in the momentous, transgressive conception of the maize god. When called insistently by the hunter in the guise of the abandoned Centeotl, all deer invariably stopped and listened. Charmed, seduced, and subjugated by the image of the child god and his mother's vehement desire to find it, the male deer-father would submit to the hunter-Centeotl's resolve to arrow it and carry it back home. The flesh of a deer hunted in this way and with this nahualtocaitl was then never just ordinary food. It was the venison of the revered animal of Mesoamerica that surrendered in order to pay a debt of love. This debt was initially contracted by the sacrifice of its very own hide, which enabled the illicit conception of the maize god who would feed the humans of the Fifth Sun.

Turning briefly to the nahualtocaitl for hunting deer with snares, Centeotl is the hunter in this incantation as well. The inscribed voice of the orphan god conjures a "cosmic complot" (Dehouve 2010, 308–12) of all the entities involved in the hunt to help him capture the male deer. The maize god speaks in that nahualtocaitl about his poverty, hunger, and lack of energy (because he is an orphan?) and also makes reference to Xochiquetzal's tears as well as his own.[32] As Dehouve convincingly argues, Centeotl is able to gain the favor of all the entities he invokes by eliciting compassion for his undeserved, miserable fate. But Chicomexochitl Teotlalhuah is tricked into the noose by the Orphan, who then makes fun of him: "Where is [Seven] Flower? Where is he? A game of fortune has been played. Ha, ha! People have captured things. . . . It is already over with" (Ruiz de Alarcón 1984, 102). In other words, the male deer hunted with snares is caught inattentive, unknowing, by surprise.

In the nahualtocaitl for archers I analyze here, the deer is also duped in the sense that the hunter disguises himself using Centeotl's voice. However, the animal is captured less by deceit than by the taming, powerful, and—for the deer—fatal attraction of love. Agustín Jacobo's unapologetic claim of the infallibility of this nahualtocaitl bespeaks a belief in the sacrificial economy of transgressions, sustenance, debt, and payment, characteristic of a Postclassic Mesoamerican civilizing imagination. Yet this economy can also embrace love and expiation as forces to be contended with. For whenever a deer stops to listen to the names called out by the archer disguised as Centeotl, then waits for the shot of death, the culpable transition to the maize civilization of Tollan is cleansed again with the sacrificial flesh and blood of the atoning animal of Mesoamerica.

— 2 —

Jacobo's statement about the powers of the nahualtocaitl for hunting deer with arrows has visual support in the first page of the famous Mapa Quinatzin.[33] This map was commissioned and painted in 1542 to defend Texcocan dynastic lands against the Spanish Crown (Douglas 2003, 285–89). In the upper middle left of its first page is an unnamed lordly Chichimec ancestor with long, loose hair, dressed in hide, and wearing sandals (*cactli*) and a crown of grass (*pachxochitl*). He is

FIGURE 3. Detail of the first panel of the Mapa Quinatzin. A Chichimec lord shoots a deer.
Courtesy of Dorothy Sloan Rare Books.

hunting a deer with bow and arrows. The animal, already struck by the deadly weapon, appears mesmerized (figure 3).

Although I do not claim any direct connection to the nahualtocaitl I analyze here, this image in the Mapa Quinatzin offers a striking visual analogy to the goal of the nahualtocaitl: namely, that (by voicing the conjuro) the archer may be able to persuade the deer to obey his command to stop, look back at him, and give itself up to the shot. In her analysis of the images on this map, Luz María Mohar Betancourt (2004, 216–17) suggests that the scene depicts a deer-hunting ritual to feed the sun and the earth; that is to say, the deer is hunted not for sustenance but for ritual purposes.[34]

I argued earlier that Ruiz de Alarcón's and Serna's reports of the prescribed practices in preparation to meet deer in the forest indicate that "hunting [deer] is a ritual whose symbolic importance far exceeds its contributions to subsistence" (Schaefer and Furst 1996, 17). It is as if the deer, as a wild animal capable of giving itself up in sacrifice, stirred in the human hunter a civilizing knowledge and sensibility that, if nothing else, tames and improves his ways. In the first section of this chapter I described how for twentieth-century Huichols, the blood of the deer makes offerings and objects sacred (Myerhoff 1974, 200). In addition, in some

Huichol myths, blood from hunted deer repays agricultural deities for providing maize to humans, a crop the deer itself taught them to cultivate. Consequently, the killed animal is treated with reverence and dread. However, not only Huichols but also the deer hunters from the Balsas River—descendants of those who lived in the region where Ruiz de Alarcón did his investigations—take the corpse of the animal home, place it in front of the family altar, and burn incense and pray to its body (Hémond 1996, 276). Dehouve (2008, 15–16) has observed similar ceremonies among the nearby Tlapaneca in Acatepec, adding the tender and delicate detail that a collar of eight flowers is placed around the neck of the male deer, or one of seven flowers around the neck of a female. Another significant, related practice is that corn balls are placed in the mouth of the dead buck or doe. Following Braakhuis (2001) on contemporary Mayan hunting practices, Dehouve also claims that the Tlapaneca observe a strict protocol for the consumption of the venison. The hunter must make sure to return all the bones of the deer to the Master of the Species, so that new animals can be born. Brown and Emery (2008) state that game and prey species are active and conscious participants in the hunt. They allow themselves to be captured only if the hunter has fulfilled all his or her ritual obligations. According to Pedro Carrasco, Chontal hunters abstain from sexual contact for nine days prior to the hunt, eat only once a day during this time, and refrain from drinking alcohol or smoking. After performing a propitiatory ritual in a spring, they fast for three additional days before setting out to face the (hypersensitive) Owner of the Animals so that he will allow access to his protégées (Carrasco, quoted in Olivier 2014, 132). Even the postmodern, non-indigenous western hunter today is warned on the Internet that good marksmanship is not enough to hunt a white-tailed deer. There is also a clear requirement of character: he or she must be patient and perseverant in order to merit the reward of a deer or of a "truly unforgettable hunting experience" (Berres-Paul 2013).

Needless to say, all these practices point toward the reverence in which the deer is held—at least in these parts of the Americas. Not unlike its sacrifice in the nahualtocaitl, which both enabled and expiated the transgression that originated maize civilization, the delicate, non-aggressive animal that gives itself up as a gift of the wild keeps trying to teach us humans how to conduct ourselves properly in a sentient, highly vulnerable environment in order to conserve the intelligence of its balance for us all.

CHAPTER SIX

Light, Mirror, and Knowledge in a Nahualtocaitl for Divining with Maize Kernels

In this chapter I examine a nahualtocaitl for the practice of divination. Valued as a foundational source of knowledge by the indigenous peoples in Central Mexico and its surrounding valleys, divination was strictly prohibited by the intrusive worldview of Christianity. In the preamble to the fifth treatise, entitled "About Seers and Superstitions of the Indians as Regards Divination" Ruiz de Alarcón expounds on the Christian condemnation of the practice. He quotes classical passages from the Bible and doctors of the church in which it is firmly proscribed. Ruiz de Alarcón acknowledges that the use of divination has been commonplace among all nations of the world. Christianity detests it, however, because unless authorized by God, "being by essence a pure contingency" it is reckless to depend on it for resolving serious matters (Ruiz de Alarcón 1984, 141). He further complains that although everybody knows that divination is a fortuitous affair, his indigenous flock was uniquely ignorant because they believed that "fortune told without an invocation will not have the desired effect" (142). Specifically, Ruiz de Alarcón claims that his indigenous charges thought invocations could influence the prediction and outcome of what (Christianity believed or experienced) was only accidental.

Because casting lots with maize is the subject of the nahualtocaitl in this chapter, it is useful to examine some aspects of what Thomas Aquinas had to say about divination. His views were especially respected in the Counter-Reformation Catholic Church, and Aquinas was one of the authorities Ruiz de Alarcón invoked on the issue. By examining Aquinas's position, if only very briefly, we will have a better understanding of why the Christian explication was incompatible with an extant Postclassic Mesoamerican epistemology about so-called fortune-telling practices. We will also see why Ruiz de Alarcón's depiction of the indigenous peoples as singularly confused regarding these arts was inaccurate. For if only in their refusal to give up divination, the Tlalhuica and Coixca from the Marquisate and the Chilapa province closed ranks with multitudes of Christian indigenous and non-indigenous peoples in Mexico, Peru, and all over Europe.

Thomas Aquinas (*Summa Theologiae,* part 2-2, question 95, article 8) says with regard to divination that there are three categories of casting lots: sortilege of allotment, sortilege of consultation, and sortilege of divination. For Aquinas, all involve either random chance or the interference of (superhumanly smart) demons, because "the actions of man that are required for sortilege are not subject to the disposition of the stars." That is, in the majority of cases, the effect of a sortilege is not caused by occult, natural cosmic astral forces. Thus, when Christians consulted soothsayers, in the best-case scenarios the diviner's guidance would be groundless or based on pure contingency.[1] Or much worse, wittingly or unwittingly, diviners would seek to communicate with preternatural beings and draw on their superior conjectural knowledge in order to help people gain control over difficult and uncertain worldly situations. By resorting to diviners Christians erred not only because they withdrew their trust in the providence of God, but also because they entered into the dangerous province of occult knowledge where they became extremely vulnerable to demons that could easily deceive them. As was discussed in chapter 1, in Christian theology angels and demons are higher species that can always outsmart human beings. By conjecturing with their superior angelic cognition, demons were able to lead humans astray by feigning to know about contingent future things or events involving the free will of humans, occurrences that nobody except God was truly able to know.[2] Six centuries before Aquinas, Eligius, Bishop of Noyon, had worked tirelessly to convert pagans from Flanders to Christianity from 639 until his death in 660. He warned his anxious and afflicted flock against divination: "No pretext, no illness, nothing whatsoever can permit of the presumption of your approaching or questioning lot casters or seers or soothsayers or enchanters." He urged Christians "not to place devilish charms at springs or trees or crossroads. The one who is ill should trust in God's mercy alone and receive the sacrament of the body and blood of Christ in faith and reverence" (quoted in Flint 1991, 89).

It goes without saying that many would-be or even recent converts to Christianity did not follow these admonitions. Even the long-Christianized masses in the medieval and early modern periods did not pay much heed to Eligius's warnings or to Thomas Aquinas's reasoning, especially when they found themselves in desperate situations. I have already mentioned in previous chapters how people turned to wise men and women when they were struck by adversity, such as serious illnesses or losses that could be catastrophic for them and their families. To persuade people that their habit of resorting to cunning men and women for remedy was not a mere transgression or dangerous affair, but a major criminal offense against God would be one of the main epistemic transformations to be carried out in the Reformation and Counter-Reformation (Clark 2015, 228–32). Enabled by the printing press, an enormous, unprecedented output of catechistic literature in both Spain and Europe was directed at pastors and literate audiences, reiterating the imperative to perform this epistemological upheaval.[3] Stuart Clark points out that "one of the most persistent images held by European reformers was precisely that they were faced by conditions like those in the New World or the Far East" (Clark 1999, 512). Indeed, in Spain many Jesuits argued that there were "Indies in Spain" and that many people in Asturias, Andalucía, and towns near Huelva would benefit from having Jesuits in their midst since they were in dire need of doctrinal instruction. In 1568 a certain Licentiate Herrera from Oviedo wrote to a former colleague who was then a Jesuit stationed in Rome that "there are no Indies where your lordships go with so much dangers of water and other innumerable miseries, that are in more need to understand the word of God than in these Asturias" (quoted in Campagne 2009, 40; translation is mine).[4]

When we consider, however, the significant difference between early modern popular masses in Europe and in the Americas, perhaps reformers and Jesuits protested too much about the European Indies. For in spite of their alleged ignorance, malice, and deceits, cunning men and women, their clients, and zealous reforming ministers in Europe all shared at least a rudimentary cultural Christian horizon that harked back anywhere from seven to fifteen centuries. In the New World first missionaries and afterward secular priests were expected to perform an even more daunting epistemic mission among their indigenous neophyte flocks, sometimes in very remote towns and parishes. New World friars and clerics had to undertake massive linguistic efforts in order to be able even to communicate with their wards, and to exert intensive ethnohistorical labor in order to have some idea of the ontologies they were up against. Their counterparts in Spain, France, Italy, England, and Germany faced no such obstacles. Entire books have been written on such topics. Suffice it to say here that whereas in Europe the Herculean efforts of Catholic and Protestant ecclesiastics were geared toward revamping popular customs, practices, and beliefs, in the colonies of the New World missionaries and clerics were expected to utterly revolutionize the millennial habits and worldviews of masses of indigenous populations in just a few decades. It is worth keeping these differences in mind when thinking about Ruiz de Alarcón's virulent denunciations of the indigenous traditional practices he recorded. For only one hundred years after the arrival of the Spaniards in Mexico the divining practices reported to him—albeit still inflected by centuries if not millennia of Mesoamerican fallen angels lurking the land—were not much more subversive, oppositional, or offensive to the Christian faith than the ones circulating in Spain and the rest of Europe.

— 1 —

All five conjuros for divination recorded in the fifth book of the *Treatise* sought the very ends that priests and pastors in Europe complained so much about: diagnosing and healing the natural or superhuman origin of an illness, predicting the outcome of critical events, or locating missing people or lost valuables. This coincidence of objectives may reflect the nahualtocaitl Ruiz de Alarcón selected to record, be a result of self-censorship by the declarants of the conjuros, or provide evidence of extended, transcultural human strategies to deal with misfortune.[5] Be this as it may, what is more certain is that Tlalhuica and Coixca resistance to the early modern, colonial attacks on divination was rooted in a Postclassic Mesoamerican epistemology that was evinced in the declared nahualtocaitl. In particular, divining the cause of events or their future course was not sinful, debasing, or pernicious in Postclassic Mesoamerica. Quite the contrary: it meant accessing a practical, cosmic knowledge inherent in the very way time and space operated in the world. The present was tied up with the past and the future in an orderly way, fixed by a calendric system whose fundamental twenty-day count was born even before the heavens, water, and earth of the suns were created (Boone 2007, 13–14). None of the nahualtocaitl for divination that Ruiz de Alarcón recorded entails the actual use of the tonalpohualli. But, as in the rest of the conjuros, the tonalpohualli is present in the use of calendrical names to invoke entities and mobilize the godly powers that systematically converged on their birthdates. The inscribed speakers in the five nahualtocaitl for divination are priests and gods appropriately associated with time and space: a commanding tlamacazqui in the first one, the lord of the Underworld Mictlanteuctli in the second, and Oxomoco and Cipactonal in the next three.

The two main methods of fortune-telling declared by the confessants of these five conjuros were measuring the forearm of the patient and casting lots with maize kernels. In the first divination procedure, the specialist measured the left forearm with his or her right hand, and how well the fingers of patient and specialist matched up at the end revealed what needed to be known. The forearm was thus invoked metaphorically in the nahualtocaitl as a *tonahualtezcauh*, "our nahualli mirror" or as *namoxco*, "my book," where the culprit of a malady could be discovered (Ruiz de Alarcón 1984, 144, 149). The forearm was also called *tochalchiuhehcahuaz*, "our jade ladder" (1984, 145), since the palm and fingers of the specialist would climb the forearm in order to gain precious, sought-for knowledge. It was also called *Mictlanehcahuaz*, "the ladder of Mictlan" (1984, 151), because the climbing fingers of the specialist would sometimes end up aligning with the fingertips of the patient. This could mean that the patient's end was near and the person would soon be in the underworld, leading to the metaphorical and metonymical name for the forearm as ladder of Mictlan. This could also explain why Mictlanteuctli was the inscribed speaker in the second nahualtocaitl for divining through measuring the forearm: he was the reigning lord of the place to which the ailing patient could soon be departing, or not. Ruiz de Alarcón claims that fortune-telling by measuring the forearm "is the [kind] most used by the Indians" (1984, 143). The rich, tropological, highly marked, reverential language of the nahualtocaitl enunciated during this measuring act certainly evinces the great esteem in which it was held.

The practice that best embodies the foundational place of divination in the Postclassic Mesoamerican imagination and epistemology, however, is the technique of casting lots with maize. Thus, this is the conjuro I have chosen to analyze. Before turning to this nahualtocaitl, some additional discussion about its cosmogonic context is in order.

In his rendering of the Postclassic Mesoamerican cosmogony, which follows closely the *Historia de los mexicanos por sus pinturas*, Alfredo López Austin talks about three different dimensions of time. The first dimension was anterior to creation, and there dwelled Tonacateuctli and Tonacacihuatl, eternal and self-created, with no beginning (see also chapter 5). According to the *Historia de los mexicanos por sus pinturas*, these two gods "of whose beginning nothing has ever been known" engendered four gods, or four manifestations of Tezcatlipoca, and a vigesimal count or pattern (Garibay 1965, 23–24).[6] After six hundred years, a saga of actual cosmic creations began, in which "violations, broken honor, death, struggles, and the dismembering of gods gave origin to beings who would be more intimately connected with man " (López Austin 1988, 1:61) Oxomoco and Cipactonal were created during this second era. The gods gave Cipactonal "some maize kernels, so that she would cure and divine" (Garibay 1965, 25; translation is mine). Then the days were made and divided into eighteen months of twenty days plus five remaining days: the xiuhpohualli, or count of years (20 × 18 = 360 + 5).[7] There is no mention in the *Historia* of the creation of the tonalpohualli. However, the xiuhpohualli used the combination of numbers and day-signs of the tonalpohualli to name its days and years (Quiñones Keber 1995, 155; Hassig 2001, 13; Boone 2007, 17; Maffie 2014, 434–35). Therefore, the tonalpohualli should already have been in place when the count of years was established. In the *Anales de Cuauhtitlan* Oxomoco and Cipactonal receive responsibility for the year, day-sign, and twenty-day period, while in the *Florentine Codex* they are the lords or very progenitors of the division of time who created both the tonalpohualli and the xiuhpohualli (Feliciano Velázquez 1992, 3–4; Bierhorst 1992, 24; Sahagún 1950–82, 4:4, 10:191). In these three sources Oxomoco and Cipactonal are also the first diviners.

Whether created concurrently or derivatively, the counts of the tonalpohualli and the xiuhpohualli would keep track of and even regulate the emergence and duration of the four or five ensuing suns that Quetzalcoatl and Tezcatlipoca were to create.[8] At least in the present era of the Fifth Sun, the tonalpohualli and the xiuhpohualli rotated simultaneously, having a coincident point of departure every fifty-two years.[9] This time unit was known as the xiuhmolpilli, or calendar round (see chapter 3). It can be argued that the nahualtocaitl recited to Ruiz de Alarcón entailed an implicit link between the tonalpohualli and the xiuhpohualli insofar as entities were called by their calendrical names to persuade or command them to behave in optimal fashion in the world of the Fifth Sun. However, there are no allusions to the days as part of the months of the xiuhpohualli in the nahualtocaitl, although sometimes day-signs may refer to year bearers.[10] Indeed, the twenty calendrical festivities of the 360 (+ 5) vague solar-year days of the xiuhpohualli concerned state or seasonal agricultural matters pivotal to the life of the community or the polity (Nicholson 1971, 434–35; Read 1998, 223–24).

Many of the deities propitiated in these community festivities were also patron gods in the tonalpohualli. But in the words of Elizabeth Boone (2007, 17–18), "no person asked the xihuitl for guidance. People instead turned to the tonalpohualli to know the forces that affected them personally." And the ones in charge of figuring out these forces were the tonalpouhque, the wise ones who consulted the pictorial books recording the tonalpohualli cycles (Quiñones Keber 1995, 153–54). People resorted to the tonalpouhque for divining the fates of newborns according to their birthdays, as well as for all sorts of personal affairs, such as when to perform marriage ceremonies, till the land, or initiate long-distance travel; how to cure an illness; or in order to confess one's sins (154). Thus, because the nahualtocaitl had to do with manifold affairs close to home it is fitting that they should also be highly concerned with tapping the godly powers patterned by the 260-day tonalpohualli.

—— 2 ——

Unlike the nahualtocaitl recorded in the second, third, and fourth treatises, those collected in the fifth and sixth, involving divination and healing, are necessarily recited by ritual specialists. Ruiz de Alarcón (1984, 143) calls them *ticitl,* warning his readers that the term refers to doctors as well as fortune-tellers and seers. The cura is not the first Spaniard to notice the admixture of Postclassic Mesoamerican medicine with divination, however. Alonso de Molina had previously interpreted *ticitl* as "medico o agorero y echador de suertes" in his famous *Vocabulario* of 1551–71 (1992, 113). This is a pertinent point to make for the present nahualtocaitl, because it suggests Molina was aware that the indigenous peoples viewed illness in a holistic way, as a result of both natural and preternatural causes. It also suggests that, to Molina, *ticitl* originally meant a caster of lots, not one who measured with the hands. Other more specialized names for those who divined with maize kernels (or sometimes with beans) were *tlaolchayauhqui* or *tlaolliquitepehuaya* (Nicholson 1971, 439–40) and *tlaolxiniani* (Coe and Whittaker 1982, 32).

The immediate, pragmatic objective of the incantation for divining with maize kernels is a medical diagnosis and prognosis. The use of maize kernels for divination is highly significant, of course, since it establishes a deep connection between this seeing art and the staple food of Mesoamerica. And indeed, this metonymical connection was made explicit in the *Legend of the Suns,* where Oxomoco is said to have cast corn kernels and Cipactonal to have divined that Nanahuatl would strike open the Food Mountain Tonacatepetl with a lightning bolt. Inside, white, black, yellow, and red corn for human consumption was found.[11] Serna documents this connection as still being alive in 1656. He declares in his *Manual* that the Indians venerated the Sierra Nevada next to the volcano of Toluca: "They said that there was where their gods Chicomecoatl—the Goddess of Bread—were and lived; and therefore they called it Sierra Tonacatepetl, which means the hill of the grains or sustenance" (Serna 1892, 283; translation is mine).

Visual evidence also supports this tradition of Oxomoco and Cipactonal as prime diviners. Famously painted on page 21 of the *Codex Borbonicus* (figure 4), and in book 4 of the *Florentine Codex,* they cast lots with maize kernels much as

FIGURE 4. Oxomoco and Cipactonal divining with maize kernels, center image. *Codex Borbonicus* 21.
Courtesy of Special Collections, University of Miami Libraries, Coral Gables, Florida.

Alarcón describes. In the *Florentine Codex,* they are depicted using a perspectivist, naturalistic pictorial language. Thus, they are represented as humans, not quite expressing the Postclassic worldview regarding the ontology of these gods of divination.[12] Another difference is that in the *Codex Borbonicus,* the diviner is the woman of the couple, while in the *Florentine Codex* it is the man. In the *Codex Magliabechiano,* a woman diviner is also depicted casting lots with what appear to be either maize kernels or beans in order to diagnose a malady, although there are not nineteen or twenty-five beans or kernels, as Ruiz de Alarcón specifies. In sum, the maize-tossing ritual accompanying this nahualtocaitl was documented in several independent narrative and pictorial traditions in Central Mexico. This suggests, of course, that this ritual practice was widespread, not restricted to the Coixca and Tlalhuica in the regions of present-day Morelos and Guerrero.

Turning now to the nahualtocaitl itself, Ruiz de Alarcón describes some of the paralinguistic acts that preceded its enunciation. They entailed the selection of nineteen or twenty-five of the most beautiful kernels from a maize ear. The seer then bit off the nib of each of the chosen kernels and arranged most of them along a carefully stretched-out piece of cloth, keeping a few in the hand (Ruiz de Alarcón 1984, 153). Having prepared the cloth and holding the kernels chosen to be cast in his hand, the ticitl recites these words:

> [1] Tlā xihuālmohuīca, Tlazohpilli, ChicōmeCōātl. Tlā xihuālhuiān. Mācuīltōnalehqueh, Cemithualehqueh.
>
> [2] Welcome, precious man, seven snakes, come also, the five solar beings, all of you who look toward one side.
>
> [3] Come (H) Tlazohpilli, Seven Snake [i.e., the maize kernals]. Come five-tonals-owners, one-courtyard-owners [i.e., the hands]. (Ruiz de Alarcón 1984, 153–54)[13]

The illocutionary voice addresses the entity Seven Snake, calling it precious or beloved noble (tlazohpilli) in order to communicate deep reverence and affection and thus attract its power. All scholars who have translated this incantation concur that "Seven Snake" refers to the corn kernels soon to be cast for the divination (López Austin 1970a, 4; Coe and Whittaker 1982, 311; Andrews and Hassig 1984, 154). By now we know that Seven Snake is not a metaphor or trope for the kernels, but a calendrical name from the tonalpohualli. It is also the most common name for the goddess of maize, at least in the Valley of Mexico (Nicholson 1971, 417). Ruiz de Alarcón, López Austin, and Coe and Whittaker assume that the addressed entity is male (in other words, the maize god Centeotl), but this is not necessarily the case.[14]

Only in the seventh trecena does the day-sign snake (Coatl) fall in the seventh day-place. The patron of this trecena is Tlaloc, the ancient Mesoamerican god of rain, who sometimes appears accompanied by Chicomecoatl as co-patrons (Caso 1971, 338; Boone 2007, 48). Chalchiuitlicue, goddess of water, is the patroness of the day-sign Coatl (Caso 1971, 337). As discussed earlier, Centeotl, the god of maize, is always the ruling lord of the day in the seventh position of the trecena, and he is also the patron Lord of the Night for the calendrical day Seven Snake. Moreover, in Late Postclassic Mesoamerican cosmogony the snake was associated with fertility, earth, and rain (Florescano 1999, 146), and it was also related to lightning by similitude (Armillas quoted in Florescano 1999, 146). We thus have coalescing in the calendrical day of Seven Snake two series of superhuman powers that are intimately related to the maize kernels to be cast. Tlaloc was revered as the owner—or efficient cause—of all nutritional plants, the agent of all fertility (Krickeberg 1985, 148). Suitably, Chicomecoatl was believed to live close to the rain god or to his tlatoque in Tlalocan, a place of plenty (Brundage 1979, 157; Graulich 1997, 249; Maldonado Jiménez 2000, 64). Thus, Tlaloc and Chalchiuitlicue are metonymically related to the maize kernels as agents of fertility. The maize gods Chicomecoatl (Seven Snake) and Centeotl are synecdochic substitutions of the kernels as the whole for the part, or the [godly] cause for the effect. In turn, the four gods form two gendered couples of rain and maize. It is interesting to note that in the *tonalamatl* (sacred divinatory almanac) painted in the *Telleriano-Remensis* and in the *Vaticanus A*, the patron of the seventh trecena is Nahui Ehecatl "an unusual figure who displays the insignia of both the rain god Tlaloc and the wind god Ehecatl Quetzalcoatl" (Quiñones Keber 1995, 172). Quiñones Keber goes on to say that Ehecatl Quetzalcoatl was also related to the Tepictoton, or dough image mountain representing the tlatoque, or rain gods (173). Recall that in the *Legend of the Suns*, four colored tlatoque snatched the maize bounty that was revealed after lightning (Nanahuatl) opened up the Food Mountain, discovered by Quetzalcoatl (Bierhorst 1992, 146–47; Feliciano Velázquez 1992, 121). Hence, the dual image of Nahui Ehecatl Quetzalcoatl as patron may allude to this tradition. In the *Florentine Codex* Sahagún's indigenous informants state that the day-sign Seven Snake "represented our sustenance—grains of dried maize, completely edible. And so they said that the days of the seventh place were always a time of good" (Sahagún 1950–82, 4:49). The close relationship between maize as sustenance and tool of divination that we saw in the *Leyenda de los soles* is thus also confirmed in the *Florentine Codex*.

The initial day of the trecena in which Seven Snake appeared was considered unfortunate, however. One Rain (Ce Quiahuitl) was one of the five terrible days when malevolent forces from deified women who had died in childbirth (the Cihuateteo) descended upon the earth (Krickeberg 1985, 78–79; Burkhart 1989, 63; Quiñones Keber 1995, 154; Boone 2007, 119). In the *Florentine Codex* it is stated about this day that "it was in no way a good sign. It was full of evil, vice, misery, orphanhood, affliction. . . . This was because during this day sign, then descended those known as the Goddesses, inhuman ones, mockers of the people" (Sahagún, 1950–82, 4:41). Parents did not allow their children to go out during the day One Rain because they feared the children could become crossed-eyed, suffer deformities of their lips, or be possessed. In addition, "inhuman" form-changing, evil nanahualtin were born on this day (4:41). Thus, the negative force of One Rain conspired against the benevolent, bountiful Seven Snake, representing sustenance and seeing, and against the fertility powers of Tlaloc and Chalchiuitlicue.

The fingers that will cast the maize kernels are summoned next. They are invoked as if they were entities operating independently from the ticitl. The fingers are the Macuiltonaleque, or "five solar beings, all of you who look toward one side" (Ruiz de Alarcón 1984, 152). Ruiz de Alarcón writes in a previous chapter with regard to divining using the forearm that when he objected to his informants that a match or mismatch between the patient's and ticitl's fingers depended on the whim of the seer "they answer that it is not thus but that, without being able to avoid or prevent it, the hand becomes larger or shorter and goes straight or twists in the measurement" (1984, 146). The informants' reply suggests the use of *ololiuhqui* (peyote) in these divination sessions. The plant could have given the ticitl visions of his hand twisting or growing larger in order to meet with the fingers of the patient and yield the divinatory knowledge. Note in this regard that in the first chapter of this fifth treatise, Ruiz de Alarcón (1984, 148) states that "for better success in their fraud" fortune-tellers would drink ololiuhqui in addition to pronouncing the nahualtocaitl and applying divination techniques. Be this as it may, the insistence on twisting hand or fingers supports their invocation as entities not controlled by the ritual specialist.

Alfredo López Austin (1967b, 27) translates *Macuiltonaleque* as "owners of the five solar heats," identifying the solar heats as the lunules of the fingernails "that represent the disks with which the Sun is symbolized."[15] In the specific context of this nahualtocaitl, López Austin renders *Macuiltonaleque* not as a proper name but as a common noun: "los de cinco destinos," "those of five destinies" (López Austin 1970a, 4). In their modernized Nahuatl version of the incantation, Andrews and Hassig translate *Macuiltonaleque* (plural of Macuiltonale) as "five-tonals-owners," paralleling López Austin's (1967b) translation. However, they claim that *Macuiltonaleque* is a ritual name for the hands, not the fingers (1984, 230).[16] Somewhat more vaguely, Coe and Whittaker (1982, 213) translate the voice as "those of the Five Signs."

But none of these translations adequately underscores the fact that the Macuiltonaleque were considered to be at least minor masculine deities associated with courtly activities. The best known of them, Macuilxochitl, was god of flowers, song, and dance (González Torres 1995, 109; Boone 2007, 107; Dehouve 2010, 314). The calendrical name-signs of the Macuiltonaleque bear the numeral 5—a number signifying excess. They appeared in those trecenas of the tonalpohualli associated with the south, a direction that was neither good nor bad. They were also closely related to the maize cult (Nicholson 1971, 417–18). Cautioning that the Macuiltonaleque deities are still not fully understood, Elizabeth H. Boone (2007, 233) notes that they were connected with activities performed with the hands, such as hunting, fashioning luxury crafts, and stealing.[17] In the *Codex Borgia, Vaticanus B,* and *Aubin No. 20,* the Macuiltonaleque are paired directly with the five fearsome, monstrous Cihuateteo.[18] Pohl (1998, 194–97) argues that both series of entities were equated with the Tzitzimimeh, or castigating sky spirits and avatars. He points out that in the *Codex Borgia* a white human hand ornaments the mouths of the Macuiltonaleque, and suggests this image may signify that the Tzitzimimeh were the spirits of diviners (1998, 196 n. 7). Finally, Pohl (1998, 194, 197, 200) also notes that, at least in Tlaxcala, the Macuiltonaleque and Cihuateteo were a predominant iconographic theme in the twenty-plus movable feasts of the tonalpohualli, which were celebrated in palaces and characterized by excessive drinking, violence, and chaos.

The fact that the powers of the kernels, fingers, and hands were summoned in the nahualtocaitl for divination implies that they were believed to be intelligent, communicative, volitional mantic agents.[19] Because of the Macuiltonaleque's relation to the maize cult, music, and dance; their inclination toward excess and youthful pleasures; and their symmetry with forces of destruction, the owners of five destinies were at least ambivalent actors. On the other hand, although the kernels' calendrical name involved the evil force of One Rain, it also tapped the bountiful nourishing powers of the goddess of maize and the very favorable influence of the number 7. Most likely then, because all these powers—positive, ambivalent, or negative, good or ill-fated, some with more impact than others—were called upon to intervene in the tossing of the maize kernels, the divining act involved from the outset the possibility of disquieting knowledge. But this act was not anxiety-provoking because forbidden demoniacal forces were tapped for their far superior conjectural powers with which they could easily deceive humans, as the Christian pastors constantly warned, nor even because the outcomes of divination could only be contingent, and thus the act itself unreliable and meaningless. Rather, the anxiety resided in that known favorable and unfavorable, positive and negative superhuman forces were unleashed in the very entities involved in casting lots. Thus, a fortunate reading or diagnosis about the outcome of the situation consulted on could never be expected or guaranteed. The good, ambivalent, and destructive powers converging in Seven Snake and the Macuiltonaleque would mirror in the divination act the heterogeneous forces that circulated in the world.

Having solicited these various powers to come forth, the speaker then demands to find out immediately what afflicts the client:

> [1] Āman yēquen eh. Tlā tiquittatih in īncamanāl in īnetequipachōl. Cuix quin mōztla? Cuix quin huīptla? Ca niman āman.
>
> [2] Now is the time when immediately we will see the cause of the pain and affliction of this one. And this is not to be put off until tomorrow or the day after, but immediately, at this moment, are we to see it and to know it.
>
> [3] It is the instant at last [i.e., now is the time to act]. Let us go in order to see their joke that is his worry. Will it perhaps be by-and-by tomorrow? Will it perhaps be by-and-by the day after tomorrow? It will indeed be immediately at this instant. (Ruiz de Alarcón 1984, 154)

Ruiz de Alarcón translates the element of mockery as the very cause of the affliction that is to be divined. López Austin (1970a, 4) considers "in incamanal, in inetequipachol" as a doublet and translates it as "their mockery, his anguish."[20] This is close to Andrews and Hassig's rendering of a joke causing worry, albeit that theirs, like Ruiz de Alarcón's, is in continuous prose form. Coe and Whittaker (1982, 213) translate the phrase as "their mockery / their troublemaking," also implying mockery as the likely cause of the affliction. In all cases, however, because jokes and mockery were culturally associated in the Late Postclassic with the overwhelming, arbitrary powers and constantly changing moods of Tezcatlipoca, they were no laughing matter. In the first book of the *Historia general* Sahagún (1989, 1:38) famously records that Tezcatlipoca could give riches, health, and wealth, then take them away immediately afterward, at his whim and pleasure. Guilhem Olivier has written that the notion of Tezcatlipoca's mockery was linked to a construction of the human being as "both crushed under an unavoidable destiny and [a] powerless toy in the hand of mocking gods" (2003, 16). Ortiz de Montellano points out that one of the deities usually deemed responsible for causing illness was precisely "the omnipotent, unpredictable creator god Tezcatlipoca" (1990, 131). In the present nahualtocaitl then, we can at least posit that the allusion to mockery as the origin of what afflicts the patient underscores the element of uncertainty, even malevolence, regarding the origin of the malady and the course it could take.[21]

The exhortation to entities to perform their duty immediately is one prominent semantic feature that is articulated throughout all the nahualtocaitl reported in the *Treatise*. The implication is that the words of the nahualli had the power to summon not only very efficacious action from the entities they addressed, but to make this force materialize in the very instant it was called forth. Seemingly to underline further this authority, the illocutionary voice in this nahualtocaitl discloses its identity in the next lines:

> [1] Nohmatca nehhuātl. NiCipactōnal. NiHuēhueh. Ye iihtic nontlachiaz in nāmox, in notezcauh, in tlā quināmiqui pahtzintli, ahnōzo motlanahuītia.
>
> [2] I command it thus, the powerful one, I who am the light, the Old Man, I who have to see in my book and in my enchanted mirror which medicine will do him good or whether he is continuing on his way.
>
> [3] It is I in person. I am Cipactonal. I am Old-Man.[22] Soon I will look inside my book, my mirror [i.e., the thrown maize kernels] [to see] if a medicine will match him [i.e., be appropriate to him] or if he will get worse. (Ruiz de Alarcón 1984, 153–54)

The accurate transformational words of the nahualli allowed the ritual specialist to assume or access the identity of the great seer and giver of light, note-keeper, lord composer of time, organizer of labor, and first diviner Cipactonal, if only by speaking like him.[23] Thereby, the ticitl tapped some of the divining powers of the god and doubled them in the present moment of human time, whose counter and keeper was Cipactonal himself or herself.

According to López Austin (1988, 1:238), some sources posit that Cipactonal and his partner, Oxomoco, were considered more as gods or archetypical figures than as human beings. Some elements supporting this supposition are that the couple was contemporary to or even earlier than the creation of the heavens, the suns, the earth, and the underworld. No source mentions that a specific line of their descendants populated the earth (although the *Historia de los mexicanos* does state that *macehualtin* [common people] would descend from them [Garibay 1965, 25]). López Austin (1988, 1:238) also points out that Oxomoco and Cipactonal were the inventors and patrons of herbal medicine, and that in Mesoamerican thought patrons or inventors were always considered gods. Boone (2007, 24) has called them "prototypal diviners." More recently, James Maffie (2014, 438) has refined Enrique Florescano's contention that time did not emerge until Oxomoco and Cipactonal created the calendar. Maffie argues that before the First Sun–Earth Age there was another kind of non-countable time, which was not patterned according to the tonalpohualli or the xiuhpohualli. This was the time of the gods, in which Oxomoco and Cipactonal were created.

It is of note that many sources make clear reference to the old age of both Cipactonal and Oxomoco. The appositive to Cipactonal's name in the present nahualtocaitl for divining with maize kernels—NiHuehueh, "I am Old-Man"—is a direct allusion to his longevity. In the *Annals of Cuauhtitlan*, it is explicitly stated not only that Oxomoco and Cipactonal were very old, but that "since then, old men and old women were called by those names" (Bierhorst 1992, 24). Fittingly, the time-keepers were also prototypes, godly ancestors or patrons of those who had achieved old age.[24] Indeed, the knowledge of Oxomoco and Cipactonal was vast and expansive. They knew not only of heaven and hell; of the counting of the days; of the present, past, and future; but also of medicine and healing. The *Florentine Codex* states that besides being diviners, day-keepers, and interpreters of dreams, they were "the wise [ones] who discovered, who knew of medicine, who organized medicine art" (Sahagún 1950–82, 10:167).[25] Recall that the *Historia de los mexicanos por sus pinturas* also alludes to this couple's close connection to the healing arts when stating that the female partner of the couple—in this source Cipactonal—received the kernels of maize for curing as well as for divining and doing sorceries. In addition, labor was gendered through them. He was to toil the land and she was to weave (Garibay 1965, 25).

In the second nahualtocaitl for divining with the forearm, the illocutionary voice also articulates the powerful knowledge of Oxomoco, Cipactonal, or both. Identifying itself as both Oxomoco and Cipactonal, it conveys their powers and knowledge as "Nicmati Huēhueh [or] nicmati Ilamah [if it is a woman]. Ni Mictlānmati, ni Topanmati." Ruiz de Alarcón translates this couplet as "[I am] a wise experienced old man or wise experienced old woman, who knows even what there is in Hell and in the heights" (1984, 151). López Austin (1970a, 4) interprets the passage as, "I know the world of the dead, I know the world that is above us. I know the old man. I know the old woman." Coe and Whittaker's translation reads, "I know the old man, / I know the old woman; / I know the Land of the Dead, / I know the Beyond" (1982, 211). Finally, Andrews and Hassig's rendition is "I know Old-Man [or] I know Old-Woman. I am knowledgeable about Mictlan, I am knowledgeable about Topan," interpreting the last as the celestial realm ("Above-us") or the transcendental (1984, 151). These versions all point to the vast, encompassing knowledge of Cipactonal and Oxomoco as Old Man, Old Woman, or both. Old age is thus metonymically linked to knowledge of the above and the below: of what lies in life as well as in death. Jacinto de la Serna also mentions that the Indians venerated and respected Oxomoco and Cipactonal as diviners who knew and saw everything (Serna 1892, 389) and who taught the Indians knowledge of the stars (396). The transcendental, divinatory medical and healing knowledge of Cipactonal and his partner, Oxomoco, enhanced the possibilities of conserving time and granting humans a longer life.

The conjuro concludes with Cipactonal saying that he will soon look "inside my book, my mirror . . . [to see] if a medicine will match him [i.e., be appropriate to him] or if he will get worse (Ruiz de Alarcón 1984, 153–54). Boone has discussed the correspondences between reading a book, the divinatory act of seeing, and the mirror: "As seeing instruments, or mirrors, divinatory codices allowed the diviners to see things that are ordinarily obscure: the future, for example, or situations causing illnesses" (2007, 20). And, in fact, these divinatory codices were the tonalamatls, or sacred picture books, that represented the mantic elements of the different time units in the tonalpohualli (Quiñones Keber 2002; Boone 2007, 20). Cipactonal's *disfrasismo* "my book, my mirror" in the incantation is also registered in book 5 of the *Florentine Codex*. When somebody went to consult the tonalpouhqui about an omen, the latter would say: "You came to see yourself in the mirror; you came to consult the book."[26] Although the divinatory act that concerns us in this nahualtocaitl is not performed by a tonalpouhqui (reader of day-signs) but by a specialist in divining with maize kernels, Cipactonal had nonetheless participated in inventing both divinatory techniques. In the present nahualtocaitl then, the picture book in which destinies are read and the mirror in which they are reflected are metaphors for the expanse of cloth on which the maize kernels were to be cast. There, at the behest of Cipactonal, a power shape would be produced by the tensions between the bountiful Seven Snake; the destructive One Rain; the ambivalent Tlaloc, and the unruly, youthful Macuiltonaleque. In this shape it would be possible to see, read, or bring to light the origin and future course of the malady that afflicted the patient. Once the Cipactonal-impersonating, shape-shifting nahualli pronounced the incantation and "traversed the space that he has created with the stretched-out cloth at full speed with the hand in which he holds the kernels" he cast them at the center of the cloth. Based on the way they fall, "he judges the fortune" (Ruiz de Alarcón 1984, 154).

— 3 —

The array of fundamental, foundational activities, creations, and discoveries for which the semi-godly human prototypes Oxomoco and Cipactonal were responsible show the prominent role of their body of knowledge in the imagination of Postclassic Mesoamerica—at least in Central Mexico and its surroundings. Divination using the powers of the noble Chicomecoatl, the excessive

Macuiltonaleque, the beloved Centeotl, and the fearsome One Rain was a very sensitive art that would not always yield a positive outcome. It did however allow the ritual specialist as Oxomoco, Cipactonal, or both to determine whether medicines existed to cure a particular illness, to see if something could be done about whatever loss troubled the client, or to help him or her prepare for the fate that was to come. The creators of divination with maize kernels were also said to be the inventors of the count and divisions of time; patrons of medicine, healing, and the gendering of labor; discoverers of sustenance; and wise progenitors of old age. Hence, the nahualtocaitl for divining with maize kernels stood side by side, in a firm metonymical bond, with those foundational, civilizing arts that helped the people to shape, maintain, and control their lives in the unsteady, shifting earth of movement that was the Fifth Sun.

—— 4 ——

When one thinks about how theologians, pastors, and priests all over Europe denounced turning to blessers, conjurors, and fortune-tellers as spiritual apostasy and a betrayal of God (Clark 2015, 228–32), it is not surprising that Ruiz de Alarcón and Jacinto de la Serna would not accept the divining knowledge enacted by the nahualtocaitl as a legitimate aid to humanity or as a great legacy of Postclassic Mesoamerican culture and knowledge. Such resistance to divination was to be expected within their epistemological horizons as historical subjects. The raging religious wars in Europe with their merciless persecution of people from different confessions, the eschatological beliefs, the witch hunts that led to scandalous burnings of alleged witches in Logroño, Spain—an event which paled in comparison with those in Cologne and in Switzerland—the thousands of prosecutions registered in the archives of the Inquisition and European civil courts, all indicate that religion, heresy, and apostasy were experienced and politicized as very urgent, very real, very consequential threats to the people, the community, and even the emerging nations in early modern Europe. The reach of this early modern European worldview, of course, would encompass Ruiz de Alarcón in his remote parish of Atenango del Río in the first three decades of the seventeenth century.

So we can excuse the creole priest for not placing the knowledge of Cipactonal and Oxomoco on an equal ontological footing with Thomas Aquinas's "Question on the Nature and Intellect of the Angels" in the *Summa Theologiae*, as perhaps we can do now, four hundred years after the fact. However, Ruiz de Alarcón concludes his chapter on divination with maize by berating his indigenous charges, lamenting that "the ignorance and blindness of these wretched people reaches so far that they consult such fortune-tellers in order to know who is a wizard or a sorcerer" (1984, 155), a sentiment that Serna (1892, 304–5) echoes. Again, the cura comisionado was not alone in considering such divinations dangerous since a lot of panic and resentment ensued when seers wrongly accused innocent people of being perpetrators of maleficent sorcery. Noemí Quezada (1991, 46–47) has written that those who denounced curanderos as sorcerers to the Holy Office in New Spain were usually former patients, and they most likely turned in their healers due to resentment over failed treatments, or fear or remorse when things did not work out well. And this was not the case only in New Spain. Historians of early modern Europe have also pointed out that most accusations against maleficent witches came from below; namely, from laypeople who suspected their neighbors or relatives and wanted to have them punished (Henningsen 1980, 17; Blécourt 1994); Marcos Casquero and Riesco Álvarez 1997, 38, 100; Clark 1999, 517; 2015,225–28). In a 1996 study of German witchcraft Wolfgang Behringer wrote that one major shift in the field has been "the recognition of a massive desire for persecution stemming from the general population" (quoted in Clark 2015, 226), rather than from elites who sought to secure control. This popular persecution did not occur because people had any interest in theological issues of idolatry, however. Rather, they were terrified about the harm they believed was inflicted by witches, such as epidemics, bad harvests, illnesses, and other misfortunes (Levack 2006, 9–10; Clark 2015, 227).

Thus, in his capacity as ecclesiastical judge or comisionado, the criollo cleric should have known that one recurrent reason why indigenous and nonindigenous people all over Europe and in Mexico City consulted their local diviners and soothsayers was precisely because of their presumed capacity to determine or confirm whether the cause of their misfortune was witchcraft and, if so, who was responsible (Blécourt 1994; Thomas 1971, 257–58; Henningsen 1980, 1–25; Clark 2015, 225). Wise men or women in Europe "had oracles and methods of divination which enabled them to discover who had bewitched a man or his possessions" (Henningsen 1980, 10). Closer to home, an illustrative case is reported by Laura Lewis in *Hall of Mirrors* (2003). In 1624, Hernán Sánchez de Ordiales, a priest from faraway Cuacoman, finally elevated his case to the Inquisition in Mexico City, since local inquisitors had ignored his accusations. He wrote to the higher authorities that an Indian woman diviner had confirmed to him that he had been bewitched by another Indian named Miguel Lázaro. The Indian woman, Marichi, informed the wretched priest that she would be unable to heal him unless Lázaro gave his consent. Sánchez reminded the inquisitors in his letter that "witches can do evil with witchcraft and if they do not agree to cure it, it is difficult to undo" (Lewis 2003, 125). His case has various interesting ramifications—especially the fact that a priest had sought the proscribed help of a diviner to alleviate his suffering. Whether Sánchez suffered consequences for having resorted to the indigenous diviner is unknown. What is relevant to the argument at hand, however, is that this case shows the generalized belief, transcultured from Europe—or at least also widespread on the continent—that the witch who cast a particular spell was the most adept at undoing it (Cirac Estopañán 1942, 92–95; Blécourt 1994, 297). This was the main reason why diviners were called upon to expose the culprits (rather than being expected to do the healing themselves).[27] But even more ironic was that not too far away from Cuauhnahuac, in the town of Tenantzinco, Serna himself would call in a renowned ticitl named Francisca in 1626 to have her discover who had bewitched his indigenous servant Agustina (1892, 302–3). Therefore, if Ruiz de Alarcón should not be chided for being unable to wield our current postmodern and postcolonial epistemological openness to all ontologies, he can certainly be held accountable for singling out his indigenous flock as uniquely ignorant for wanting to find out from fortune-tellers and diviners who the evil sorcerers were.

If Archbishop Manso y Zúñiga ever did leaf through the fifth book of the *Treatise*, perhaps he may have felt more pastoral patience and compassion for his flock than the cura from Atenango del Río did. Although for him it was undoubtedly a sin for the indigenous peoples to use Mesoamerican fallen angels to divine cures or find missing persons, valuable animals, or stolen food, the good archbishop might have considered that conversion took time and that these admittedly worrisome practices would eventually go away as the Christian faith took deeper root in the land and the Indians learned to put all their trust in the only true God.

As for seers from the towns of Oapan, Comala, Xoxouhtla, and Ozomatlan, along with their clients, the Spaniards in Yautepec, creoles, mestizos, castas, and blacks in Mexico City and all over New Spain and Peru, as well as people in Spain, Germany, France, England, Denmark, the Netherlands, Scotland, and even faraway Sweden, all divined or consulted diviners for guidance and advice in times of affliction. All of them shared the same incapacity, or unwillingness, to give up resources that they thought or experienced could ease the wretchedness and suffering of their lives. And in the admittedly local Postclassic Mesoamerican colonial case of casting lots with maize kernels in the province of Chilapa, the act of seeing was furthermore justified by the authority of the nahualtocaitl. For the nahualtocaitl anointed all its speakers with an ancient, empowering memory of knowledge, as they became Cipactonal or Oxomoco, the consummate models for the Mesoamerican magi, ancient patrons and inventors of divination, medicine, and healing; finders of sustenance; light of heaven and hell; venerable first ancestors and benefactors of humanity, who could read in their book and mirror, *in nāmox, in notezcauh,* all the signatures, shapes, and latitudes of time.

Conclusion

A creation of Mesoamerican Postclassic civilization of Central Mexico and the regions of present-day Morelos and Guerrero, the nahualtocaitl collected in the *Treatise on the Heathen Superstitions and Customs That Today Live among the Indians Native of This New Spain* in 1629 deployed the view that the world was saturated with intelligent, volitional superhuman and nonhuman entities that were responsive to human address. The recorder of this remarkable indigenous oral genre, the criollo cura comisionado Hernando Ruiz de Alarcón, set out to transcribe and translate the nahualtocaitl in order to denounce their existence to Archbishop of Mexico Juan Pérez de la Serna. Not surprisingly then, the parish priest from Atenango del Río offered a very negative view in the *Treatise* of this oral genre and of its users. Because the intelligent, superhuman forces invoked in the nahualtocaitl were not Christian, Ruiz de Alarcón classified them as demons or as the very devil himself, according to the tenets of the demonological thinking of his time, which I discussed in chapter 1. Consequently, he portrayed his informants as subaltern, malicious, recalcitrant backsliders who in spite of one hundred years of Christianization still held fast to their false gods and beliefs. Meanwhile, the indigenous declarants of the nahualtocaitl, surely not unaware that the cura comisionado wanted to extirpate the practice that he zealously sought to record, may very well have chosen to withhold from him other nahualtocaitl that they judged could be more incriminating. It almost seems as if word had gone around that the priest from Atenango del Río would be less angry at confessed incantations that benefited the people in spite of their proscribed engagement with Mesoamerican deities.[1] Drawing from Latin American postcolonial theory, I hypothesized that this apparent cautious restraint involved a competence in border epistemology and plural world dwellings. It should be added that these culturally mobile skills would be well suited to users of the language of the form-changing, interspecies-versed nanahualtin.

I then suggested that this practice of border epistemology did not gain much sympathy from Ruiz de Alarcón or Jacinto de la Serna, author of the derivative *Manual for Ministers*, judging by the way they represented the indigenous peoples in their works. The possible reticence of the informants may however have resonated with the pastoral silence of the highest ecclesiastical authority in the archdiocese at the time, Archbishop Francisco Manso y Zúñiga. If he ever read or paid any attention to Ruiz de Alarcón's *Treatise*, he is not known to have given any special instructions to investigate its findings. No records have been found of any trials conducted by Ruiz de Alarcón, by other commissioned judges, or by visitadores on the indigenous peoples identified in the *Treatise* as ritual specialists or as frequent users of the incantations (Tavárez 2011, 76). Even the nahualtocaitl for enhancing the practice of divination, clearly prohibited in the decrees of the Mexican Third Provincial Council, were overlooked by the archbishop himself or by his assistants.[2] And although Manso y Zúñiga appointed Jacinto de la Serna visitador general in 1631 or 1632 (Coe and Whittaker 1982, 53; Tavárez 2011, 90), Serna did not visit Atenango del Río until 1646, as visitador for Archbishop Juan de Mañozca. It was there, not in the ecclesiastical halls of Mexico City, that Serna reportedly came across the *Treatise*—seventeen years after it had been dedicated to Manso y Zúñiga. And, in a puzzling historical omission, neither the *Treatise* nor the much more learned *Manual* was published during the colonial centuries (Gruzinski 1993, 148). Both works for extirpating indigenous idolatrous practices were commissioned or encouraged to be written, but then they circulated only in manuscript form. Perhaps they were dismissed or intentionally silenced; either way, they were seemingly forgotten. No concerted action was taken against the indigenous peoples based on the findings in the *Treatise* or the *Manual*, an outcome that Alarcón's coerced informants must have desired.

I also suggested that Manso y Zúñiga's silence or inaction vis-à-vis Ruiz de Alarcón's denunciations of idolatry in the *Treatise* was not that different from the measures Serna proposed to Archbishop Mateo Sagade Bugueiro in his *Manual* two decades later. I pointed out in the introduction that the principal remedy Serna proposed in the last five chapters of his work was not public persecution or exemplary punishment of idolaters or even of the sly ticitl who were all over the land. Serna (1892, 457, 467–73) recommended that parish priests or ministers should be in charge of handling the kind of idolatrous "crimes" he had reported. He argued that they would know their flock better than any judge; had time to conduct long, unhurried, conscientious investigations; and would not require additional monies to carry out extirpation activities. Most importantly—and this is the proposed remedy pertinent to our study—the cure was to be "the continuous preaching of the Gospel, the teaching of good customs, and the refutation of these errors, which is the principal thing."[3] Such continuous preaching and rebuttal of the "errors of idolatry" would nourish the faith and enable it to take eventual root in the hearts of the Indians. Change was not to be expected soon, however, and much work and patience from the pious, hardworking parishioners would be necessary (Serna 1892, 462). Thus, the three-time rector of the Royal University of Mexico, *racionero* of the Cathedral of Mexico, and visitador general proposed quite modest remedies that pointed toward a long, difficult road still to be traveled, instead of an immediate, spectacular, final solution.[4] The ministers of the expansionist, universalizing, globalizing powers of Christianity in the Archdiocese of Mexico had no other choice but to keep negotiating patiently, indefinitely, with hope, faith, and courage, in a form of provisional, strategic coexistence with the "idolatrous," colonial Nahuas. The Indians did not reject Christianity, and could even practice it with devotion, but they refused to give up certain of their practices and beliefs—however syncopated, reduced, or transformed—inherited from a long indigenous past that would not be forgotten anytime soon. Indeed, the nahualtocaitl recorded in the *Treatise* and reproduced in the *Manual* are compelling, immensely rich sources evincing a vigorous, extant Mesoamerican Postclassic worldview in the southwest of Central Mexico. By the seventeenth century the ritual specialists and lay users who recited the nahualtocaitl may or may not have been fully aware of its layers of meaning. But the analyses in this book suggest that the conjuros that have come down to us protect and conserve deep layers of sophisticated Mesoamerican thought and knowledge that harked back at least one hundred years before the arrival of the Spaniards.

Because the nahualtocaitl are the names of the nahualli and therefore a form of his or her language, I discussed this metamorphic figure at some length in chapter 2. In a nutshell, the nahualli is an individual who is thought to be able to transform himself or herself at will into animal or other nonhuman forms, and therefore to have a unique, close relationship with entities in the environment. Operating especially in the realm of dreams, the nahualli projected his or her soul force onto an object or animal disguise. Because of its non-ordinary powers, the nahualli has usually been both greatly respected and feared. The *Florentine Codex* registers a sharp distinction between good and bad nahualli, with the former being considered "a caretaker, a man of discretion, a guardian" (Sahagún 1950–82, 10:31), and the latter a destroyer of the people. As I discussed in chapter 2 and also in chapter 4, to Serna and in the Christian worldview that he represented (more learnedly than Ruiz de Alarcón did) the preternatural, interspecies fluidity of the nahualli was inherently incompatible with the Christian belief in the exceptionality of the human form. Serna (1892, 367) explicitly wrote that assuming the form and perspective of what Christians considered lower species in the world, erased the image of God in human nature, which was the primary reason the transformation was sinful. Serna's position, albeit articulated in quite a patronizing manner, expressed a very important, perhaps irreconcilable difference between Christianity and the Postclassic Mesoamerican epistemology underpinning the conjuros; namely, the latter allowed and even encouraged crossing boundaries between entities and species as a source of knowledge and power, whereas this was (and is) forbidden by the former.

This leads me to recap some of the chief constituent elements deployed in the names of the nahualli recorded in the *Treatise*. I chose to do close semantic readings of four, quite diverse nahualtocaitl, in order to show their range. My methodology for approaching these complex, sophisticated productions of Postclassic Mesoamerican epistemology was interdisciplinary and eclectic. I worked with the original transcriptions in Nahuatl and with all available translations in Spanish and English, especially with the superb annotated edition by J. Richard Andrews and Ross Hassig. I engaged a wide variety of material from Mesoamerican ethnohistory and anthropology—and from Latin American colonial cultural studies, history, and literature—to explain and substantiate what I interpreted as I closely followed the texts. The nahualtocaitl, I believe, were very responsive to this approach. They allowed more of their powerful tropological imagination, time depth, narrative coherence, and will to accomplish with excellence to be tapped into and beheld. I think the readings in the book warrant my claim, but needless to say, they do not exhaust all that can be glossed from the invaluable record of this genre, still circulating widely not that far away from Mexico City, one century after the arrival of Christianity to the land.

As the four analyzed conjuros in this book show, the nahualtocaitl were deeply imbued with traditions of cosmogonic time and the creation of the Fifth Sun and its beings. Such traditions are registered in the *Codex Borbonicus*, the *Codex Telleriano-Remensis*, *Historia de México por sus pinturas*, *Florentine Codex*, *Historia de los indios de Nueva España*, *Leyenda de los soles*, *Annals of Cuauhtitlan*, and *Histoyre du Mexique*, to mention some of the more important sources I worked with in this book. Often the inscribed speakers of the nahualtocaitl are the very gods who generated the domain of the activity the conjuro seeks to influence or ones who are closely related to those activities. And when the speaker does not represent a god, he or she is usually a priest or tlamacazqui, a nahualli lord, or an impersonal, knowledgeable speaker of the names. The inscription of these authoritative godly, powerful subjects of knowledge bolsters the assumption—or image—of the operative capabilities of the nahualtocaitl. Any user could take cover under the cloak of the illocutionary voice of these subjects in order to impersonate them and access some of their godly or priestly competence—as long, of course, as they performed the proper, attendant material actions.[5] Herein the species mobility allowed (or imagined) by the names of the form-changing nanahualtin can be considered a source of power.

Nevertheless, the efficaciousness of the nahualtocaitl was not based solely on the fact that their inscribed speakers were gods, priests, or nahualli lords. It was also supported by what these figures knew. One salient feature of their knowledge was the calendrical names of the entities populating the conjuros. A calendrical name registered a regulated series of superhuman godly forces that converged in one of the 260 day-signs of the tonalpohualli, or divinatory calendar. In my readings of the nahualtocaitl, I analyzed the deep coherence of this series and the tightly knit relations that it held with the entities that emerged on a particular day-sign. Thus, when the inscribed speaker Quetzalcoatl addressed One Water, when Centeotl summoned Seven Flower Piltzinteuctli, or the impersonal subject of knowledge called out Eight Flint Woman, the intelligent, superhuman constellation of forces that came together in the birth day-sign of the club, the deer, and the maguey were being expertly called out by the authority of the knowing deity, priest, nahualli lord, or impersonal subject. What (the image of) this authoritative invocation was supposed to achieve was the optimal performance by the pertinent entities so that the material results sought via the incantation could be obtained. Fittingly, the inscribed illocutionary voices in the conjuros constantly solicited the entities to immediately fulfill their duties. In many cases, they even declared that the desired, anticipated outcome had already happened. In this way, the nahualtocaitl merged the time of origins with the present time of the speech act, which in turn called out the future event as already fulfilled. This was the notion (or practice) of condensed temporality discussed by Davíd Carrasco (1982, 77). Such dissolution of temporal boundaries—quite compatible with the interspecies fluidity of the nahualli—enhanced the image of the power of the conjuro and its capacity to produce effects.

The close readings confirm the elaborate tropology of the conjuros, which led Ruiz de Alarcón to complain of the difficulty and complexity of their metaphorical fabric. This tropology, in turn, wove dense webs of connectivity among the entities of the world. Thus, we saw how entities were bound in the conjuro by metaphoric resemblances like the copper spoon for the Red Chichimec, the forearm of the patient as the ladder or mirror of the God of the Underworld, and Xochiquetzal's balls of thread as the rocks of the neutralized enemy. Entities were linked by metonymic associations such as godly inhumanity with insensibility and dead flesh; or the agricultural maize god turned hunter to chase his father-deer. Through synecdoche Matl, or the Hand, stood in for Quetzalcoatl because he was patron god of merchant traders and a warrior wielding well his weapons. By analogy and metonymy the sacrificial white blood represented the pulque that would be offered to the sacrificial victim at the death stone where his or her blood would be shed. The metonymic concatenation between divination and sustenance was linked by their common patron, Cipactonal, who divined with maize kernels how the Food Mountain would open up. Many other forms of connections will surely be teased out as other scholars analyze the nahualtocaitl. But the point is that dense yet discernable relations of tropological correspondences are enacted or performed in the nahualtocaitl, and that voicing this knowledge was expected to produce calculated effects. Mirroring how the world was wrought was a way of tapping into its power.

I believe each one of the sixty-plus conjuros resists and allows the kind of careful, close readings I have undertaken.[6] Some nahualtocaitl, however, do plumb different temporal depths, as Andrews and Hassig (1984, 27) have indicated. A topic of research that can be advanced in the future is a mapping of the layers of cultural references in the nahualtocaitl in the *Treatise*—or perhaps others that may still be found in the archives.[7] In an additional topic of research, the nahualtocaitl may engage cosmogonic traditions existing at any time from the Early Postclassic in Morelos and the Valley of Mexico (circa 950 C.E.) to the time of the Chichimec migrations after the fall of Tollan (circa 1150 C.E.) and most likely before the definitive conquests of the area by the Triple Alliance in 1468 (see Smith and Berdan's [2003, 5] Postclassic chronologies and cultural areas). That is, the earliest nahualtocaitl in the *Treatise* may have condensed Postclassic cosmogonic narratives and traditions that were already circulating in the regions that would be settled by the Tlalhuica and the Coixca in the early thirteenth century, mixed with traditions they brought with them.[8] As was discussed in chapter 3, Andrews and Hassig (1984, 20) have noted the conspicuous absence of Huitzilopochtli as one of the invoked or speaking deities in the nahualtocaitl of the *Treatise*. By 1468 Guerrero and Morelos had been brought under firm Aztec rule, so it can be assumed that a significant portion of the nahualtocaitl documented in the *Treatise* was circulating or had already taken form before this time. For after the (re)conquest of the territory by Motecuhzoma Ilhuicamina, fifth tlatoani of the Tenochca (Coe and Whittaker 1982, 7), surely Huitzilopochtli would have been much better known, feared, and respected in the region. Consequently, if the reported nahualtocaitl had been codified during this time, it is likely that this powerful god of the Mexica would have been invoked in at least a few of them.

Of possible interest for further research regarding the *Treatise* is that scholars have believed these nahualtocaitl to have circulated in a relatively vast zone (López Austin 1967b, 1969; Coe and Whittaker 1982; Andrews and Hassig 1984; Gruzinski 1993; Tavárez 2011). This fact suggests that these incantations expressed an inflexion of Postclassic epistemology still at work at a macro level in a significant geographic area surrounding the Valley of Mexico in the seventeenth century. The translocal circulation of the nahualtocaitl could give us a better idea of the ongoing processes of indigenous cultural negotiations with the imposed globalizing, modernizing colonial forces of epistemological change. It could also document that the recitation of nahualtocaitl for a wide array of activities was not constrained to an isolated town or group of towns. This is significant for discerning an indigenous awareness about the cultural production, transmission, and conservation of the nahualtocaitl as an "intellectual enterprise" (Tavárez 2011, 282), especially given the fact that Ruiz de Alarcón and undoubtedly other clerics were attempting to suppress the conjuros. At least during the years of Ruiz de Alarcón's extirpating activities commissioned by Archbishop Pérez de la Serna, the Tlalhuica and Coixca users of the nahualtocaitl would certainly have been cognizant that this mainly oral ritual practice was not acceptable to Christians. But that did not stop them from keeping it alive.

Along the same line of research, it may also be of interest that many colonial indigenous voices can be heard in the *Treatise*, and even in Serna's derivative and more mediated *Manual*. For although their declared nahualtocaitl were coerced, Alarcón's indigenous confessants speak with less institutional constraints than were present in ecclesiastical trials. Thus, I have argued that indigenous voices in the *Treatise* were not fully controlled by the cura comisionado. Indeed, the users of the nahualtocaitl are not depicted as distressed, anomic, or even melancholic subjects, paralyzed by the traumatic loss of their culture and their people. In spite of Ruiz de Alarcón's constant subordinating remarks, his declarants enter the historical record as full-fledged agents: alert and aware but unafraid of the perils of practicing their border epistemology as they faced risks of arrest and even conviction. It is not unlikely that Ruiz de Alarcón represented or inflated such attitudes as evidence to construct an image of the Indians in his parish as obstinate and ignorant. But the more Ruiz de Alarcón, and later Serna, reiterated the willful recalcitrance of the declarants, the more powerfully they come forth to us in their firm claims of the efficacy of their indigenous practices to fend off misfortune and in their unshakeable refusal to given them up. Some of the individuals Alarcón identified as frequent users of the nahualtocaitl were prominent members of the pueblos where he did his inquiries, their high status indicated by the titles of don or doña. So even community leaders continued using the difficult, disguised names of the nanahualtin, and claiming quite resolutely and unabashedly that the results were infallible. Confronted by the powers of the colonial environment of Christianity, the declarants of the nahualtocaitl in the *Treatise* and also later in the *Manual* appear as de-centered but unbroken.

Ruiz de Alarcón's bilingual, bicultural, profoundly heteroglossic text seeks to eradicate what it transcribes but ironically makes it more available by translating it and fixing it in writing. The quality of the cura's translation of Nahuatl into Spanish is another topic that could be examined more closely. As I discussed in the book, although he and Serna miss the very important cultural element of the calendrical names in the nahualtocaitl, the way they both interpret these references says a lot about the possibility, impossibility, and paradoxes of cultural translation. The adjectives chosen, the verb dynamics, the apostrophes, the synonyms, and the parallelisms that are present in the Spanish translations provide evidence that these translations, although clearly lacking in certain respects, were not dashed off carelessly. I broached this subject in my short discussion about the mistranslated yet delicate, noble, chivalric name of the Lord of the Seven Roses for Chicomexochitl Piltzinteuctli in chapter 5. In spite of Ruiz de Alarcón's and Serna's constant metadiscursive denunciatory interventions, their care for the language of the translation and their occasional lyrical exegeses in the Spanish translation of the conjuros can be read, *malgré lui*, as a form (or performance) of cultural acknowledgment of and homage to the original.

I also suggested that some of the elements deployed in the nahualtocaitl had affinities with the principal forms of resemblance Michel Foucault laid out in *The Order of Things*. The French philosopher and cultural critic argued that resemblance was a form of cognition in Europe until at least the end of the sixteenth century (Foucault 1973, 17–44). Indeed, similitude served as an operative knowledge of connectivities in the natural occult workings of the Renaissance magi, as discussed in chapter 2. Similarly, the inscribed, authoritative speakers of the nahualtocaitl wielded knowledge of correspondences between origin stories, birth names, resemblances, iterations, and contiguities. But perhaps most importantly, they all shared the belief that nature was alive, sentient, and communicative. Without glossing over the geocultural differences and peculiarities that mark the boundaries of cultures, it is of interest to point out these subtle affinities between the good nahualli and the Renaissance magus, especially as represented by the Florentine philosopher Marsilio Ficino. For both Late Postclassic relational epistemology and learned early modern Neoplatonic magic recognized and engaged with animate, occult, and marvelous powers that were not imagined as inherently evil. More research in this direction could show such epistemological resemblances at work, below the surface, at unexpected points and interstices in the embattled contact zone. And then, perhaps, we might come to consider the possibility that such sympathies and consonances were able to mitigate, if only in some small measure, the terrible shock waves of early modern globalization and subordination suffered by the indigenous peoples in Mexico.

Furthermore, it is of interest to note that elements of the relational epistemology deployed in the nahualtocaitl survive today in indigenous communities in Guerrero and Morelos, as well as in other regions of Mexico and Guatemala. Especially in chapters 4 and 5, where I analyze nahualtocaitl for harvesting and hunting, I discuss how ethnographers have recorded many contemporary nonmodern cultural practices in which Mexican and Guatemalan Indians perceive and ritually engage with the environment as teeming with sensitive, intelligent, and volitional beings. Humans offer special foods, candles, bones, drinks, and offerings they believe, or have discovered, the entities they address desire, expect, or appreciate. Humans may also speak, sing, and dance to them in order to solicit, attract, or compensate them for their consent to provide for humans, lest they become angry, unresponsive, or even dangerous if they are mistreated. Certain crops and game animals are addressed and engaged as spouses (Braakhuis 2001, 2009; Dehouve 2008). Of course, this relational epistemology is not exclusively Mesoamerican. But the ways in which it has been elaborated, codified, imagined, and facilitated by the non-ordinary, morphing fluidity of the figure of the nahual, and the companion nonhuman entity of the tonal, certainly are. And as I have shown in chapter 2, beliefs and experiences of the nahualli and the tonalli are still extant in many communities of Mexico and Guatemala today.

Perhaps because they truly feared the anger of the Christian God or because they were following the instructions of the *tlamatinime* (wise ones), the confessants in the *Treatise* may have only revealed those nahualtocaitl spoken for "justa causa," or just cause (term quoted in Martínez González 2011, 507), in an effort to appease the zealous Ruiz de Alarcón. Perhaps many others were left unsaid because they belonged to radically unfathomable elsewheres, forever inaccessible to any western, "Greco-Abrahamic" subject (Rabasa 2011), including the well-meaning, epistemologically open, postmodern, postcolonial critic and reader of Latin American studies. But as I hope I have demonstrated with my reading practice in this book, those nahualtocaitl that were deemed to be revealable to a nonindigenous audience and that have come down to us continue arousing and meriting our finest critical attention. For the polished, super-intelligent tropological language of the nanahualtin recorded in the *Treatise* and the *Manual* constitute a great, self-conscious body of cultural achievement from Postclassic Central Mexico and regions to the southwest. Even under their Spanish and English cloaks, the nahualtocaitl deliver powerful testimonies of the knowledge and unflinching resolve of the people to negotiate, resist, and survive in the precarious, ever-changing, globalized world of the Fifth Sun.

Notes

Introduction

1. Three major, devastating *cocoliztli,* or epidemics, occurred during the sixteenth century: in 1520–21 during the siege of Tenochtitlan, in 1544–48, and in 1576–81 (Gibson 1964, 136; Israel 1975, 12–13, 27). See Gibson (1964, 448–51) for a list of the most horrific epidemics in Central Mexico during the colonial period. By the early seventeenth century some estimates are that almost 90 percent of the preconquest indigenous population had died (Gibson 1964, 138).
2. In the interest of avoiding fastidious repetition, I will use the words *conjuros, conjuratiwons, incantations,* and *spells* interchangeably with *nahualtocaitl* throughout this book. Admittedly, none of the former terms captures the meaning and ideology of nahualtocaitl, because incantations and spells carry negative connotations from an orthodox Christian point of view that nahualtocaitl do not have from the perspective of their Tlalhuica and Coixca users. In addition, nahualtocaitl have many points in common with Christian prayers, especially with regard to seeking favors from superhuman holy beings. "Prayer" is not a satisfactory translation for *nahualtocaitl,* however. In a prayer the supplicant communicates with a divine or holy entity to implore or beseech favorable mediation, concession, or even actions. Although always communicating politely, the speaker of a nahualtocaitl usually commands and expects the intervention of the entities addressed, even if the command cannot be guaranteed to produce the expected result. Most of the nahualtocaitl Ruiz de Alarcón recorded are instrumental, authoritative, and directive, whereas prayer tends to be devout and submissive to the will of the godly or saintly entity addressed. This important difference in the power structure of the nahualtocaitl to my mind brings them closer to the notion of conjuro than to that of prayer.
3. Jacinto de la Serna finished his *Manual de ministros de indios para el conocimiento de sus idolatrias y extirpacion de ellas* in 1656. He wrote the text to orient new ministers to the ostensibly superstitious and idolatrous practices of their parishioners-to-be. Serna took a great deal of content from the *Treatise,* but his scope is more extensive and ambitious. He

showed knowledge of a variety of indigenous religious beliefs and local practices of which Ruiz de Alarcón was unaware. He also demonstrated a good understanding of the unique Mesoamerican 260-day divinatory cycle although, much like Alarcón, he missed important references to its names in the nahualtocaitl. For a good discussion of Serna and his *Manual*, see Sáenz de Santa María (1969) and, more recently, González Martínez (2006).

4. Mexican nahuatlato Alfredo López Austin has written important articles on the *Treatise* and has translated several nahualtocaitl into modern Spanish (López Austin 1969, 1970a). The most notable recent works on the *Treatise* are a chapter by Gruzinski (1993) and articles by Tavárez (1996, 1999). Tavárez (2011) also dedicated a full chapter to Ruiz de Alarcón and Serna. Other significant essays engaging the *Treatise* are by Dehouve (2010), Raby (2006), and Díaz Balsera (2007, 2011a, 2011b, 2017).
5. Sahagún had already warned about these continuities and about unrealistic expectations of culture change based on the millenarian hype of the first contingent of Franciscan missionaries to Mexico, the famous Twelve. See especially his *relación*, or quasi-testimony, about the state of the Christianization of the "naturales" in New Spain in book 10, chapter 27 of the *Historia general*. This part does not correspond to the *Florentine Codex* because it is Sahagún's personal disruptive intervention and rant in the text as author and witness of the (for him) tenuous Christianity of the converted indigenes (1989, 2:628–36).
6. See Alberro (1988, 1992) for excellent accounts of how widespread "idolatrous" practices were among non-indigenous populations in Mexico City, including sometimes Spanish governors and their wives. Her extensive and thorough research on the Mexican Inquisition amply supports this claim. See also Aguirre Beltrán (1963), Perry and Cruz (1991), and Griffiths and Cervantes (1999). Other relevant sources are Lewis (2003), Jaffary (2004), and Bristol (2007). On European popular magic and superstition, see Thomas (1971); Clark (1999, esp. 472–88); and Cameron (2010). For standard studies of magical practices among both popular and elite classes in early modern Spain see Cirac Estopañán (1942), Caro Baroja (1992), and Christian (1989), a classic work. See René Taylor (1967) for Juan de Herrera's interest in correspondences between architecture and magic. Herrera was the architect and mathematician who completed Philip II's famous monastery-palace of El Escorial. For love magic and superstition in Italy, see Ruggiero (1993) and O'Neil (1984). See also Owen Davies (2003 and esp. 2009), for a collection of charms, incantations, and instructions for fabricating talismans and other magical objects. For the Protestant Church's struggle to control popular interpretations and practices of Christianity, see Scribner (1987). I could list numerous other sources, but I hope the cited studies suffice to support the claim that indigenous people of Mexico were not the only people in the Spanish kingdoms who resorted to remedies shunned by the Church.
7. Original in both sources reads "Adiuinio, sabio y Hechizero, y que tiene pacto con el Demonio."
8. "El conocimiento de la enfermedad por graue, y occulta, y no conocida que sea, y que puede applicar el remedio conveniente para curarla."
9. Philip II's *protomédico*, Francisco Hernández, wrote this compendium of the plants and animals used for medicinal purposes. In 1570 the king charged him to undertake a scientific

expedition in order to study medicinal plants and animals in New Spain. Hernández traveled for four years in Central Mexico, collecting specimens and conversing with indigenous herbalists and healers about what plants and animals they used to treat illnesses. From 1574 to 1577 he organized the material he had collected and tried to prove experimentally their efficacy with patients at the Hospital de Naturales in Mexico City. He returned to Spain in 1577 and died the next year, without seeing his work published. For a detailed account of Hernández's life and the significance of his work, see Somolinos D'Ardois (1960).

10. In chapter 6 I will explore further how clerics and pastors all over Europe condemned divination as an extended superstitious practice and habit.
11. Noemí Quezada has published the most important document pertaining to these accusations against Ruiz de Alarcón (see Quezada 1980, 323–50).
12. In a personal communication to Coe and Whittaker, Woodrow Borah wrote that as ecclesiastical judge, Ruiz de Alarcón "could ask for imprisonment, try, impose penance, and sentence to various punishments such as flogging . . . , shearing off hair, service in an obraje, or . . . imprisonment of some other kind" but that he always had to rely on the secular arm for arrests and to inflict punishment (quoted in Coe and Whittaker 1982, 21). Thus, the ecclesiastical judge did not have the authority to punish or act directly against the natives he accused or found guilty of idolatry.
13. John Chuchiak (2002, 146–47) argues that all ecclesiastical documents in Spanish America transmitted to higher authorities had to state whether confessions had been made under torture, with permission of the civil officials present. There are no extant records documenting idolatry trials as a result of Ruiz de Alarcón's interrogations, nor any document from civil authorities granting him permission to apply torture in order to extract confessions from natives. Given that Alarcón had already been accused of unduly encroaching on episcopal and inquisitorial authority (and by a Spaniard, not an indigenous official) in his small-scale autos de fe, it is unlikely—although certainly not impossible—that he would have risked using torture without proper, documented authorization, or that he would have gotten away with it. Zaballa Beascoechea (2005, 66) also reports that it was forbidden to torture Indians in order to obtain confessions.
14. The priest reported that the indigenous people greatly resisted revealing what they knew or actually did, especially regarding the nahualtocaitl: "Those who desire to help do not have sufficient information about this subject, and those who have it are offenders in it; either they do not want to reveal or, already having been caught in the act, hide completely what they can" (Ruiz de Alarcón 1984, 40).
15. Dialogism is associated in literary and cultural theory with Mikhail Bahktin. His classical formulation of the term appears in *Discourse and the Novel*: "The living utterance having taken meaning and shape at a particular historical moment in a socially specific environment, cannot fail to brush up against thousands of living dialogic threads, woven by socio-ideological consciousness around the given object of an utterance; it cannot fail to become an active participant in social dialogue" (Bahktin 1981, 276). Dialogism posits that there is an aspect of utterances that is unavoidably relational. No word can be pronounced in a cultural and social vacuum; that is, without involving its history and anticipating some

future response from the present addressee. In the case of the nahualtocaitl being stated at the demand of the colonial cura comisionado, the declarants could not fail to anticipate some of the consequences of their utterances. These anticipated consequences, in turn, would or could modify the utterance itself. I propose (at the moment and in this book) that the modifications they chose had less to do with the content of the nahualtocaitl itself than in the choice of *which ones* they would utter. For discussions of the term *dialogism* in literary theory see Todorov (1984) and Holquist (2002).

16. Because of their status as "nuevas plantas de la Iglesia," the *naturales* were spared from the Inquisition. Indians were investigated and prosecuted for idolatry by bishops and their *provisores* (administrative assistants). Although the Inquisition and the ecclesiastical tribunals headed by bishops had many procedural similarities, Richard Greenleaf points out that the indigenous flock may have understood that the bishops "were less stringent than the Inquisition and acted accordingly when they became involved in pagan accusations" (1965, 166). Thus, the confessants likely had more room for discursive control before commissioned judge Ruiz de Alarcón than they would have had in the scarier, much more institutionalized, secretive, and regulated trial procedures of the Inquisition.

17. Except perhaps for the *tecochtlazqui* (sleep-thrower) (Nicholson 1971, 442) in the second chapter of the second book of the *Treatise*, hardly any of the nahualtocaitl recorded involve evil ritual practitioners. However, Ruiz de Alarcón seems to have found this nahualtocaitl in written form because he mentions in passing that after the words of the conjuro "we found in the page in *nomini domini*" (1984, 80). Therefore, this nahualtocaitl for the very suspect end of inducing sleep does not seem to have been declared orally to him.

18. For a brief discussion of the theological difference between heresy and sortilege in determining degrees of religious transgression, see Mentzer (1984, 37–38) as well as the case of Marsilio Ficino in Walker (1975, 42). Also see Clark and Kaske's excellent introduction to the 2002 edition of Ficino's *Three Books on Life* (2002), a work discussed in detail in chapter 1. For now, suffice it to say that sometimes when Ficino could not claim the agency of natural occult forces in his defense from charges of invoking demons, he would argue that the learned, Renaissance Magus never worshipped demons, whether good, indifferent, or evil. The Magus had a strictly "unworshipful, businesslike relationship" with them (Ficino 2002, 64). Because the demons were deemed to be in some sense corporeal, they could be "allured by mere sympathy with natural objects into a business relationship" (69). In any case, whether aimed at worshipping or manipulating them, the invocation of spiritual entities not recognized and approved by the Church would have been considered idolatrous by most church reformers and theologians in Europe.

19. The original Spanish reads: "Y pues que esta es la verdad: qualquiera hombre o muger que por estos ensalmos [spells] quiere sanar: consiente secretamente en querer auer la sanidad por mano del diablo. . . . Esto es grauiissimo peccado de ydolatria contra el primero mandamiento" (Ciruelo 1978, 83–84). The influence of this treatise can be gauged by its numerous reprints. It was first published in 1538, followed by at least eight reprints during the sixteenth and seventeenth centuries, the last one being in 1628 (Ebersole 1978, 9). Two twentieth-century editions were published in 1952 and 1978, the latter of which I am citing in this book.

20. For more detailed discussions of maleficent ritual practitioners in both colonial and precolonial times see Aguirre Beltrán (1963, 99–105); López Austin (1966, 1967a). In his article "Cuarenta clases de magos del mundo náhuatl" López Austin (1967a) lists forty evil ritual practitioners who surely used incantations to support their power. See Nicholson (1971, 441–42) for a list of specialized ritualists characterized by their malevolent practices. See also Nutini and Roberts (1993, 80–131) for an analysis of malevolent practitioners in rural Tlaxcala during the sixteenth and seventeenth centuries.
21. Sahagún records in book 10 of the *Historia general* his informants' belief in a good nahualli as "he who is knowledgeable in things of sorcery and is sharp in their usage, helping and not harming" [*aprovecha y no daña*, 1989, 2:598; translation is mine]. I will discuss the good nanahualtin who were believed to protect the people in chapter 2.
22. One informant who recanted when she realized that her declaration was incriminating was a woman healer in the district of Tepequaquilco. According to the priest she was denounced and arrested for using cures where she applied cupping glasses while pronouncing "certain incantations and superstitious words" (Ruiz de Alarcón 1984, 176). After confessing the procedure and the nahualtocaitl she used conjointly, she "turn[ed] around and denied it after she perceived how full it was of heathenism" (176). Ruiz de Alarcón had to intervene again to make her confirm her initial confession, which she was finally compelled to do. However, she showed agency and self-censorship in managing her admission, and even accused Ruiz de Alarcón to her parish priest of unjustly persecuting her.
23. In her introduction to *Negotiation within Domination*, Susan Kellogg also argues for natives' ability to negotiate within the colonial regime. She writes that "while colonial rule led to many negative consequences for native peoples, resistance occurred, and cultural vitality and creativity existed and have a lengthy history." Although Mesoamerican peoples fought back and rebelled, "communities and individuals often turned to negotiation to deal with conflicts and ameliorate the conditions and consequences of colonial rule" (2010, 3).
24. William Taylor points out that being active in extirpating idolatry was one way for parish priests to climb the ecclesiastical ladder, as they vied for the office of half-racionero (lesser canon) in the cathedral chapter, "the usual entry-level position and the one most open to curas" (1996, 121). Ruiz de Alarcón (1984, 66, 73) mentions twice in the *Treatise* his special commission from Archbishop Juan Pérez de la Serna to investigate idolatrous practices, perhaps as if emphasizing the distinction. The creole priest also underscores in the dedicatory epistle and prologue to the *Treatise* (now directed to Pérez de la Serna's successor, Manso y Zúñiga) the enormous difficulties he had surmounted in putting into writing the conjurations of the backsliding idolaters, as if seeking recognition for his (quasi-heroic) recording efforts. But if he had hoped producing the manuscript would promote his career, he was disappointed. Coe and Whittaker (1982, 15) and Tavárez (2011, 90) both stress that Ruiz de Alarcón had no great success in rising above his position as a *beneficiado* (permanently appointed) priest in the not so lively parish of Atenango del Río.
25. Archbishop Juan Pérez de la Serna was finally able to publish and promulgate the decrees from the Third Provincial Council of Mexico in 1622, thirty-seven years after it came to a close (Poole 1987, 200–202; Pérez Puente 2005, 23). The council, which among other

things decreed submission of regular clergy to examinations and visits by the bishops, not surprisingly had always been bitterly opposed by the religious orders. In order to affirm and justify secular authority, Pérez de la Serna was especially interested in displaying the competence of the episcopacy to pursue the purity of the faith and the reformation of customs of its indigenous charges. Under Pérez de la Serna's tenure from 1613 to 1627 there were several idolatry accusations against different indigenous towns, although no convictions were made (Traslosheros 2002).

26. The archbishop's silence is even more remarkable if one considers that it is not unlikely Ruiz de Alarcón may have visited Mexico City at least a couple of times during Manso y Zúñiga's tenure as archbishop, if only to visit his notable brother Pedro Ruiz de Alarcón (Coe and Whittaker 1982, 15). The latter had risen in the ecclesiastical hierarchy to become chaplain of the Royal College for Children in Mexico City (Tavárez 2011, 73–74). If only by virtue of his distinguished brother, Hernando Ruiz de Alarcón should not have been a totally unknown figure in the ecclesiastical circles of Mexico City.

27. The erudite Jacinto de la Serna served as *visitador general* to Manso y Zúñiga in 1631. Thus, Serna "was rising far faster in the Church hierarchy than Ruiz de Alarcón" (Coe and Whittaker 1982, 53). The visitador was responsible for conducting periodic visits to rural parishes, convents, and monasteries in the bishop's or archbishop's stead, in order to make sure "they complied with all aspects of canon law" (Schwaller, 1987, 23). In 1646 Jacinto de la Serna visited Atenango del Río under the commission of Archbishop Juan de Mañozca y Zamora. There, Serna came across a copy of the *Treatise*, which he later revamped for his *Manual for Ministers*, a work that was not published either.

28. Serna's manuscript had a limited, yet intricate circulation. The Jesuit Marcos de Yrala wrote to Jacinto de la Serna on August 22, 1656, offering compliments on the *Manual*. According to some notes by the historian of Mexico José Eguiara y Eguren (1695–1763) the famous Mexican savant Carlos Sigüenza y Góngora (1645–1700) at some point had in his possession Serna's original manuscript. Sigüenza passed it on to a cleric by the name of Valverde, who then passed it on to a certain Don Rodrigo Diego Valdés, who in turn lent it to the canon of Mexico, Dr. Barreda. Eguiara's note was published by bibliographer José Mariano Beristáin (1756–1817) in volume 3 of his *Biblioteca hispano-americana septentrional* (1817). Francisco Paso y Troncoso then reproduced the note as part of his introduction to Serna's *Manual*, which he published in the *Anales del Museo Nacional de México* in 1892. I consulted this introduction for the story of how Paso y Troncoso finally accessed Serna's manuscript in the Fuente Cultural edition of the *Manual for Ministers* (1953, 21–23).

29. Much like his predecessors, Archbishop Mateo Sagade y Bugueiro—to whom Serna dedicated his *Manual*—may have been too busy with his own jurisdictional wars against the viceroy (the Duke of Alburquerque) to pay much attention to indigenous idolatry. See Pérez Puente (2005) for a discussion of this bitter rivalry between temporal and ecclesiastical powers.

30. I will address the definition of superstition as the expectation of something unnatural happening in chapter 2, where I discuss the Christian preternatural.

31. "Como por ser estos delictos de calidad, que requieren mucho espacio para inquirirse, y averiguarse" (Serna 1892, 470).

32. Note that at least five of the incantations Ruiz de Alarcón found and included in the *Treatise* were written down by ritual specialists. However, these few instances do not undermine the argument that informants could have censored themselves when forced to confess face-to-face.
33. The term *disfrasismo* was coined by Angel Garibay in 1954 and it entails the pairing of two or even three metaphors or metonyms in order to express the significance of a third term. Because of the abundance of couplets and triplets or disfrasismos in the nahualtocaitl, Coe and Whittaker (1982, 40) argue that the incantations operate in discrete semantic and syntactic units that call for organizing the original text and its translation in verse form. However, the argument that the ever-present, highly marked disfrasismos in the nahualtocaitl support the reading of the conjuros as poetry is not fully warranted. After all, couplets and triplets are used in the oratory genre of the huehuetlatolli as frequently as in the lyrical genre of the *in cuicatl, in xochitl* (song and flower) (Lockhart 1992, 394).
34. In the introduction to their accomplished translation into English of Ruiz de Alarcón's bilingual *Treatise*, Andrews and Hassig explain that the pantheon of gods extant at the time of the Conquest was "the result of long accretion, the movement of various peoples, and the political fortunes of empires" (1984, 9). The names of the deities invoked in the nahualtocaitl recited one hundred years after the arrival of the Spaniards belong to the Late Postclassic period (circa 1350–1521 C.E). The gods themselves, however, sometimes hark back to Classic and even Preclassic or Formative times in Mesoamerica. It is pertinent to clarify now that throughout this book, when I refer to Postclassic Mesoamerica (850–1521 C.E.) (or more precisely Late Postclassic culture), it is with the understanding that many of its religious and intellectual constructs may have originated with the Olmecs more than three thousand years ago (Coe and Koontz 2008, 59–91). When this precision does not seem helpful or necessary, I use the more familiar term *Mesoamerica* to denominate the extended geocultural area that ran from Central Mexico to the Maya Lowlands and south to Central America. Although the term *Mesoamerica* has been critiqued (Creamer 1987), it is still widely used because of its expediency.
35. López Austin (1967b) lists many of these strategies as "rules of construction" in his classic article on the nahualtocaitl.
36. It is however pertinent to remember that this close-knit sociality does not mean that human-environment relations are always necessarily harmonious or that no distinctions are made between humans and nonhuman entities such as the village and the forest. Three examples will suffice for the moment. In their study of Guatemalan hunting communities Laura Brown and Kitty Emery argue that "crossing thresholds from community to forest is considered precarious and sometimes dangerous. The forest is occupied by sentient non-human agents who are capable of taking action against human interlopers" (2008, 303). Robert Laughlin (2000, 106) has also reported that in contemporary Maya culture, plants can get angry and become dangerous when they are cut down. Finally, the nahualtocaitl against ant pests politely admonishes "'nahualli obsidian-teeth-owners'" (Ruiz de Alarcón 1984, 110) to stay away from the crops or face utter destruction from the speaker.
37. Serge Gruzinski (1993, 165–66) also observes that deference is a strategy used in the nahualtocaitl to procure desired behaviors from the entities petitioned.

38. Nahuatl has an elaborate linguistic apparatus to express deference, honor, affection, and respect. In his *Arte de la lengua mexicana* of 1645, still used today by students of Nahuatl, the Jesuit Horacio Carochi explains:

> This Mexican language has something that heightens it much, and with which it has advantage over the languages of Europe, and this is that not only names, pronouns, prepositions, and many adverbs are made reverential . . . but also verbs by only altering and changing a bit its roots.
>
> The reverential verb has the same signification as the primitive from which it is derived, and it only adds respect and reverence for the agentive person, or patient, and for the person with whom one talks or of whom one is talking. But the one who talks, even though he may be of higher authority, if talking about himself or herself, does not use the reverential verb, if not obliged by the patient." (Carochi [1645] 1983, f. 66; translation is mine)

39. Ruiz de Alarcón was not the first or only individual to transcribe nahualtocaitl, however. At least once he mentions that he had found some nahualtocaitl that ritual specialists themselves had put into writing (see book 2, chapter 4). In his *Book of the Gods and Rites* (finished circa 1576–79), Diego Durán (1971, 152) had already noted that many of these incantations circulated in writing.

40. See Zhang Longxi (2007, 2009), Vilashini Cooppan (2009), and Emily Apter (2013) for three different stances on the debate over the possibilities and impossibilities of cultural and literary translation. Longxi advocates for finding deep connections and common metaphors across cultures far distant in space and time. At the other end of the spectrum, Apter alerts us to the existence of cultural, temporal, and linguistic untranslatability, and denounces assumptions of universal intelligibility as complicit with western privilege and domination. Somewhere in between Cooppan reminds us that we must engage with different cultures, languages, and historical periods, but with the knowledge that we can never have full access to the other. My practice in this book is closer to Cooppan's and Longxi's than to Apter's forbidding position.

CHAPTER ONE. The Christian Preternatural

1. The erudite Jesuit Martín del Río wrote in his *Disquisitiones Magicae*: "Those who follow the Sadducees, Democritus, Aristotle, Averroes, and Simplicius in asserting that evil spirits do not exist also say that this form of magic does not exist. But this opinion of theirs is impious and heretical. Evil spirits do exist and so does the magic that involves them. Such a magic is not based upon the industry or inventiveness of human beings, nor does it rely on natural causes. It rests, rather, on some kind of non-material, separate power [virtus]" (Del Río 2000, 68). Del Río held chairs of philosophy, moral theology, and scripture at various renowned European universities, among them the University of Louvain and his alma mater, Salamanca. He wrote extensively, but his most influential work is his treatise on magic (Fisher 1908; Maxwell-Stuart 2000, 2–8).

2. I am referring to the famous eight omens of book 12 of the *Florentine Codex*. While the omens are a historical reconstruction by Nahua bilingual informants of marvelous and

frightful events that had happened ten years before the intrusion of the Spaniards, the discursivity of these signs gives us an image of the way the informants self-represented their people's communicative experience with the gods. For instance, the indigenous informants declared with regard to the third omen, "[It] was that a temple was struck by lightning, hit by a thunderbolt. It was just a building of straw at the temple complex of Xiuhteuctli, called Tzonmolco. The reason it was taken for an omen was that it was not raining hard, just drizzling. It was said that it was struck when the sun was shining, nor was thunder heard" (Lockhart 1993, 52). James Lockhart believes that the omens in book 12 are "a typical attempt of a vanquished group to explain, after the fact, what has happened," not necessarily evidence of how people really experienced the events (17). Although the images of the eight omens most likely are reconstructions decades after the fact, and already altered by the hegemonic discourse of Christianity in the bargain, they still convey culturally specific forms compatible with other books of the *Florentine Codex* and with what is known of Late Postclassic epistemology and histories.

3. Thomas Aquinas held that although demons belonged to hell, they were allowed to wander on the earth, in the air, and in sublunar space in order to tempt humans "for our trial." Humans should exercise themselves "by fighting against opposition," thus growing stronger and better by the effort. Demons thus had a purpose "lest they should cease to be of service in the natural order" (Aquinas, *Summa Theologiae*, part 1, question 64, article 4).
4. Pedro Ciruelo was possibly the most influential demonologist in Spain. His short treatise—*Reprobation of Superstitions and Sorceries*—was printed several times and established the guidelines for the Spanish Inquisition in its dealings with witchcraft. On Ciruelo, see Ebersole (1978), Campagne (2003), and María de Jesús Zamora (2014, 188–90).
5. In his introduction to *The Cornell Witchcraft Collection*, Edward Peters lists significant examples of fifteenth-century tracts about demonic magic, including *Ut magorum et maleficiorum errores* by the Briançonnais judge Claude Tholosan (1437); Johaness Nider's *Formicarius* (1437, first printed 1475); *Errores Gazariorum* (author unknown, circa 1440), *Flagellum Haereticorum Fascinariorum* by the Dominican inquisitor Nicholas Jacquier (1458); *Fortalitium Fidei* by Alfonso de Spina (1471), the *De Lamiis* of Ulrich Molitor (1489), and the *Malleus Maleficarum* (1487), which I discuss in the text.
6. On witchcraft panic in different regions of Europe see, among many other authors, Ankarloo and Henningsen (1993); Certeau (1973); Larner (1981); Henningsen (1980); and Sharpe (1996).
7. In Spain, superstitions in the form of vain observances, which implied ignorance by the perpetrators, were punished by confiscation of goods, fines, public shaming, and imprisonment, but not death (Montaner and Lara 2014, 159). The fact that such punishments were considered "minor" because they did not entail the ultimate penalty shows how vulnerable healers and cunning folk could be to both civil and ecclesiastical authorities. Willem de Blécourt (1994, 293) has written that in northern Germany and the Netherlands, cunning folk, diviners, soothsayers, and fortune-tellers were banished whenever they fell into the clutches of the law, even during the eighteenth century after witches were no longer sent to the stake.
8. The *Corpus Hermeticum* or *Hermetica* is a very diverse group of writings in Greek about monotheism, the creation of the world, mind, and nature. These writings were attributed to the Egyptian sage Hermes Trismegistus, who was supposed to have been more or less

contemporary to Moses. Ficino believed that Hermes had been a major source for Plato, hence his enormous interest in translating the *Hermetica*. To the dismay of the admirers of Hermes Trismegistus, in 1614 the philologist Isaac Casaubon convincingly redated the *Hermetica* to the second century C.E. See Walker (1974); and Copenhaver (1992) for a discussion on the history of this text. Ficino's translation of the *Hermetica* would be the prevailing version in Europe of writings attributed to Hermes Trismegistus until the nineteenth century (Copenhaver 1992, xlviii).

9. Foucault's well-known "Prose of the World" in *The Order of Things* aptly and succinctly represents the regimes of similitude and resemblance operating in the early modern episteme. He identifies this epistemic period as running from the late fifteenth century to the great disrupter Descartes and his acolytes in the mid-seventeenth century (Foucault 1973, 17–45, 51). The similitudes and resemblances that Foucault stakes out as shaping the Renaissance body of knowledge are *convenientia* and *aemulatio*, or analogy and sympathy/antipathy. These, however, were not believed to be merely contemplative or philosophical resemblances that were repetitive and monotonous, as Foucault (1973, 30) suggests. They were assumed to be operative and instrumental, and to constitute the cornerstones of natural magic. These powers of deep resemblances were dispersed all over the world in signatures, knowledge of which could bring entities together. They would have many affinities with the various pragmatic knowledge deployed in the nahualtocaitl, as we will see in following chapters.

10. As Cornelius Agrippa (1486–1535) "the Renaissance magus par excellence" (Szőnyi 2004, 110) wrote in the opening paragraph of his (admittedly controversial) *De Occulta Philosophia*:

> Seeing there is a threefold world, elementary, celestial, and intellectual, and every inferior is governed by its superior, and receiveth the influence of the virtues thereof, so that the very original, and chief Worker of all doth by angels, the heavens, stars, elements, animals, plants, metals, and stones convey from himself the virtues of his omnipotency upon us, for whose service he made, and created all these things: wise men conceive it no way irrational that it would be possible for us to ascend by the same degrees through each world, to the same very original world itself, the Maker of all things, and First Cause, from whence all things are, and proceed. (Agrippa 1993, 3)

Cognizant of the Platonic chain of being and the Neoplatonic hypostases, and unconstrained by fears of overstepping the boundaries of licit human knowledge, the Magus supposedly climbed up the ladder of worlds, from the earthly to the celestial realm and onward from there to the supra-cosmic—beyond the eternal, yet still a material cosmos—and lastly perhaps he glimpsed the very One itself, from which supra-cosmic intelligences themselves spurted forth.

11. I use "exalted" following the cultural historian György Szőnyi (2004, 16), who employs *exaltatio* as a metaphor to describe the early modern learned Christian magician's desire "to understand the divine plan of creation and God's intentions with the cosmos and man."

12. Kaske and Clark (2002, 49), the editors and translators of *De triplici vita*, explain that Ficino introduced into the Plotinian universe the world spirit so as to offer a substitute for demons. They, along with D. P. Walker, believe Ficino felt that natural attractions by virtue of forms alone were not always powerful enough.

13. "The ancient sages arranged certain long series of mundane gods, as they call them, and of the demons and spirits who follow them in order; under each star certain demons, who dwell in that part of the heavens, and under them in the air various other demons, all endowed with the same quality and family name as the superior ones—Saturnian ones under Saturn, Jovial under Jupiter . . . and others likewise; and also Saturnian and Jovial men under the Saturnian and Jovial demons; and then, as well as men, animals pertaining to one or another celestial or other demon, and not only animals, for they thought that even plants and metals and certain stones had the properties of the higher beings" (Ficino, Commentary on St. Paul's Epistle to the Romans, quoted in Walker 1975, 49–50).
14. This was obviously not true of Giovanni Pico della Mirandola, who did aspire to ascend to and converse with angelic intelligences. By combining Cabalist magic and Hermeticism, he sought to connect with higher spiritual powers than those lurking in the natural, physical world. For Pico, natural magic was weak and almost inefficacious if super-celestial spirits from beyond the stars were not attracted to perform operations (see Yates 1964, 84–116). At the end of his life, however, he recanted from all his angeolological attempts and from his interest in Egyptian and Chaldean oracles.
15. Understandably, Ficino feared trouble from the Church. According to Paola Zambelli (2007, 22), *De triplici vita* received so much criticism—as well as fame, judging by its numerous printings—because it was published in 1486, only a year before the frightening and influential tract *Malleus Maleficarum*. In the apology Ficino had to publish for his book, he formally declared that his magic was not demonic (Walker 1975, 52) and that the magic "which joins medicine with astrology, must be kept" (Ficino quoted in Zambelli 2007, 23). See Kaske and Clark (2002, 55–70) for a more detailed discussion of Ficino's self-defense in his apology.
16. The quotation comes from Erasmus's *A playne and godly exposition or declaration of the commune crede . . . and of the X commaundments of goddes law* (London, 1534?). The original in Latin appeared in 1533 in Basel and Antwerp.
17. See Marcos Casquero and Riesco Alvarez's (1997) introductory study to Pedro de Valencia, whose opinion la Suprema had asked regarding the controversial auto de fe. For the specific instructions sent to the inquisitional tribunal of Logroño for use in future investigations see appendix IV in this volume. The very title of Pedro de Valencia's *informe, Discurso sobre los cuentos de las brujas* (Discourse about Fables of Witches), gives the reader an immediate clue as to his position regarding the reality of the confessed crimes. See also Henningsen's classic *The Witches' Advocate* for a thorough study on the Basque witch hunt and the author's emphasis on inquisitor Alonso Salazar and his level-headed intervention in this lamentable affair.

CHAPTER TWO. The Nahualli

1. This term was codified in 1933 by Robert Ricard in his influential book *La "conquête spirituelle" du Mexique* (Spanish-language edition 1991).
2. Unlike the Christian God and Satan, Mesoamerican deities were never totally good or bad. As Kay Almere Read (1998, 15) wrote, "Mexica deities had split personalities, multiple

identities they could take off and put on . . . all depending on the powers required at the moment." They could exert a favorable or nefarious influence, be creative or destructive, good or evil, orderly or disorderly, depending on the aspects of their manifestation at a particular time. Moreover, because each of the five suns had emerged from the destruction of its predecessor, the destructive powers of the gods were deemed violent, terrifying, and deadly, but also fundamentally creative (Burkhart 1989, 37–38; Cervantes 1994, 42; Read 1998, 69).

3. See, for example, the *Doctrina cristiana*, published in Mexico in 1544 and one of the first books published in the New World; in it the Dominican friar Pedro de Córdoba writes, "These bad angels who are demons are the ones who have deceived you, and who have made you believe that they were gods, and made you to worship them and build them cues, teocallis and temples" ([1544] 1988, 59; translation is mine). Describing the calendrical feasts abolished by the Franciscans, Motolinía writes that the Indians enacted a form of Communion with tamales made of corn and other seeds. While the tamales cooked, children played some small drums, "proclaiming in song that those loaves were changing into the flesh of Tezcatlipoca, the god or demon whom they held in special veneration and to whom they attributed greater dignity" (Motolinía 1951, 97). In the *Colloquios* the first twelve Franciscans who came to Mexico declared to the Nahua lords that we "know for sure that none of those whom you adore is God or giver of life, rather they are all infernal demons" and again, shortly after, "those whom you worship and have as gods, lords and governors . . . always procure you harm and evil because they are awful demons" (Sahagún 1986, 92–93; translation is mine). For other statements identifying the Amerindian gods as demons see the *Tratado de hechicerías y sortilegios* by Andrés de Olmos; book 5 in José de Acosta's *Historia natural y moral de Indias* (Mignolo 2002); and book 2 in Mendieta's *Historia eclesiástica indiana*. See also Sahagún's interventions in book 2 of the *Florentine Codex* and Diego Durán's *Libro de dioses y ritos* for occasional references to the indigenous gods and priests as demons. See also Juan de Torquemada's *Monarquía indiana*, especially books 6 to 10.

4. Apparently, Ruiz de Alarcón was unaware of a very similar case of wounds inflicted on animals being simultaneously perpetrated on humans that was recorded in the *Malleus Maleficarum* (Kramer and Sprenger [circa 1486] 1971, 126–28). A workman was chopping wood one day when suddenly he was fiercely attacked by three big black cats. He defended himself by beating one on the head, another on the legs, and the third on its back. One hour after the incident he was arrested for having beaten three "respected matrons" who were now lying in bed unable to move, each showing blows in the very same places he had beaten the cats. Much like the townspeople in Ruiz de Alarcón's story, the authors of the *Malleus* determined that the three women were witches (128). An anonymous eighteenth-century Spanish reader of a manuscript copy of Serna's *Manual* made a note in the margin regarding loberos (werewolves) in Spanish villages to make the point that the nahualli was not a uniquely Mexican phenomenon (Sáenz de Santa María 1969, 551–52).

5. *Tonalli* appears in many contexts, and is therefore an extremely polyvalent term. It can refer to an animating soul or spirit force located in the head and spreading through the body. It is conceived of as an irradiation or solar heat (López Austin 1988, 1:204–27; J. Furst 1995,

63–70, 96–102; Martínez González 2011, 44–52; Maffie 2014, 270–74, 423–24). Because the tonalli is linked to the day of birth and destiny of the individual, it can refer also to his or her animal companion born simultaneously. Although stating that it is a verb, López Austin (1988, 1:204) uses *tona* for the animal companion. I prefer López Austin's usage because it creates a distinction between *tonalli* as a heat and life soul force, and *tona* as a companion animal.

6. The ihiyotl, like the tonalli, spread throughout the body. Conceived of as a luminous gas, the ihiyotl had the virtue to attract beings to the person or animal from which it emanated in the form of flatulence or body vapors. When it emanated in a restrained, proportionate fashion, it was a beneficial source of energy. When it was liberated without control or with the intention to hurt someone, it was maleficent (López Austin 1988, 1:235). The ihiyotl was also linked with power, smell, and speech during the sixteenth century (Martínez González 2011, 54–55).
7. Confusion is nonetheless understandable because the nahualli, as transforming witch, and the tona, as animal companion, entail very close, deep interspecies relationships between human and animal. Perhaps the most crucial one is that when the nahualli or tona perishes or is hurt, its human counterpart will also die or evidence the injury in his or her body. Other shared features are that the social status of the person is reflected in his tona or nahualli, and that both entities are contacted in the realm of dreams (Musgrave-Portilla 1982, 37, 46–47; Martínez González 2011, 140–45).
8. For a discussion of seven years as the age of reason in the Catholic Church, see http://www.newadvent.org/cathen/01209a.htm.
9. And providential it was indeed. Coe and Whittaker calculate that "over forty percent of the text [of *Manual for Ministers*] is taken almost verbatim from Ruiz de Alarcón, sometimes but not always acknowledged" (1982, 53). They adduce that if "substantive material" were taken into account, the figure would be around 75 percent.
10. "De manera les borre el Demonio la imagen de Dios, á cuya semejança fueron criados, que siendo la criatura del hombre la mas Hermosa, que salió de las manos de su Criador, quieren ser mas Perros, Leones, Tigres, Caimanes, y otros animales inmundos como son Sorillos, Murcielagos, &c." (All translations of Serna into English are mine.)
11. "A los que lo ven los pone assi el Demonio aquella appariencia, para que parescan Caymanes ó Leones."
12. "Que todas las naturalezas de las cosas absolutamente las sabe, y poderosamente las mueve."
13. Colonial and contemporary sources register indigenous beliefs in both bodily and non-bodily nahualli metamorphoses (Musgrave-Portilla 1982, 45–47; Martínez González 2011, 422–26). Interestingly, those magicians or sorcerers who were said to undergo actual bodily transformations were and still are usually considered to be maleficent. Perhaps many indigenous groups appropriated the Christian belief that the devil could not effectuate changes in substantial form, interpreting that those sorcerers who utterly defied God's edicts were inherently evil. See Martínez González (2011, 444–51) for a list of contemporary ritual specialists, sorcerers, and magicians who are believed to undergo actual corporal transformations into their animal companions. Although a few beneficent nanahualtin are believed to undergo physical metamorphoses, the majority are maleficent.

14. This belief that present-day animals had been humans in previous eras is also expressed in the Popol Vuh, where people were transformed into different animals due to their incapacity to give appropriate service and praise to the gods, and hence to keep the world or sun going. The *Chilam Balam*, which can be translated as Jaguar-Priest, also serves as an instance of this belief. And of course, it is also expressed in the cosmogony of the five suns and in humans being transformed into present-day animals at the catastrophic end of each period. The Zoque Chima from Oaxaca also believe that animals living today were humans in previous eras (Lisbona Guillén 1999). See also Viveiros de Castro (2004, 2012).
15. Living humans and animals were not the only ones who had nanahualtin: dead people had them, and so did the gods themselves (Caso 1967, 189; López Austin 1988, 1:368). To name a few examples, among the Mexicas, Huitzilopochtli's nahualli was "el colibrí de la siniestra" (the hummingbird from the left side); Tezcatlipoca's nanahualtin were the jaguar, the coyote, and the skunk (Krickeberg 1985, 133–35; López Austin 1988, 1:369). The eagle was the nahualli of the god Tetzauhteotl (López Austin 1993, 236), who in turn was closely linked to Tezcatlipoca (Graulich 1997, 217). The deer was the nahualli of Mixcoatl (Krickeberg 1985, 140), and the dog that of Quetzalcoatl (Brundage 1982, 133).
16. Andrews and Hassig (1984, 313 n. 12) dispute all three verbs proposed by Ruiz de Alarcón as the source of *nahualli*. In the end, however, their proposed meaning is not that far off from Ruiz de Alarcón's meaning of "to hide oneself by covering oneself with something" (Ruiz de Alarcón 1984, 48). Andrews (who is the linguist of the two) proposes that *nahualli* is a patientive noun derived from the verb *tla(nāhua)*. This verb signifies "to interpose something (between self and public, skin and outer clothing, man and gods, the natural and the supernatural and so forth)". Thus, the authors conclude that *nahualli* means something that can be interposed, namely, "a mask, a disguise, a sorcerer" (Andrews and Hassig 1984, 246). See also Martínez González (2011, 81–88) for another etymological discussion of the voice *nahualli*. He concurs that it derives from the root *nāhua* and approximates the notions of "disguise" and "cover" (88).
17. For explicit mentions of the nahualtocaitl as metaphors (*nombres arrebocados*, "muffled-up names") see Ruiz de Alarcón (1984, 40, 124, 148; and 1892, 127–28, 176, 189, for the Spanish original). Serna (1892, 430) refers to metaphors or "disguised names."
18. Scholars have claimed that some were-images depict not jaguars, but snakes, crocodiles, a maize god, and an Olmec god, among many other things (see Tate 2012, 17–18, 33–34). As I will discuss later in the chapter, Tate herself posits that the axe images represent human embryos, representing a gestational stage in which humans are still not differentiated from other species and forms of life (2012, 34).
19. In contrast, Duverger argues that the baby were-jaguars were sacrificial victims linked to the cult of rain deities. Making a connection with Motolinía's and Sahagún's accounts of children who cried as they were taken in procession to be sacrificed to Tlaloc, Duverger (2007, 228–29) proposes analogically that the baby were-jaguars are depicted as shedding tears (water) and thus are most likely sacrificial victims-to-be of the rain god.
20. Staller and Stross (2013, 150–53) also note that co-essences are not limited to animals, but can also be whirlwinds, lightning, or comets. They add that if humans can have animal familiars, it is reasonable to assume that gods or deities who controlled natural forces would

also have animal familiars. These points suggest a lot of interspecies mobility: between humans and animals; between gods or their assistants and animals; and also, of course, between gods, humans, and meteorological phenomena.

21. And also it was said that he who was then born a nobleman became a sorcerer, an astrologer. . . . He changed himself into something [else]; because of it he turned himself into something [else]. Perchance he had as a disguise a wild beast, etc. (Sahagún 1950–82, 4:42).

22. Besides being predestined by the calendar to become a nahualli, an individual could inherit those powers from his or her parents. Other ways of accessing transformational powers was through the use of drugs, or by offering candles and copal to the gods, or by snatching the powers away from Tezcatlipoca in a confrontation. Still another way of obtaining the powers of the nahualli was by performing a ritual in which the person rolled over ashes (López Austin (1988, 1:372).

23. The ideas that a human meets his or her tona or nahualli in dreams, and that dreams are nightly divagations of the tonalli or the very language of the nahualli, has also been presented by other Mesoamericanists studying this phenomenon. See Vogt (1969) and Pitt-Rivers (1970) for this belief among the Tzotzil and Tzeltal from Chiapas, and more recently Galinier (1990) for the phenomenon among the Otomi people. See Lipp (1991) for the Mixe belief that individuals can meet their co-essence in dreams.

24. Note that Musgrave-Portilla and Martínez González do not agree with Aguirre Beltrán's and López Austin's claim that the ihiyotl is the soul force that nanahualtin manipulate. Musgrave-Portilla (1982, 37–40) states that López Austin's sources are not sufficient to warrant this opinion, and Martínez González (2011, 55, 500–501) opines that there are so many common features between the ihiyotl and the tonalli soul forces as to make confusion likely. Both also tend to favor the theory that the day of birth, or tonalli, is the major enabling element in the case of the nanahualtin.

25. Not surprisingly, this commendable construct of the good nanahualtin is less celebratory in Sahagún's Spanish version of the *Florentine Codex*. After defining the nahualli as a *brujo* who scares people and sucks the life out of children, Sahagún writes of the good nahualli that "he understands anything that has to do with sorceries, and to use them he is sharp and astute, he is useful and does not harm" (1989, 2:598; translation is mine). Sahagún acknowledges the usefulness of the nahualli and the fact that he or she does no harm, but refrains from recognizing him as discreet, devoted, respectable, and knowledgeable, as the Nahuatl version does.

26. The origin story of the Title of the Lords of Totonicapan is an instance of nahualli patron deities protecting the K'ich'e community (see Musgrave-Portilla 1982, 13). Another case in point is that of Quetzalmazatzin, nobleperson from Amaquemeca. In his seventh *Relación*, (187r–187v), Chimalpahin recounts how Quetzalmazatzin did battle in Huexotzinco in the form of his nahualli, which was a fire serpent (cited in Martínez González 2011, 328).

27. Indeed, Martínez González (2011, 108) reminds us that the interdependent destinies of a human being and his or her nahualli entail that any harm perpetrated against the animal or the human being will also affect the other. Citing plenty of supporting sources, Martínez González argues that contemporary Mesoamerican peoples keep their nahualli secret because they fear that someone wanting to hurt them may attack their nonhuman counterpart.

CHAPTER THREE. Quetzalcoatl Fights Highwaymen

1. For more on the history of the Chilapa province see Gerhard (1972, 111–14); Harvey (1971, 300); and Coe and Whittaker (1982, 5–11).
2. Tavárez (2011, 73–77) posits that Ruiz de Alarcón must have received his benefice during the first decade of the seventeenth century, but no documents of the appointment are extant. The conclusive evidence that he was already a beneficiado by 1613 comes from a document accusing him of conducting autos de fe among the Indians without authority from the archbishop (see Gruzinski 1993, 148–49).
3. See Creagh (1907) on the definition of benefice and Schwaller (1987, 81–109) on its establishment in late sixteenth-century New Spain. On Ruiz de Alarcón's benefice, see Coe and Whittaker (1982, 13–16).
4. The *Historia de los mexicanos por sus pinturas* is a summary of valuable annotations from the sixteenth century on sacred narratives of origins most likely derived from indigenous commentaries on pictorial codices. The annotator is believed to be Fray Andrés de Olmos. The *Histoyre du Mexique* is a sixteenth-century translation into French by André Thévet possibly of lost papers by Marcos de Niza and Olmos (Garibay 1968, 9-16). The *Histoyre* was published in 1905 by Edouard de Jonghe. The *Leyenda de los Soles* (1558) along with the *Anales de Cuauhtitlan* (1570) were both written in Mexico City. They form part of the manuscript named *Códice Chimalpopoca* in the nineteenth century. See Velázquez (1992, vii–xxi) and Bierhorst (1992, 10–14) for a history of the codex and its whereabouts.
5. Note that the Culhua also worshipped Xochiquetzal. According to the *Anales of Cuauhtitlan*, some Culhuas sought asylum in Cuauhtitlan for 300 days, to escape the devastation of Culhuacan by the Tepanec-Mexica in 1348. During this time they started making an earth altar to "set up their gods, known as Toci and Chiucnauhozomatli and Xochiquetzal" (Bierhorst 1992, 68).
6. Illocutionary force is a particular attitude or intention in making an utterance that the speaker expects his or her audience to recognize. The illocutionary force of the nahualtocaitl is best described as the requirement type of directives. In illocutionary acts of requirement, the speaker expresses explicitly or implicitly the belief that his or her authority is sufficient cause for the hearer to perform the commanded action (Bach and Harnish 1979, 47). Perhaps the clearest claim to authority in the nahualtocaitl is the fact that the inscribed position of the speaker is that of a Postclassic god, nahualli-lord, tlamacazqui, or impersonal subject of knowledge. On illocutionary acts and their taxonomies see, among many other authors, Searle (1976); Bach and Harnish (1979, esp. 39–83); Allan (1999); and Hornsby (1994, 2006).
7. In 1579, it was reported that thirty-two adult male Indians from Iguala were drafted weekly to work in the mines (Coe and Whittaker, 1982, 10). Because their forced service time was relatively short and spaced throughout the year, the mining tasks of the repartimiento Indians most probably consisted of carrying bags of ore out from the shafts and other basic duties (Haskett 1991, 458).
8. A doctrina, the most widely used term for a parochial jurisdiction in the colonies, consisted of a main town (altepetl), called the *cabecera*, where the friars or priests resided, and clusters of surrounding subordinate towns or villages called visitas, to which the priests from the cabecera went to celebrate Mass and administer the sacraments. Some clergymen blamed

the incompleteness of indigenous Christianization on the fact that visita towns were far away from the cabeceras and saw their priests only twice a year (Gibson 1964, 101, 114). James Lockhart argues that the visita priest "as an outsider neither identified himself with the parish community . . . nor fully understood its languages and ways. . . . In visita churches, the [indigenous] staff was in complete charge of day-to-day operations" (1992, 210).

9. Mining towns—and Taxco certainly among them—attracted a significant number of free wage-earning Indians from many different regions, who were highly skilled in mining and refining and who, because of better salaries, often stayed to live permanently at the haciendas (Bakewell 1997, 186) or in the towns. These mining towns became centers of urban, commercial activity that connected adjacent indigenous rural towns to translocal economic worlds that propagated intense cultural exchange, albeit seldom to indigenous advantage (Bakewell 1997; Haskett 1991).

10. I am using José Rabasa's felicitous terminology of "plural-world dwelling" to denote a particular feature of colonial indigenous epistemic plasticity. According to Rabasa, this plasticity allowed the tlacuilo from the *Codex Telleriano-Remensis* (as well as Juan Vernal, I would add) to inhabit both the new, early modern Christian habitus imposed by the Spanish globalizers and the Postclassic Mesoamerican worldview of the homeland, without incurring disruptive, distressing, or paralyzing feelings of contradiction (see Rabasa 1998, 2011). The construct of plural-world dwelling has affinities with Mignolo's indigenous "border epistemologist" discussed in the introduction (Mignolo 2002). Both confer on the indigenous subject the privilege of wielding an epistemic porosity, flexibility, or mobility inaccessible to the colonizers because of their universalist mindset.

11. As I stated in the introduction, my citations of the nahualtocaitl throughout the book come from Andrews and Hassig's critical edition of 1984. I quote first their modernized Nahuatl version; secondly their translation of Ruiz de Alarcón's renderings into Spanish of the nahualtocaitl. Finally, I quote their translation into English of the modernized Nahuatl version of the incantation.

12. Although Juan Vernal is reciting a nahualtocaitl, he does not represent himself as a shaman, sorcerer, or ritual specialist. Thus, I use the basic, non-marked term "user" to refer to him. For her part, Dominique Raby (2006, 297) prefers the more general name of *oficiante* (officiant) because, as she rightly states, several users of the nahualtocaitl in the *Treatise* were not ritual specialists or shamans, but merely individuals who knew a few incantations. However, *officiant* still denotes a person who performs a religious service or ceremony, and in this sense, is a specialist of sorts. Whereas individuals who use nahualtocaitl for divining or healing would be appropriately called ritual specialists, conjurers, or officiants, in the case of this nahualtocaitl, *user* is probably a better choice.

13. *The Book of the Gods and Rites*, or *Libro de los ritos y ceremonias en las fiestas de los dioses y celebraciones de ellas*, was one of three books written by the Dominican Diego Durán. Finished circa 1576–79, it remained unpublished until 1880. Much like Sahagún's *Florentine Codex*, Durán's book was intended to inform Spanish missionaries about extant ancient indigenous practices and ceremonies so that they could detect them, discreetly shrouded under Christian ceremony.

14. Durán writes that the Cholultecas celebrated a costly feast for Quetzalcoatl, in order to show off the wealth and greatness of their city:

> Thus the idol we deal with in this chapter was the god and patron of Cholultecs... since the Cholultecs were merchants and wealthy people, they celebrated a superb, a costly feast for the god called Quetzalcoatl, the deity of the merchants.... *Today the natives of Cholula continue their trade and commerce with different merchandise, traveling through the most remote and distant parts of the land,* such as Cuauhtemallan and Xoconochco, all along those coasts and mines, with their loads of peddlers' trinkets, just as they did in ancient times. (Durán 1971, 128–29; emphasis is mine)

15. Proposed by Celestino Solaguren in his introduction to Sor Maria de Agreda's famous *Mística ciudad de Dios* (Mystical City of God, 1655–60), the genre of the literary prophetic implies that the authorial voice "does not write in her name, but in the name of a celestial voice that guides her; that is, prophetically" (Solaguren 1970, xliv; translation is mine). Still, there is a clear difference between the guiding and the guided subjects. Sor Maria claims her book is her abstraction/translation into human language of things that God himself, Christ, the Virgin Mary, and the angels communicated to her in the way they usually communicate with each other, which is beyond language (Agreda, 1970, 7–44). Sor Maria also represents herself as addressing both God and the Virgin in her visions and recording their discourse, but she never represents herself as having actually assumed or performed their identity.
16. For more on the dissolution of human identity in Teresa de Jesús's mystical experience see, among others, Howells (2002); Tyler (2013); and García (2015). Further interesting inquiries and epistemic comparisons could be made on the posited relationship between utterer and utterance in Teresa de Jesús's and San Juan de la Cruz's mystical discourse versus the nahualtocaitl.
17. "Que es lo mismo que el Dios de las manos, el Dios de las obras."
18. The *Annals of Cuauhtitlan,* a fundamental native colonial source for Mesoamerican cosmogonies in Central Mexico, state about Quetzalcoatl as creator god of the Toltecs: "And they said that the one they called their god made them, created them out of ashes. This they attributed to Quetzalcoatl" (Bierhorst 1992, 25). Later on is the following description of Topiltzin Quetzalcoatl as Toltec king and priest:

> What is more, in his life and in his time he introduced great riches, jade, turquoise, gold, silver, redshell, whiteshell, quetzal plumes....
>
> In addition, he introduced cacao of different colors and different-colored cotton.
>
> And he was a great craftsman in all his works: his eating dishes, his drinking vessels, his green-, herb-green, white-, yellow-, and red-painted pottery. And there was much more. (30)

For the expertise of the Toltecs in arts, crafts, and sciences, and on Quetzalcoatl as their priest see the *Florentine Codex,* book 10, chapter 29 (Sahagún 1950–82, 10:165–70). For a summary of Quetzalcoatl as cultural hero see, especially, Carrasco (1982), Florescano (1999), and Nicholson (2001).

19. Coe and Whittaker translate "àmo nezço àmo / nitlapallo" as "I am not bloodied / I am not reddened" (1982, 105).
20. Mesoamerican gods were however represented anthropomorphically, with their distinctive insignia (for example, Boone 2007, 39). Gods were deemed to be constantly involved in the human world, stamping their particular powers on entities in rotating cycles or units of time (López Austin 1993, 117; Read 1998, 150). Their specific spheres of operation are recorded in complex cosmogonic myths or origin narratives that have reached us in archaeological, documentary, and pictorial forms (Nicholson 1971, 396). For a recent discussion of Aztec deities as clusters of anthropomorphically represented energies unfolding in a continuum of a single, original, unitary, and all-permeating ocean of cosmic power (*teotl*), see James Maffie (2014). In addition to an interesting hypothesis, the author offers a good, updated background on the nature and representation of the Mesoamerican gods in known documentation.
21. The twenty-day count was a fundamental Mesoamerican time cycle in which each of the twenty days had its own sign and regent deity. In her cosmogonic reading of a renowned eighteen-page section of the *Codex Borgia*, Elizabeth Boone proposes that the second event depicted in this section is the "creation of the day count and thus of time itself" (2007, 181). If this is the case, the twenty-day count clearly must be considered as predating the emergence of the tonalpohualli and the *xiuhpohualli* (365-day solar year), both of which share the twenty-day count. In the tonalpohualli, the repeating sequence of twenty signs rotated with units of thirteen days—each also having a regent deity—throughout the 260-day cycle. Thus, the second trecena always started with the fourteenth day-sign, the third with the seventh day-sign, the fourth with the twentieth and last day-sign, and so on. For more detailed explanations of the twenty-day-count and the tonalpohualli see Caso (1967, 1971); López Austin (1988, 1:204–7; 1993); J. Furst (1995, 63–130; 176–78); Read (1998, 211–35), Hassig (2001, 7–17); Boone (2007); Duverger (2007); and more recently Maffie (2014, 270–79; 419–77; 495–502). Note, however, that the sequence of days varied regionally. Consequently, at times a different day with a different iconography could appear.
22. The Mexica celebrated the feast of Huey Tozotli during the dry season and dedicated it to the rain god Tlaloc in order to stimulate the regeneration of the earth. One tree was placed in each of the four corners of the courtyard of Tlaloc, with one in the center called "Tota" (Our Father), which was another name for Xiuhteuctli. At the conclusion of the ceremony, this large tree (wood) was fixed in a lake (water) so that it would impregnate the earth (Limón Olvera 2001, 64–65). Of course, we do not know whether this calendrical feast was celebrated in Tlalhuicatlalpan or Coixcatlalpan previous to the conquest of the Triple Alliance. Even so, Limón Olvera's analysis offers an important clue on the links between the tree, the day-sign Water, and its regent deity, the god of fire Xiuhteuctli through the concept of renewal.
23. The New Fire, or Binding of the Years, ceremony took place when the end of 52 (365-day) solar cycles and 73 (260-day) divinatory calendar cycles coincided on the same day, or every 18,980 days. All fires were extinguished awaiting the appearance of the Pleiades in the midnight sky. When the constellation rose, a new fire was drilled in the chest of a war

captive, regenerating the cosmos for another fifty-two years (see Carrasco 1999, 96–103, for a detailed description of this ritual.

24. Elizabeth H. Boone explains that the surviving manuscript versions of the tonalpohualli show gods and mantic forces consistently linked to the same units of time. She writes, "The divinatory codices do not seem to present local or regional realities; rather they participate in a broadly shared ideological system that concerns the cycles of time and the gods and forces linked to these cycles" (2007, 231). Therefore, a calendar priest-reader (*tonalpouhqui*) from one region "would . . . have found it easy to divine from a manuscript that was painted in another region" (232). Thus, the calendrical names used in the nahualtocaitl (One Water, One Death, Seven Flower, Five Snake, and so on), would generally have been associated with the same patrons and mantic forces as in the *Codex Borbonicus* (perhaps from Culhuacan), the *Telleriano-Remensis* (from Mexico City and Puebla), the *Tonamatl Aubin* (from Tlaxcala), the *Borgia* (from the Cholula area), and the *Vaticanus B* (from the Mixteca Alta). See Boone (2003, 213–17; 2007, 231–33) for a list of these divinatory codices and comments about their commonalities and differences.

25. In this letter, which functions as a prologue, Ruiz de Alarcón complains to the archbishop about the difficulty of fulfilling the latter's mandate to record the idolatrous practice of the nahualtocaitl given its "difficult and almost unintelligible language" as a long, continuous stream of metaphors that "at times passes into being a sustained allegory" (1984, 40). While cognizant of the intricacy of the nahualtocaitl, Ruiz de Alarcón was not fully aware of how much he was missing.

26. In the introduction I argued that because the nahualtocaitl were coerced, the informants may have selected the least offensive conjuros to confess. The claim that they did not tamper very much with the ones they did confess does not contradict this argument.

27. For an account of this incident, which took place at Teotihuacan right before the emergence of the Fifth Sun, see the *Florentine Codex*, book 3. For contemporary versions of the Tecciztecatl myth, see Graulich (1997, 118–19). See Spranz (1973, 161–72) for the iconography of this god, whose most distinctive accoutrement is a conch.

28. Toltec-Chichimecs conquered Cholula circa 1200 and established the cult of Quetzalcoatl there (Carrasco 1982, 133–40).

29. Regarding insensibility as a godly power in this segment of the incantation, Coe and Whittaker (1982, 105–6) translate the Nahuatl original (*onichualhuicac nomiccama nomiccanayo*) as "I bring forth / My dead hand / My dead body." In contrast, Andrews and Hassig (1984, 77) translate "Ōnichuālhuīcac nomiccāma, nomiccānacayo" more literally as "I have brought my dead-man hands, my dead-man flesh." Both translations differ substantively from Ruiz de Alarcón's: he makes a conceptual and metonymical leap by equating the dead hand and body with insensibility: "I bring my hands and my insensible body." Specifically, he metonymically substitutes the image of a corpse as the cause, and insensibility as its effect. Coe and Whittaker and Andrews and Hassig highlight the deliberate bearing of a dead hand and body as a godly or priestly power. Since the voice speaks of invoking a dead body and a dead hand in order not to feel human blows, the speech act of the nahualtocaitl seemingly marks itself as enunciated by a knowing, intelligent godly power, insensible to physical death.

30. See Pete Sigal (2011, 105–6) for an interpretation of Xochiquetzal's pleasure-giving cotton fluff and ball of thread in this nahualtocaitl as a metaphor for sexual subjugation linked to blood, death, and violence in warfare.

31. These four day-signs, or year carriers, are Rabbit (Tochtli), Reed (Acatl), Flint (Tecpatl), and House (Calli). Each received a numeral from 1 to 13, representing the order of the year in the Mesoamerican "century." Thus, because 13 × 4 = 52, the solar years in a century added up to this number, and was called *xiuhmolpilli* (tying of years) (Caso 1971, 347). The number of days in 52 solar years coincided with the number of days in 73 rounds of the tonalpohualli. Thus, the xiuhmolpilli conjoined the solar and divinatory calendars.

32. In an e-mail communication on October 23, 2015, Burkhart expresses a preference for Coe and Whittaker's translation of *tla ximixtlapachtlaça* as "please stretch out" (1982, 107) over Andrews and Hassig's sterner "throw yourself down" (1984, 78). However, she asserts that neither translation conveys the command (or request) that the earth shift position from face-up to face-down. In Burkhart's more nuanced reading, the illocutionary voice would appear to be commanding the erection of obstacles against the incoming attackers, rather than the removal of obstacles to facilitate strikes by the staff and knife. The two interpretations are not necessarily contradictory; they merely express different means for achieving the desired outcomes. See Burkhart (1986, 113–15) for a discussion of the year One Rabbit.

33. The historical location of Tollan is debated. While some scholars contend that Teotihuacan was the original, historical Tollan founded by Topiltzin Quetzalcoatl (Carrasco 1982; Coggins 2002), others believe that it was Tula, founded in the state of Hidalgo in the ninth century. Enrique Florescano (1999, 44) argues that Topiltzin Quetzalcoatl founded Tula, "the first Mesoamerican state built by a mixture of invading northerners and sedentary populations from the Central High Plains, probably descended from Teotihuacan." Whether Tollan corresponded with Teotihuacan, Tula, or a mythical city, there is consensus it represented the epitome of urban, civilized life in Mesoamerica. All Postclassic regional capitals, including Tula, Cholula, Xochicalco, Culhuacan, Chichen Itza, and Tenochtitlan, adopted Tollan's model of the city as an axis mundi of integrated political, socio-religious, and military orders. And Quetzalcoatl, in his many incarnations as creator god, plumed serpent, deified ruler, epic hero, and historical leader, was the paragon of the godly priest-king-warrior, wielder of legitimate authority and patron of all sciences, arts, commerce, and military technologies that would ensure human survival and prosperity. For different theories about the historical and mythical existence of Tollan see, among many others, Nigel Davies (1977, 1980); Carrasco (1982); Florescano (1999); and Coggins (2002).

34. David Carrasco (1982, 80) points out that scholars have often overlooked the early part of Quetzalcoatl's career as a warrior. Indeed, in the *Historia de los mexicanos por sus pinturas*, Quetzalcoatl underwent seven years of penance in which he drew blood from his body in order to become a warrior. After he became an outstanding one, the Toltecs sought him out to become their king (Garibay 1965, 37–38).

35. In the *Book of the Gods and Rites*, Diego Durán (1971, 101) writes that two of the gods whom warriors "implored" to give them victory in war during the Feast of Toxcatl were Tezcatlipoca and Quetzalcoatl. Olivier (2003, 273–77) cites this instance as an example of the similarities, not merely contrasts, between the two gods. Even though Olivier states

that he knows of only one instance where Quetzalcoatl is called Yaotl (which is precisely the nahualtocaitl being discussed in this chapter) he sees many intersections between the two figures.

CHAPTER FOUR. Requesting White Blood Tears of Sacrifice

1. Friars Domingo de Betanzos and Tomás Ortiz posited in the early sixteenth century that the indigenous peoples from the Caribbean and Mexico did not have the capacity to receive the Christian religion. See Adorno (2007, especially 101–8) on the dispute about Indians' capacity for rational thought.
2. The issue is obviously much more complex than I have stated here, as it requires—among other things—an examination of how those higher operations of cognition and understanding are culturally mediated as particularities and specificities of the rational soul. But the important point for my purposes is that it would be inaccurate to say that medieval and early modern Christianity did not attribute a soul to all living things, as if all creatures except humans were soulless living machines. For Thomas Aquinas's authoritative (for Christianity) description of the soul, see *Summa Theologiae*, part 1, questions 75–79.
3. In his book *Corn Is Our Blood*, Alan Sandstrom reports similar cosmological beliefs among twentieth-century Nahuas in the village of Amatlán, Veracruz: "The four major realms of the Nahua universe, earth, sky, underworld and water, are more than simply places where human beings and various spirits reside. They, too, are aspects of a deified universe, and in this sense these locations are spirit entities in their own right. For the Nahuas, any thing and any place has a significance in that it partakes of the universal sacred natural order" (1991, 238). This conception is not unlike the *anima mundi*, or world soul, proposed by Ficino in book 3 of his *De triplici vita*. On the specific significance of colors as powers in the nahualtocaitl, see Raby (2006).
4. For a deeper discussion of the theology of the Incarnation and of Christ as the Second Person of the Trinity, see Aquinas's "Treatise on the Incarnation" in the third part of the *Summa Theologiae*, questions 1–26. Aquinas, of course, does not exhaust the topic, but he serves as an authoritative point of reference for Catholic theology after the Council of Trent. In their article for the *New Catholic Encyclopedia*, Wallace, Weisheipl, and Johnson write that Pope Leo XIII (1810–1903; pope 1878–1903) accurately described the influence of Thomas Aquinas on the Council of Trent as follows: "the Fathers of Trent, in order to proceed in an orderly fashion during the conclave, desired to have opened upon the altar, together with the Scriptures and the decrees of the supreme pontiffs, the *Summa* of St. Thomas Aquinas whence they could draw council, reasons, and answers (Aeterni Patris)." Although the *Summa* was never placed upon the altar, the authors write that "for all practical purposes it might as well have been" (Wallace, Weisheipl, and Johnson 2003, 23). This suffices to justify my characterization of Aquinas as a trustworthy source for Catholic theology and epistemology in the sixteenth and seventeenth centuries, even though his positions did not go uncontested and were not necessarily the only ones in early modern Catholic Europe.
5. In his influential *Tratado de supersticiones y hechicerías* Pedro Ciruelo gives a terse definition of superstition as a vain observance: "The rule is this: in every action which man performs

to bring about some good or avoid some evil, if the things that he uses or the words that he employs possess neither natural nor supernatural power to bring about the desired effect, then that action is vain, superstitious, and diabolical; and the effect which is produced comes from the secret operation of the devil" (Ciruelo 1978, 42; English quotation is from Clark 1999, 482). Sometimes vain, futile observances could be unwittingly demonic. That is, the perpetrators of superstitious acts did not necessarily have the conscious intent of dealing with the devil. The danger resided in that people's deluded expectation that the acts would produce results offered the devil an opportunity to intervene with his preternatural powers and disturb the course of nature. This would only confuse people and make them go astray from God's established order (see Clark 1999, 472–88).

6. In his classic study, William Taylor (1979, 28–72) argues that in colonial Central Mexico there were dramatic changes in pulque drinking practices simply because of its commercialization and availability to peasants who formerly were prohibited from consuming the beverage. Taylor (1979, 30) notes that restrictions on pulque consumption in pre-Hispanic Central Mexico were centered on the time, place, and people who could drink it, rather than on the amount consumed. Those who were allowed to drink on specified occasions could do so even to the point of losing consciousness without incurring public censure. The *Codex Mendoza* records that elderly men and women were allowed to become intoxicated due to their advanced age. At the top of folio 71r in the codex, figures of two young men and one young woman are painted as victims of unauthorized drinking of pulque. The young woman and one of the male youths appear well dressed, indicating that neither high status nor gender was an impediment to the scourge. In their explanation of this folio, however, Berdan and Anawalt (1997, 235) point out that in some ritual events drinking was mandatory, and even small children were given alcohol. This was the case at the feast of the Pillahuana—recorded in the *Codex Magliabechiano* and held in the very area of the present-day state of Morelos where Ruiz de Alarcón did his investigations (Nicholson 1991, 164). Brundage (1979, 160) also mentions this feast. In book 6, chapter 14 of the *Florentine Codex* there is a long *huehuetlatolli* (speech of elders) admonishing the people against the dangers of pulque. See Nicholson (2001) for the traditions about the incestuous transgression of Topiltzin Quetzalcoatl due to the drink. In sum, pulque was considered a drink that had to be handled with utmost caution. Consumption of the beverage was highly valued and considered a privilege but was criminalized when done outside of proper prescribed festivities and contexts.

7. According to Mastache, Cobean, and Healan (2002, 260), some scholars have estimated that there may be as many as 150 varieties of maguey growing at different altitudes and adapted to very diverse weather conditions. Nine or ten species have been identified as useful for producing pulque. These species are cultivated in high, semi-arid zones in the Central Highlands, and at an altitude of 2,000 meters (Mastache, Cobean, and Healan 2002, 261).

8. Andrews and Hassig insert an (H) in the text of the nahualtocaitl to indicate an honorific form. These forms are a basic feature of Nahuatl and are used to show respect and deference to the listener or to a third person.

9. Sweeping the house or temple was more than cleaning a space. As Michael Smith has pointed out, it had a cosmographic dimension insofar as "the power of brooms . . . linked

women and priests in a common battle against the forces of disorder and darkness" (2012, 134). Also see Louise Burkhart (1997) on sweeping.

10. Coe and Whittaker (1982) eliminate this comment altogether in their translation.

11. In an e-mail of October 23, 2015, Louise Burkhart points out that *noconnotlālilīz* and *mēhuītihtiyez* are reverential verb forms, used for people in positions of authority, like noble lords or even God in heaven. While she thinks "seated in majesty" would be too strong a translation for these verbs, "seated in honor" is a more faithful rendering of the original Nahuatl.

12. According to the *Codex Vaticanus 3738* there were thirteen heavens and nine tiers of the underworld, all inhabited by deities. The *Vaticanus 3738* is the only extant pictorial representation of this vertical layering of the cosmos of the Fifth Sun, which seems to have been standard at the time of contact with Europeans (Nicholson 1971, 406–7). Nicholson indicates however that there are also extant references to a nine-tiered heaven that may refer to an earlier notion. Indeed, in the *Treatise* nine upper layers of heaven are identified in the incantations for inducing sleep and for curing scorpion bites (Ruiz de Alarcón 1984, 79, 205). Andrews and Hassig (1984, 21) wonder whether these nine heavens in the *Treatise* represent a retention of previous traditions from pre-Hispanic times or are a corruption. They point out though that nine is the highest ritual number found in the nahualtocaitl collected in the *Treatise.* Turning to the earth, its surface was rectangular, surrounded by marine waters that ascended, forming a wall that contained the first four heavens and then supported the rest of the celestial floors. The surface of the earth itself was divided into four –color, patron deities, a bird, and occasionally, animals, although these varied by region. In each corner or direction of the earth plane stood a cosmic tree through which the cyclical influences of the gods traveled and manifested on the earth plane (López Austin 1988, 1:66). See Nicholson (1971, 403–8); López Austin (1988, 1:52–68); Carrasco and Sessions (1998, 44–47); and Maffie (2014, 504–13), among many others, for more discussion about the shape of the Mesoamerican cosmos in the Late Postclassic.

13. Parsons and Parsons (1990, 21) note that "maguey may be planted in rows on the main surface of the field or on the sides of raised linear embankments (*bordos*) that are built up to a height of 50 to 100 cm, and measure up to 3.0 meters wide at the base." Usually, 2.5 to 5.0 meters are allowed between the plants in the rows (22). However, the distribution in which maguey is planted is not the basis of the meaning of the calendrical name.

14. Coe and Whittaker also correct Ruiz de Alarcón and translate Eight-Flint as "Lady Eight-Flint." As has been mentioned earlier, Coe and Whittaker use a more polite and reverential tone in their translation of the nahualtocaitl than Andrews and Hassig do. The tone used by Alfredo López Austin in his translation is also more reverential than Andrew and Hassig's. Ruiz de Alarcón's rendering lies somewhere in between. Because he had no knowledge of the calendrical names, his mistranslations often result in complex metaphorical roundabouts. This gives his renderings of the calendrical names a disconcerting but beautiful touch of unwitting lyricism.

15. In the *Codex Borbonicus* and *Codex Vaticanus A* Mayahuel is represented as emerging from a maguey. In the pictorials *Aubin Tonalamatl 8* and *Vaticanus B 56*, and *Borgia 6*, the maguey plant is depicted behind her. Mayahuel is represented in the *Codex Laud* in a squatting

position holding a cup of pulque, highlighting her attributes as a fertility goddess. In the *Fejérvary-Mayer*, she appears in a maguey plant suckling a child. For more on the sources depicting Mayahuel, see Gonçalves de Lima (1956); Quiñones Keber (1989); and Nicholson (1991).

16. In a nahualtocaitl for hunting bees (second treatise, chapter 7) the maguey plant is invoked because it is used to make the net (Ruiz de Alarcón 1984, 92). However, the maguey as a provider of fiber is not referred to by a calendrical name but by a beautiful metaphor: *tlālocxōchitl*, or land-wine-flower (Andrews and Hassig 1984, 330 n. 6).
17. Coe and Whittaker (1982, 173) translate this passage as: "Well now, please bring yourself forth, / Red Chichimec / Please scour it now." Again, their tone is more reverential and polite than Ruiz de Alarcón's or Andrews and Hassig's.
18. In his *Manual for Ministers*, Jacinto de la Serna explains that the spoon is called a Red Chichimec because of its coppery color and because it actually "ate" the cavity of the meyollotl that it scraped just like Chichimecs "eat and suck blood and human flesh as if were from animals" (Serna 1892, 429; translation is mine). This gory, demeaning explication is not the best rendering of the metaphor.
19. Writes Foucault: "The nature of things, their coexistence, the way in which they are linked together and communicate is nothing other than their resemblance" (Foucault 1973, 29). Now this mode of communication, these resemblances could be made efficacious by the intervention of the natural philosopher (Magus), who could draw the power of higher things to lower ones by virtue of their similitudes in the corridors of being.
20. Licenses to sell pulque in Mexico City and other urban centers in the Valley of Mexico were increasingly petitioned from the 1580s on. The requirement to request a license evinces the desire of the Crown to regulate and control the commerce in liquor, because it was deemed to be a cause of social disruptions. The permits were not difficult to obtain, however. City officials throughout the seventeenth century encouraged the trade because the tax on pulque sales provided an important source of revenue for public works. William Taylor (1979, 36) reports a petition in 1629—the exact year when Ruiz de Alarcón finished his *Treatise*—which declared that many villages near Mexico City depended on the sale of pulque as their main means of support.
21. Immediately after the conjuro for the cultivation of maguey I have analyzed, Ruiz de Alarcón reports a second one addressing Tlalteuctli, the lord-lady of the Earth. Suffice it to say for the moment that the speaker in this conjuro does not identify himself as a priest, a nahualli lord, or a god. Most likely it would be a male speaker since tlachiqueros and maguey farmers are usually men. Tlalteuctli is a addressed as a female earth manifestation, although it was also considered a god. See Eduardo Matos Moctezuma's article "Tlaltecuhtli" as an excellent introduction to this deity (1997, 15–40). In the conjuro in question, the speaker exhorts "my mother Tlalteuctli" to be attentive to his voice and to embrace Eight-Flint-Woman because he will soon come back to see her. I will leave for another occasion a closer reading of this short, beautiful nahualtocaitl. What I do want to point out now is that this second nahualtocaitl for planting maguey does not demand either any non-ordinary action from the earth—other than calling her mother and lady and expecting her to behave as a communicative subject.

22. The *Silva de varia lección* (A Miscellany of Several Lessons) is an encyclopedic collection of intellectual curiosities and humanistic subjects. It was an extremely popular work, with more than one hundred editions in several languages published in less than two hundred years (Lerner 2003, 12). The author, Pedro Mexía (1497–1551), was cosmographer of the Casa de Contratación de Indias in 1527, and official chronicler of Emperor Charles V in 1547.

23. In his prologue or preface to the *Silva*, Mexía writes:

> Regarding the truth of the history, and of the matters about which this work treats, it is certain that I do not say or write anything that I have not read in a book of great authority.... Therefore it will be a fair matter that, before anybody condemns what he reads, he should consider first the authority and reason that is given. Because not everything a man does not know or does not understand he must deem untrue. (Mexía 2003, 4; translation is mine)

According to Isaías Lerner (2003, 23–24), these claims of truth are not merely rhetorical. The beliefs documented in the *Silva*, based on texts and figures of recognized authority, are supposed to give us some insight into the "intellectual universe" of Spain and Europe, given the success of its numerous translations.

CHAPTER FIVE. Fatal Attraction

1. Of course, this nonmodern, animistic worldview is not unique to the Amerindian peoples of the Amazonian, Andean, and Mesoamerican cultural areas. It is a way of knowing, perceiving, and understanding common to hunter-gatherer and agricultural peoples all over the globe (Callicott 1982; Berkes 2012).
2. William H. Fellowes (1985) also analyzes the Nahuatl version of this incantation for hunting deer with snares, since it is one of the three or four that Ruiz de Alarcón reported had been put into writing separate from his interrogations. Fellowes's analysis is very difficult to follow, and in many instances, his explanations are not sufficiently grounded in or supported by evidence.
3. Sanders, Parsons, and Santley (1979, 476) state that the optimal habitat of white-tailed deer in Mesoamerica is the pine-oak woodlands of the Basin of Mexico, Puebla, Toluca, Oaxaca, and Guerrero.
4. The nahualtocaitl for hunting deer with snares is one of the few conjuros that Ruiz de Alarcón found already transcribed by the indigenous users themselves. Lamentably, Ruiz de Alarcón does not give any detail regarding the provenance of this transcribed incantation, nor how he came across it. The fact that he found it in writing, however, may point to its importance among the indigenous people, as well as explain its unusual length.
5. According to the tribute list for Tepequaquilco recorded in the *Codex Mendoza*, the Coixca province was to provide the Triple Alliance with two thousand cotton mantas of different sizes and designs every six months. Annually, it was to provide twenty-two warrior costumes; one bin each of maize, chia, beans, and amaranth; and five strings of chalchihuitl. Every eighty days the province had to give 100 small axes, 1,200 yellow gourd bowls, 400 little baskets of white copal for incense, 8,000 balls of unrefined copal, and 200 little jars of

honey (Berdan and Anawalt 1997, 79, f. 39r). See also Dehouve (1994, 40–48). This shows that the province was a tributary source of rich and varied agricultural products, and did not depend on hunting for sustenance. Paso y Troncoso ([1892] 1953), however, claims that Tepequaquilco also had to give some wild game to the Triple Alliance (quoted in Berdan 1996, 127).

6. Burkhart (1997, 29) explains that when a new house was built, the fire that would give warmth to it could not be taken from a neighbor or relative, but had to be drilled anew on the home's hearth. Brian Stross (1998, 35) observes that two essential elements in present-day Maya rituals for ensouling or animating a house are placing three hearthstones in the center of the house floor and starting the fire. David Freidel, Linda Schele, and Joy Parker also point out that three hearthstones "have been used in Maya homes for over three millennia" (2001, 67). These hearthstones surround the fire (Xiuhteuctli) for cooking and establish the center of the home.
7. "'And when you have done your shooting, lay them in the hands of Xiuhteuctli, the Old Spirit, whom these three are to guard: Mixcoatl, Tozpan, and Ihuitl. These are the names of the three hearthstones.' Thus Itzpapalotl taught the Chichimecs" (Bierhorst 1992, 23).
8. Andrews and Hassig do not translate the appositive in this or any other instance where appositives appear in the *Treatise*. They explain that Icnopiltzintli is another name for Centeotl, and that in the *Treatise* it "vacillates between being a god name . . . and simply a common noun" meaning "poor orphan" (Andrews and Hassig 1984, 228). Because it is an appositive and refers to the idea of having been abandoned by the father, I think Coe and Whittaker's decision to translate it as "the Little Orphan" is preferable, at least for this nahualtocaitl (1982, 145). Louise Burkhart also prefers that *Icnopiltzintli* be translated as "Little Orphan" or "Orphan Child." However, *nicenteotl* as "the Single God" is less felicitous. She writes that "icel teotl" was "the standard expression for 'single' or 'only god'" (e-mail communication, October 23, 2015). Thus, in this case, Andrews and Hassig's rendering of *nicenteotl* simply as "Centeotl" is more accurate.
9. Regarding the Maize God's dancing and singing, Braakhuis writes that a basic feature of the Maize Hero is "his boundless vitality and gaiety" (2009, 20). Indeed, in pre-Hispanic Nahua sources Centeotl is associated with the youthful solar fertility deities—among them Xochipilli and Piltzinteuctli—who were patrons of painting, writing, sculpting, dancing, games, and music, and the latter the progenitor of Centeotl himself. All these arts are in turn metonymically linked to Centeotl, who enabled the emergence of agricultural civilization in which such arts would thrive.
10. These contemporary traditions have been recorded in the Gulf Coast region of the Huasteca. In them, the male maize child-god or corn spirit is called Chicomexochitl. As we will see, this name for the maize god establishes an important connection between these traditions and the seventeenth-century nahualtocaitl from the district of Oapan that we are examining in this chapter.
11. Interestingly, in Kakquichel rituals in preparation for hunting in twenty-first-century Guatemala, recently collected ethnographical information has suggested that weapons are treated as "animated social actors" (Brown and Emery 2008, 313). Since the weapons will be inflicting death blows on the animals, the weapons are brought into the rituals to

solicit permission and later to ask for forgiveness. The hunters dance with their guns in the hunting shrines and tell them how lovely they are in order "to help sway them into hitting their targets" (313). Thus, this belief and experience that inanimate entities have a dimension that is sentient and intelligent, and can therefore be persuaded to act, is part of the animistic, relational epistemology shared by some Mesoamerican indigenous peoples from at least the Late Postclassic and colonial periods up to the present day, as Ruiz de Alarcon's nahualtocaitl and contemporary ethnographic research evidences.

12. According to the annotations in the *Codex Telleriano-Remensis* pertaining to the trecena presided over by Itzpapalotl, the gods who fell from heaven with her and Xochiquetzal were Quetzalcoatl, Huitzilopochtli, Tezcatlipoca, Tonacateuctli, Yohualtecuhtli, and Tlahuizcalpantecuthli (Quiñones Keber 1995, 182–83).
13. Specifically, they are related by virtue of continuity: by sharing the same space of transgression.
14. In her reading of the nahualtocaitl for hunting deer with snares, Dehouve (2010) proposes that the Mixcoatl origin story undergirds the incantation. I hope to show that this is not the case, at least not for the nahualtocaitl I am analyzing here.
15. In the previous conjuration for hunting deer with snares, an abandoned Xochiquetzal also yearns for her husband, and Centeotl states, "I have been sad because of him. I am poor. I suffer poverty. I am tired" (Ruiz de Alarcón 1984, 98).
16. This famous episode appears in *El ingenioso hidalgo Don Quijote de la Mancha*, part I, chapter 6. See Juan Manuel Cacho Blecua's excellent introduction to *Amadís de Gaula* (1987). Ángel Rosenblatt's (1987) and Alicia Redondo Goicoechea's (1987) shorter introductions are also useful.
17. Written between 1581 and 1584 and unpublished until 1871, the *Historia de Tlaxcala* by historian Diego Muñoz Camargo is the main colonial source for the origin story of Tezcatlipoca's seduction of Xochiquetzal.
18. Olivier (2003, 215) explains that the commonalities between Tezcatlipoca and Xochipilli as lovers of music and flowers are enacted in the ritual of the Toxcatl, the major calendrical feast dedicated to Tezcatlipoca. In this feast his *ixiptla*, or impersonator, led for a full year the life of a nobleman, playing the flute and smelling flowers, before being sacrificed. See Carrasco (1999, 115–39) for a detailed description and cultural analysis of this ritual celebration.
19. In endnote 10 I mentioned that in some contemporary Huasteca traditions the divine maize child is called Chicomexochitl (Hernández Bautista et al., 2004; Sandstrom and Gómez Martínez, 2004), not his progenitor. There are many other variations of these traditions similar to the seventeenth-century nahualtocaitl for hunting deer from Guerrero. However, the fact that in the Gulf Coast tradition the orphan maize child bears the same name, Chicomexochitl, as his absent father-deer in the nahualtocaitl establishes a significant link between them.
20. Writes Klein: "Xochipilli-Piltzinteuctli appears twice . . . in Codices Vaticanus B 96 and Borgia 53. . . . Here the god assumes the disguise of a deer, an act that surely refers to the Mexican legend that Piltzinteuctli turned into a deer on the day 7 Xochitl (7 Flower), the day of the annual festival held in honor of his beloved, the moon goddess Xochiquetzal" (Klein 1976, 6). *Codex Borgia 53* and *Vaticanus B 96* show flayed deerskins that are 20-day almanacs. Elizabeth H. Boone (2007, 107) observes that in *Borgia 53*, the open mouth of

the dead deer depicts "the face mask of Xochipilli or Macuilxochitl, gods of the flowers, song, dance and pleasure." This mask is shown face-on. Boone points out that the face in the deerskin in *Vaticanus B 96*—also shown frontally—is also linked to Xochipilli and Macuilxochitl "being heavily jeweled, with turquoise lips, copious turquoise jewelry . . . and a black eye mask with four clustered disks (a "sun" symbol characteristic of the costume of these gods)" (2007, 107). Similarly, Klein (1976, 6) states that "[Xochipilli-Piltzinteuctli] is associated . . . with the phenomenon of frontality in two-dimensional art." Given the merging of Xochipilli and Piltzinteuctli in many traditions, the fact that they appear in *Borgia* 53 and *Vaticanus B* on the splayed-out deerskin supports the contention that the ritual name Chicomexochitl Piltzinteuctli establishes a relationship among the feast day of Xochiquetzal, Piltzinteuctli, and the deer (or its hide).

21. Xochiquetzal speaks first, stating that she comes from Tamoanchan. In the second strophe, Piltzinteuctli is shedding tears, looking for the goddess (see Garibay 1958; Seler 2014).

22. Interestingly, Burr Brundage claims that the Tlalhuica celebrated Xochiquetzal's festival "to introduce the young to drink and to sex in a ceremonial and therefore a controlled way" (1979, 160). He posits that the Tlalhuica most likely adopted this feast day from the Culhua, but does not specify that it took place on the day Seven Flower. In contrast, Henry Nicholson (1991, 164) notes the feast of the Pillahuana, or Drunkenness of Children, was celebrated during the veintena of Huey Pachtli. He mentions that the annotations to this feast in the Codex Magliabechiano state that it was celebrated by the Tlalhuica. Xochiquetzal is painted in the codex as the patron goddess of the feast. Neither Brundage nor Nicholson establish any identity between the Pillahuana and Xochiquetzal's movable feast on the day Seven Flower. However, the facts that she was patroness of both celebrations (if they were not the same one) and that both involved sexual acts suggest some connection with the goddess's own seduction on Chicomexochitl, the day of her great feast, by Lord Prince Piltzinteuctli, who disguised himself as a deer. This, in turn, is additional evidence that this seduction is the cosmogonic event resonating in the ritual name for the male deer in the present nahualtocaitl for archers, also of Coixca-Tlalhuica provenance.

23. "The gods descended to a cavern where a god named *Pieciuntentli* [Piltzinteuctli] lay with a goddess named *Choquijceli* [Xochiquetzal] of whom a god named *Ciutentl* [Cinteotl] was born" (Thévet 1905, 31; translation is mine).

24. Coe and Whittaker (1982, 146) translate Mixcoacihuatl literally as "Cloud Serpent Woman." Andrews and Hassig (1984, 231) read the name as a compound noun, which suggests "woman of Mixcoatl," or female deer.

25. This interpretation is supported by the nahualtocaitl for hunting fowl, in which the speaker refers to himself as "Nicnopiltzintli, NiCenteotl, NiQuetzalcaotl" (I am Icnopilzintli. I am Centeotl. I am Quetzalcoatl) (Andrews and Hassig 1984, 89). Namely, the orphaned child Centeotl and Quetzalcoatl come together as identities of the speaker of this incantation.

26. A name-form "is a special form of a noun that may be used as a personal name. It is marked by the replacement of an absolutive number suffix by zero (i.e., a silently present constituent)" (Andrews and Hassig 1984, 307). That is, non-possessed nouns take absolutive number suffixes, but in the name-form, the number suffix is suppressed. This enables the name-form to be used as a personal name.

27. Andrews explains that the adjunctive (optional) particle *in* "automatically adjoins the following element (or group of elements) to a nucleus" (1975, 33). The adjoining of a noun to a matrix using *in* makes it a definite noun. This relation can be expressed approximately in English by the definite article "the" (Andrews 1975, 199–200).
28. "La flor de la carne de Mixcoacihuatl" (López Austin 1967b, 18) and "carne florida de mi hermana mayor Mixcoacihuatl" (Dehouve 2010: 316, 327). Or, "My elder sister Cloud-serpent Woman's / Flesh-flower" according to Coe and Whittaker (1982, 137).
29. In an e-mail communication of October 23, 2015, Louise Burkhart agrees with Andrews and Hassig that *Acaxoch* as "reed flower" is more likely than *nacaxoch*, or "flesh flower."
30. Andrews and Hassig (1984) also support their translation of *Acaxoch* as "deer" by referring to the occurrence of this voice in book 11 ("Earthly Things") of the *Florentine Codex*. In chapter 1, paragraph 6 of this book, which tells of "four-footed animals," it says about the deer: "Deer: Its name is also acaxoch and forest deer. It is a forest dweller, tall, with sinewy, well-formed legs" (Sahagún 1950–82, 11:15).
31. In the first book of the *Treatise*, Ruiz de Alarcón says that his informants did not understand what *tahui* meant (1984, 72). Andrews and Hassig (1984, 322 n. 6) state that in his famous vocabulary, Alonso de Molina (1992) defines *tahui* as an interjection used to call someone. But regardless of whether or not indigenous hunters in the seventeenth century knew the meaning of *tahui*, had they believed that bellowing this single word or the name Mixcoacihuatl was what made the deer stop, the nahualtocaitl for hunting deer would have been superfluous. Hunters would have needed only to cry out "Tahui" or "Mixcoacihuatl" to make the game appear. Thus, it is safe to assume that Agustín Jacobo meant the full nahualtocaitl is what made the deer stop and turn around.
32. "Since yesterday and even the day before . . . Xochiquetzal has been crying, because of whom she has been sad. Since yesterday and the day before I, the priest, have been crying for him, I have been sad because of him" (Ruiz de Alarcón 1984, 98).
33. Quinatzin was a descendant of the semilegendary Xolotl who had led the migrating Acolhua ethnic group from Aztlan into the Basin of Mexico after the fall of Tula. Quinatzin moved the Acolhua capital from Tenayuca after its establishment by Xolotl in the western arm of Lake Texcoco (Smith 2008, 29–30). The new Acolhua capital on the eastern shore of the lake would become Texcoco, the greatest and most culturally prestigious city of the Aztec Triple Alliance.
34. Mohar Betancourt (2004, 217) supports her reading by citing the *Relación de Michoacán* and the *Historia tolteca chichimeca*, in which there are references to hunting deer in order to offer them to the gods and to the four quarters of the world.

CHAPTER SIX. Light, Mirror, and Knowledge in a Nahualtocaitl for Divining with Maize Kernel

1. According to Aquinas the actual occurrence of contingent things cannot be foreseen because "events which proceed from their causes in the minority of cases are quite unknown, such as casual and chance events" (*Summa Theologiae*, part 1, question 57, article 3). Contingent or chance events are a product of many causes whose conjunction has no necessity of being and therefore, no determinable cause. It is in this sense that they are groundless. Even

angels and demons—in spite of their superhuman knowledge of the causes and effects of all things terrestrial, sublunar, and even celestial—cannot have knowledge of contingent future things in themselves, unless by divine permission. Namely, they cannot know the future exactly as it will happen.

2. Aquinas states that even angels cannot fully know how things will be in the future because "although the species in the intellect of an angel, insofar as they are species, refer equally to things present, past and future, nevertheless, present, past and future do not bear the same relations to the species" (*Summa Theologiae*, part 1, question 57, article 3). Things in the present have a unique materiality, a nature whereby they resemble the species in the mind of the angel. But the nature of a thing in the present is not identical to its intellectual species. This difference has to do with the corruptible and mutable causes affecting matter, and of course, accidents, which cannot be anticipated because they have no being or discernable cause. See Aquinas, *Summa Theologiae*, part 1, question 115, article 6, "Whether Heavenly Bodies Impose Necessity on Things Subject to Their Action," where Aquinas writes that "everything which has a being 'per se' has a cause, but what is accidentally has not a cause, because it is not truly a being." For a thorough discussion on the intellect of angels and their way of knowing things through the perfection and universality of their species, but not through the nature of their future actuality, see *Summa Theologiae*, part 1, question 55, article 3 of his questions on "The Angels (Spirit)."

3. For some important works on the subject of superstition and the reinterpretation of popular culture in early modern Europe see Jean Delumeau (1977) and Robert Muchembled (1985). On the widening gap between elite and popular cultures, see Peter Burke (1978) and, of course, Stuart Clark (1999, 2015) and Euan Cameron (2010). For literature against superstitious beliefs in Spain see F. Alejandro Campagne (2003). Alexandra Walsham (2008) provides a careful historiographic revision of the attributed, teleological role of the Reformation in the spiritual modernization and disciplining of popular piety. She argues that both the Reformation and Counter-Reformation sought to weed out superstition and better secure the boundaries between the secular and the preternatural.

4. See Anthony Pagden (1982, 97–99) regarding Francisco de Vitoria's and other theologians' earlier comparisons between the Amerindians and the Spanish peasantry. See Campagne (2009, 37–38) for additional comparisons between European peasantry and Indians of the Americas by ecclesiastics in France and Italy. Deserving particular attention is the pronouncement from the terrifying French witch-hunter Pierre de Lancre, who unleashed the hunt of 1610 in Logroño as a ramification of his persecution in Labourd. In 1612 Lancre lumped together global geopolitics, religion, and heresy when he declared that as demons from the Indies, Japan, and the rest of the world were forced out from their places of origin, they had emigrated to the French Basque province of Labourd. Lancre's quote also appears in Campagne (2009, 39).

5. See Barbara Tedlock's article "Divination as a Way of Knowing" (2001) for a useful discussion and extensive bibliography on the transcultural practice of divination in non-Christian cultures.

6. In her reading of the *Codex Borgia*'s notable eighteen-page section on cosmogony, Elizabeth H. Boone (2007, 173–210) posits that the creation of the twenty-day count occurred immediately after a (big bang–like) explosion of primordial energy and power, as pictured

in the second image of the codex (folio 30). Boone comments that although the cosmogonic narrative she posits has no direct correspondence with creation stories recorded in sixteenth-century colonial sources, it does contain various places and actions in common. And indeed, in the *Historia de los mexicanos por sus pinturas*, the twenty-day count was also among the very first entities created.

7. For a lengthier discussion of the xiuhpohualli see Caso (1971); Nicholson (1971); Read (1998, 211–35); Hassig (2001, 7–17); and Maffie (2014, 430–44).
8. Colonial and precolonial sources vary as to whether there were three or four suns—each with specific patron gods and dominant elements—before the present world era. Some sort of humans lived during each of the suns, but humankind in its current form emerged in the last sun. The *Leyenda de los soles, Historia de los mexicanos por sus pinturas, Histoyre du Mexique,* and *Codex Vaticanus A* mention the foods consumed in each sun. Michael Graulich (1997, 90–91) points out that in the Mexican sources, the people in the previous ages are depicted as having had hardly any culture. But in the Popol Vuh, for instance, the wood people of the Second Sun had utensils, pots, and kettles. Each past era came to an end, usually by a catastrophe or duel between agonistic forces, and the humans of that era were transformed or converted into fish, monkeys, or birds, depending on the patron god of that world, and the day and manner of its destruction (Graulich 1997, 90). For a discussion of the Aztec shift from four to five suns, see Hassig (2001, 63–69).
9. Maffie (2014, 423–77) posits that the fitting overlap or synchronization between the xiuhpohualli and the tonalpohualli comes as a result of the specific teotl interrelational pattern of the Fifth Sun.
10. See chapter 3 and the discussion about One Rabbit as year bearer.
11. Primo Feliciano Velázquez (1992, 121) translates the passage into Spanish as, "A continuación Oxomoco echó suertes con el maíz: también agoró Cipactónal, la mujer de Oxomoco." Bierhorst translates it more literally as, "Then Oxomoco counted it out, and Oxomoco's wife, Cipactonal, also counted its fate." In a note Bierhorst elaborates that "Oxomoco counted corn kernels to divine the future" (1992, 147 n. 22).
12. Quiñones Keber (2002) makes this argument regarding the pictorial representations in book 4 of the *Florentine Codex.* She argues that the paintings of the days of a trecena are empty of all representations of divinities and their mantic forces. All figures are represented in quasi-realistic fashion, following European conventions.
13. Once again, Coe and Whittaker's (1982) translation of *tla xihualmohica* as "Please, bring yourself forth" is more polite and reverential than Andrews and Hassig's version. Andrews and Hassig (1984, 239) also do not translate "Tlazohpilli" because they consider it a ritual name for maize. However, although this compound name appears in apposition with Seven Snake—a calendrical, and thus also ritual name—the literal meaning of *tlazohpilli* is a more satisfactory translation because it underscores the elements of preciousness and affection: "precious [in the sense of beloved] noble, Seven Snake." Another notable feature is that, except for failing to recognize the calendrical name Seven Snake, Ruiz de Alarcón translates this nahualtocaitl in a more appropriately reverential tone than do Andrews and Hassig.
14. In a personal e-mail communication on February 5, 2016, Louise Burkhart confirms that Tlazohpilli can certainly refer to the goddess Chicomecoatl. She writes, "Pilli is gender

neutral but when a woman is referred to, we typically see *cihuapilli*. So the unmarked *pilli* might tend to be seen as male, or more likely to be male, maybe especially by male speakers. But there is no reason why it can't refer to a female, especially in association with Chicomecoatl, as here. Pipiltin as a class are both sexes, and *pilli* means male or female child in relation to a male parent. There would be less of a bias toward reading it as male than there is in Spanish or English."

15. Andrews and Hassig (1984, 339 n. 75) also believe that "owners of the five tonals" refers to the lunules of the fingernails.
16. See Andrews and Hassig 1984, 339 n. 75 for a grammatical explanation of this translation.
17. The Macuiltonaleque are addressed in the first three chapters of the fifth treatise on divination (Ruiz de Alarcón 1984, 144, 151, 153). Their assistance is also solicited in nahualtocaitl for the hands-on activities of hunting, fishing, and healing (102, 112, 138, 168).
18. As mentioned earlier, the five gloomy days of the descent of the Cihuateteo carried the numeral 1. One Rain, the opening day of the seventh trecena, was one of these days, The day-signs of the Cihuateteo occurred in trecenas 3, 7, 11, 15, and 19, which were all associated with the west. They were coupled with the five days of the Macuiltonaleque because the latter appeared in the fifth place in trecenas subsequent to those of the Cihuateteo, namely, 4, 8, 12, 16, and 20 (Boone 2007, 120). For the Macuiltonaleque as consorts of the Cihuateteo see Pohl (1998, 195), who follows Seler and Taube on the subject. See also Dehouve (2010, 314).
19. Note that in this nahualtocaitl, the speaker invokes only the fingers or the hand itself as intelligent and volitional entities operating apart from the rest of the human body. A topic that could merit further inquiry is the role of the Macuiltonaleque as godly, ambivalent powers of the hand or fingers, not entirely controlled by humans, their association with Quetzalcoatl as Matl or hand (see chapter 3), their relation with the sophisticated, sedentary civilized arts of the Fifth Sun, and the dangerous aspects of excess associated with the number 5.
20. "La burla de ellos, la angustia de él."
21. In the nahualtocaitl for divination appearing in the first and second chapters of the fifth treatise, however, the chilling element of mockery as the motivation that may move the superhuman force to inflict harm on the patient is absent. Rather, hate or anger is given as the likely motive. The ticitl respectfully consults the patient's forearm in order to find out which is the offended superhuman force: "Who is the god, who is the marvelous being who thus breaks things, who thus shatters things, who thus destroys our jade, our jewel, our quetzal-feather [i.e., the sick person]?" (Ruiz de Alarcón 1984, 145). In a modernizing gesture in the nahualtocaitl that supports what Bernand and Gruzinski have called the "plasticity of the autochthonous cultures" (1992, 104), the seer questions the Virgin Mary and other saints to find out if they were the angry parties causing the affliction. And if the divination revealed that indeed it was a saint who caused the sickness in retaliation for some disrespectful behavior toward his or her images, the process continued to find out what could be done to make amends. In words of Ruiz de Alarcón (1984, 146), "And usually they prognosticate that they will placate them by making some image for them, or if they already have one, by making it some clothing or a veil, or by adding some ornament

to it and making some feast for them." This passage reveals the very thin line between an indigenous understanding of Catholic religious images as actual recipients of teotl, or numinous power, and the Catholic interpretation of religious images as representative objects that merit veneration. Indeed, James Lockhart (1992, 235–60) has written about how the Nahuas quickly adopted the cult of saints and reverence owed to Catholic images because it paralleled their conception of tutelary gods and of the ixiptla. Ixiptla were moving or nonmoving images of the gods, in which their powers resided and which thus were treated with utmost respect and reverence. Referring specifically to the incantation to determine whether Christian saints were the originators of the patient's illness, Lockhart (1992, 259) adds that saints had to be placated with Christian elements: images, clothing, celebrations on the saint's day, and the like.

22. López Austin (1970a, 4) translates this passage as, "Yo mismo, soy Cípac, soy Tónal" ("I, myself, I am Cipac, I am Tonal"; translation is mine). Andrews and Hassig dismiss the couplet and offer the straightforward translation "I am Cipactonal" (1984, 154). Retaining the couplet is the more accurate translation because it emphasizes the two components of the name Cipactonal; namely, Cipac[tli] and tonal. Coe and Whittaker's translation of "I am the Dragon, I am the Sign" is somewhat disconcerting (1982, 214). Dragon is too far-fetched a representation for Cipactli, the aquatic monster from which the body of the Fifth Sun was made and which constitutes the first sign of the twenty-day count.

23. Dominique Raby (2006, 296) and David Tavárez (2011, 80) mention that lay users and ritual specialists pronouncing the nahualtocaitl impersonated the deities whose voices were inscribed in the conjuros. However, both acknowledge that this deity personification was very different from the practice of the ixiptla in the calendrical celebrations. In the latter, an individual also impersonated a deity, sometimes for a long period preceding the feast. Usually, although not always, he or she was dressed in the deity's characteristic attire and sacrificed in order to reenact the original sacrifice of the deity and to replenish its powers. The impersonator might sing, but it is unclear whether it was also deemed to speak the sacred words of the god it incarnated, or to heal people or divine their future. See Carrasco (1991, 31–57) for a fuller description of the ixiptla in the actual calendrical feast of the Toxcatl. See Burkhart (1996, 42–48) and Díaz Balsera (2005, 57–64) for the contrast between an ixiptla and an actor.

24. Following Eduard Seler and Dennis Tedlock, Elizabeth Boone (2007, 24) has pointed out that Oxomoco and Cipactonal were "models for the aged couple Xucame and Xpiyacoc who appear in the Quiche Maya Popol Vuh as the first day-keepers, midwife and matchmaker."

25. Sahagún does not mention Oxomoco and Cipactonal as the discoverers or artificers of medicinal arts in his Spanish translation of the Nahuatl in book 10, however. Perhaps he chose not to link medicine with divination?

26. In his translation of book 5 of the *Florentine Codex* into Spanish, López Austin writes "viniste a verte en el espejo; viniste a consultar el libro" (1969, 21). In their translation Anderson and Dibble translate the metaphor less directly: "For so hast thou come that thou mightest come to see thy reflection, to use the sacred book for thyself" (Sahagún 1950–82, 5:152).

27. As recently as 1969, F. Herbert Fields reports that while doing fieldwork in Oaxaca, he received information about a woman in the town of San Bartolo Yautepec who was believed

to be a witch and had been forced at gunpoint "to reverse bewitchment and enact a curing" (208). The ingredients of the bewitchment had been clay "momo" pins and a secret copal ceremony. The un-bewitchment was performed with *Ipomoea violacea*, goat fat, and another unknown leaf.

Conclusion

1. In the last chapters of his *Manual*, where Serna offered his remedies for extant indigenous idolatrous and superstitious practices, he warned that commissioned judges would not be able to enter the Indian pueblos "so in silence, and so unaccompanied that it is not very public [knowledge]; and that even before setting out from this City everybody in the mountains will know it, where they [the judges] will go, which is the same as chasing away the game, and making that delinquents and offenders hide themselves" (1892, 468; translation is mine). Serna's observation suggests that word spread fast among indigenous pueblos when the intimidating visitas were on their way. Since Ruiz de Alarcón's investigations continued for more than ten years, the Tlalhuica and Coixca must surely have known that they were going on.
2. See III Concilio Provincial Mexicano, Libro V, Título VI: "De los hechiceros." (quoted in Lara Cisneros 2015, 124–25).
3. "La continua predicacion de el Evangelio, la enseñança de las buenas costumbres, y refutacion de estos errores, que esto es lo principal" (Serna 1892, 470).
4. According to Jorge Traslosheros (2002), bishops in the Archbishopric of Mexico usually tried to combat "devious" indigenous practices with pastoral care. Judicial processes were a last resort. Serna's discreet, patient, very long-term remedies for uprooting idolatry provide evidence for Trasloheros's position.
5. Recall that the nahualtocaitl did not operate independent of appropriate physical actions. Thus, the conjuro for hunting deer would not work if the user did not carry his bow and arrow and shoot at the game, nor would the one for defending oneself on lonely roads be effective if the user did not strike the enemy with a club.
6. I have analyzed other nahualtocaitl using the same analytical methodology (see Díaz Balsera, especially 2007, 2011a, and 2011b). See also Dehouve (2010), Raby (2006), Tavárez (2011), and of course, Andrew and Hassig's paraphrases and notes on the nahualtocaitl in their translation and edition of 1984.
7. As a case in point, a recent discovery is five nahualtocaitl that were used by ritual specialist Magdalena Papalo Coaxochitl and were documented in her idolatry trial in 1584, conducted by juez comisionado Francisco León de Carvajal in the diocese of Tlaxcala; see Tavárez (2011, 70) and Cruz Soto (1993).
8. Michael Smith (2012, 38) explains that Aztec migration movements registered or mapped in the native histories and accounts of Central Mexico are supported by historical linguistic evidence. Nahuatl belongs to the Nahuan group of Uto-Aztecan languages, which were unknown in Mesoamerica until the arrival of Chichimecs coming from the north. It is believed that Uto-Aztecan languages originated in the present U.S. Southwest or northern Mexico. Thus, the ancestral Aztecs are ethnic groups that came from Aztlan or Chicocomotz,

the Seven Caves—most likely after the fall of Tula or Tollan. However, the Aztlan migration to the Valley of Mexico was not the first migration from the north. Nigel Davies (1980, 82–87) argues that the so-called Chichimecs who supposedly contributed to the fall of Tollan and then invaded the Valley of Mexico were highly organized and thus most likely already possessed differing degrees of sedentary Mesoamerican cultural knowledge and practices.

Bibliography

Adorno, Rolena. 2007. *The Polemics of Possession in Spanish American Colonial Narrative.* New Haven, Conn.: Yale University Press.

Agreda, Sor María de Jesús de. 1970. *Mística ciudad de Dios. Vida de María.* Edited by Celestino Solaguren, OFM. Madrid: Fareso.

Agrippa, Henry Cornelius. 1993. *Three Books of Occult Philosophy Written by Henry Cornelius Agrippa of Nettesheim.* Translated by James Freake. St. Paul, Minn.: Llewellyn.

Aguirre Beltrán, Gonzalo. 1963. *Medicina y magia. El proceso de aculturación en la estructura colonial.* México: Instituto Nacional Indigenista.

Alberro, Solange. 1988. *Inquisición y sociedad en México, 1551–1700.* México: Fondo de Cultura Económica.

———. 1992. *Del gachupín al criollo. O de cómo los españoles de México dejaron de serlo.* México: Colegio de México.

Allan, Keith. 1999. "Meaning and Speech Acts," http://users.monash.edu.au/~kallan/papers/Speechacts.html

Allen, Michael J. B. 1984. *The Platonism of Marsilio Ficino: A Study of his Phaedrus Commentary, Its Sources and Genesis.* Berkeley: University of California Press.

———. 2002. Introduction to *Marsilio Ficino: His Theology, His Philosophy, His Legacy,* edited by Michael J. B. Allen and Valery Rees, xiii–xxii. Leiden: Brill.

Alva Ixtlilxochitl, Fernando de. 1952. *Obras históricas de don Fernando de Alva Ixtlilxochitl,* vol. 1, edited by Alfredo Chavero. México: Editora Nacional.

Anders, Ferdinand, Maarten Jansen, and Luis Reyes García. 1993. *Manual del adivino: libro explicativo del llamado Códice Vaticano B.* México: Fondo de Cultura Económica.

Andrews, J. Richard. 1975. *Introduction to Classical Nahuatl.* Austin: University of Texas Press.

Andrews, J. Richard, and Ross Hassig, eds. and trans. 1984. *Treatise on the Heathen Superstitions That Today Live Among the Indians Native to This New Spain, 1629,* by Hernando Ruiz de Alarcón. Norman: University of Oklahoma Press.

Ankarloo, Bengt, and Gustav Henningsen, eds. 1993. *Early Modern European Witchcraft: Centers and Peripheries.* Oxford: Clarendon Press.

Apter, Emily. 2013. *Against World Literature: On the Politics of Untranslatability*. London: Verso.

Aquinas, Thomas. 1920. *The Summa Theologiae of St. Thomas Aquinas*. Translated by the Fathers of the English Dominican Province. Chicago: Encyclopedia Britannica, www.newadvent.org/summa.

Aristotle, 1991. *On Rhetoric: A Theory of Civic Discourse*. Translated by George A. Kennedy. New York and Oxford: Oxford University Press.

Augustine. 1950 *The City of God*. Translated by Marcus Dodds, DD. New York: Modern Library.

———. 1955. "The Divination of Demons." In *Saint Augustine: Treatises on Marriage and Other Subjects*. Translated by Ruth Wentworth Brown. Washington, D.C.: Catholic University of America Press.

Azpilcueta, Martín de. 1556. *Manual de confessores y penitentes qve clara y brevemente contiene, la vniversal y particvlar decision de qvasi todas las dvdas, que en las confessiones suelen ocurrir de los pecados, absoluciones, restituciones, censuras, & irregularidades*. Salamanca: Andrea de Portonarijs.

Bach, Kent, and Robert M. Harnish. 1979. *Linguistic Communication and Speech Acts*. Cambridge, Mass.: MIT Press.

Bahktin, Mikhail M. 1981. *The Dialogical Imagination: Four Essays by M. M. Bahktin*. Edited by Michael Holquist. Austin: University of Texas Press.

Bakewell, Peter. 1997. "Notes on the Mexican Silver Mining Industry in the 1590s." In *Mines of Silver and Gold in the Americas*, edited by Peter Bakewell, 171–97. Brookfield, Vt.: Ashgate/Variorum.

Barlow, C. W., trans. 1969. *Martin of Braga, Paschasius of Dumium, Leander of Seville*. Vol. 1 of *Iberian Fathers*. Washington, D.C.: Catholic University of America Press.

Baudot, Georges. 1990. *Tratado de hechicerías y sortilegios por Andrés de Olmos*. México: Universidad Nacional Autónoma de México, Instituto de Investigaciones Históricas, Centro de Estudios Mexicanos y Centroamericanos.

Benítez, Fernando. 1975. *In the Magic Land of the Peyote*. Austin: University of Texas Press.

———. 2000. "Sacred Moon, Lord Maguey." In "Maguey." Special issue, *Artes de México* 51: 82–84.

Berdan, Frances. 1996. "The Tributary Provinces." In *Aztec Imperial Strategies*, edited by Frances F. Berdan, Richard E. Blanton, Elizabeth Hill Boone, Mary G. Hodge, Michael E. Smith, and Emily Umberger, 115–35. Washington, D.C.: Dumbarton Oaks.

Berdan, Frances, and Patricia Rieff Anawalt. 1997. *The Essential Codex Mendoza*. Berkeley: University of California Press.

Berkes, Fikret. 2012. *Sacred Ecology*. 3rd ed. New York: Routledge.

Bernal, Ignacio. 1994. "Durán's Historia and the Crónica X." In *The History of the Indies of New Spain by Fray Diego Durán*, translated by Doris Heyden, 565–77. Norman: University of Oklahoma Press.

Bernand, Carmen, and Serge Gruzinski. 1992. *De la idolatría. Una arqueología de las ciencias religiosas*. México: Fondo de Cultura Económica.

Berres-Paul, Jeremy. 2013. "How to Use Perseverance in Whitetail Hunting," www.wideopenspaces.com/use-perseverance-whitetail-hunting.

Bierhorst, John. 1992. *History and Mythology of the Aztecs: The Codex Chimalpopoca*. Tucson: University of Arizona Press.

Blécourt, Willem de. 1994. "Witch Doctors, Soothsayers, and Priests: On Cunning Folk in European Historiography and Tradition." *Social History* 19(3): 285–303.

Boone, Elizabeth H. 2003. "A Web of Understanding: Pictorial Codices and the Shared Intellectual Culture of Late Postclassic Mesoamerica." In *The Postclassic Mesoamerican World*, edited by Michael E. Smith and Francis F. Berdan, 207–21. Salt Lake City: University of Utah Press.

———. 2007. *Cycles of Time and Meaning in the Mexican Books of Fate*. Austin: University of Texas Press.

Bossy, John. 1988. "Moral Arithmetic: Seven Sins into Ten Commandments." In *Conscience and Casuistry in Early Modern Europe*, edited by Edmund Leites, 214–34. Cambridge: Cambridge University Press.

Braakhuis, H. E. M. 2001. "The Way of All Flesh: Sexual Implications of the Mayan Hunt." *Anthropos* 96(2): 391–409.

———. 2009. "The Tonsured Maize God and Chicome-Xochitl As Maize Bringers and Culture Heroes: A Gulf Coast Perspective." *Wayeb Notes* 32: 1–38.

Bristol, Joan Cameron. 2007. *Christians, Blasphemers, and Witches: Afro-Mexican Ritual Practice in the Seventeenth Century*. Albuquerque: University of New Mexico Press.

Broda, Johanna, Stanislaw Iwaniszewski, and Ismael Arturo Montero García, eds. 2001. *La montaña en el paisaje ritual*. México: Conaculta, INAH.

Brown, Laura A., and Kitty F. Emery. 2008. "Negotiations with the Animate Forest: Hunting Shrines in the Guatemalan Highlands." *Journal of Archaeological Method and Theory* 15(4): 300–37.

Bruman, Henry J. 2000. *Alcohol in Ancient Mexico*. Salt Lake City: University of Utah Press.

Brundage, Burr C. 1979. *The Fifth Sun: Aztec Gods, Aztec World*. Austin: University of Texas Press.

———. 1982. *The Phoenix of the Western World: Quetzalcoatl and the Sky Religion*. Norman: University of Oklahoma Press.

Bueching, Godofredus-Pr. Fridericus Hoffman. 1703. *Disputatio inauguralis medico-philosophica. De potentia diaboli in corpora*. Saxony-Anhalt, Halle: Typis Ioannis Gruneri.

Burke, Peter. 1978. *Popular Culture in Early Modern Europe*. New York: New York University Press.

Burkhart, Louise M. 1986. "Moral Deviance in Sixteenth Century Nahua and Christian Thought: the Rabbit and the Deer." *Journal of Latin American Lore* 12(2): 107–39.

———. 1988. "Doctrinal Aspects of Sahagún's *Colloquios*." In *The Work of Bernardino de Sahagún: Pioneer Ethnographer of Sixteenth-Century Mexico*, edited by José Jorge Klor de Alva, Henry B. Nicholson, and Eloise Quiñones Keber, 65–82. Albany: Institute for Mesoamerican Studies, State University of New York.

———. 1989. *The Slippery Earth: Nahua-Christian Moral Dialogue in Sixteenth-Century Mexico*. Tucson: University of Arizona Press.

———. 1996. *Holy Wednesday: A Nahua Drama from Early Colonial Mexico*. Philadelphia: University of Pennsylvania Press.

———. 1997. "Mexican Women on the Home Front. Housework and Religion in Aztec Mexico." In *Indian Women of Early Mexico*, edited by Susan Schroeder, Stephanie Woods, and Robert S. Haskett, 25–54. Norman: University of Oklahoma Press.

Byrne, Susan. 2015. *Ficino in Spain*. Toronto: University of Toronto Press.

Cacho Blecua, Juan Manuel. 1987. Introduction to *Amadís de Gaula*, by Garci Rodríguez de Montalvo, vol. 1, 19–216. Madrid: Cátedra.

Callicott, J. Baird. 1982. "Traditional American Indian and Western European Attitudes Towards Nature: An Overview." *Environmental Ethics* 4: 293–318.

Cameron, Euan. 2010. *Enchanted Europe: Superstition, Reason and Religion, 1250–1750*. Oxford: Oxford University Press.

Campagne, Fabián Alejandro. 2003. "Witchcraft and the Sense-of-the-Impossible in Early Modern Spain: Some Reflections Based on the Literature of Superstition (ca. 1500–1800)." *Harvard Theological Review* 96(1): 25–62.

———. 2009. *Strix hispánica: demonología cristiana y cultura folklórica en la España moderna*. Buenos Aires: Prometeo Libros.

Caro Baroja, Julio. 1992. *Vidas mágicas e inquisición*. 2 vols. Madrid: Ediciones Istmo.

Carochi, Horacio. [1645] 1983. *Arte de la lengua Mexicana. Con la declaración de los adverbios della*. México: Universidad Autónoma de México.

Carrasco, Davíd. 1982. *Quetzalcoatl and the Irony of Empire*. Chicago: University of Chicago Press.

———. 1991. "The Sacrifice of Tezcatliopca: To Change Place." In *To Change Place: Aztec Ceremonial Landscapes*, edited by Davíd Carrasco, 31–57. Niwot: University Press of Colorado.

———. 1999. *City of Sacrifice: The Aztec Empire and the Role of Violence in Civilization*. Boston: Beacon Press.

Carrasco, Davíd, and Scott Sessions. 1998. *Daily Life of the Aztecs: People of the Sun and Earth*. Westport, Conn.: Greenwood Press.

Caso, Alfonso. 1967. *Los calendarios prehispánicos*. México: Universidad Autónoma de México, Instituto de Investigaciones Históricas.

———. 1971. "Calendrical Systems of Central Mexico." In Ekholm and Bernal 1971, 10:333–48.

Certeau, Michel de. 1973. *La possession de Loudun*. Paris: Gallimard.

Cervantes, Fernando. 1994. *The Devil in the New World: The Impact of Diabolism in New Spain*. New Haven, Conn.: Yale University Press.

Christian, William A. 1989. *Local Religion in Sixteenth-Century Spain*. Princeton, N.J.: Princeton University Press.

Chuchiak, John F. 2002. "Towards a Regional Definition of Idolatry: Reexamining Idolatry Trials in the *Relaciones de Méritos* and Their Role in Defining the Concept of Idolatria in Colonial Yucatán, 1570–1780." *Journal of Early Modern History* 6(2): 140–67.

Cirac Estopañán, Sebastián. 1942. *Los procesos de hechicería en la Inquisición de Castilla la Nueva (tribunales de Toledo y Cuenca)*. Madrid: Diana.

Ciruelo, Pedro. 1538. *Arte de bien confesar*. Sevilla: Dominico de Robertis.

———. 1978. *Reprouacion de las supersticiones y hechizerias*. Edited by Alva V. Ebersole. Valencia: Albatros Hispanófila.

Clark, Stuart. 1999. *Thinking with Demons: The Idea of Witchcraft in Early Modern Europe*. Oxford: Oxford University Press.

———. 2015. "Witchcraft and Magic in Early Modern Culture." In *Superstition and Magic in Early Modern Europe: A Reader*, edited by Helen Parish, 215–74. London: Bloomsbury.

Clendinnen, Inga. 1991. *Aztecs: An Interpretation*. Cambridge: Cambridge University Press.

Cline, Howard F., ed. 1972. *Guide to Ethnographical Sources: Part One*. Vol. 12 of *Handbook of Middle American Indians*. Austin: University of Texas Press.

Codex Vaticanus A. 1979. *Codex Vaticanus 3738 ("Cod. Vat. A," "Cod. Ríos") der Biblioteca Apostolica Vaticana. Codices Selecti: Phototypice Impressi*, vol. 65. Graz: Akademische Druck und Verlagsanstalt.

Coe, Michael. 1972. "Olmec Jaguars and Olmec King." In *The Cult of the Feline: A Conference on Pre-Columbian Iconography, October 31st and November 1st, 1970*, edited by Elizabeth P. Benson, 1–12. Washington: Dumbarton Oaks.

Coe, Michael D., and Rex Koontz. 2008. *Mexico: From the Olmecs to the Aztecs*. New York: Thames and Hudson.

Coe, Michael D., and Gordon Whittaker. 1982. *Aztec Sorcerers in Seventeenth-Century Mexico: The Treatise on Superstitions by Hernando Ruiz de Alarcón*, edited and translated by Michael D. Coe and Gordon Whittaker. Albany: Institute for Mesoamerican Studies, State University of New York at Albany.

Coggins, Clemency. 2002. "Toltec." *RES: Anthropology and Aesthetics* 42: 34–85.

Columbus, Christopher. [1493, 1498–1500] 1986. *Los cuatro viajes. Testamento*, edited by Consuelo Varela. Madrid: Alianza Editorial.

Cooppan, Vilashini. 2009. "The Ethics of World Literature: Reading Others, Reading Otherwise." In Damrosch 2009, 34–43.

Copenhaver, Brian P. 1984. "Scholastic Philosophy and Renaissance Magic in *De Vita* of Marsilio Ficino." *Renaissance Quarterly* 37(4): 523–54.

———. 1986. "Renaissance Magic and Neoplatonic Philosophy: 'Ennead' 4.3–5 in Ficino's *De vita coelitus comparanda*." In *Marsilio Ficino e il ritorno di Platone. Studi e Documenti*, vol. 2, edited by Gian Carlo Garfagnini, 351–69. Florence: Olschki.

———. 1990. "Natural Magic, Hermetism and Occultism in Early Modern Science." In *Reappraisals of the Scientific Revolution*, edited by David C. Lindberg and Robert S. Westman, 261–301. Cambridge: Cambridge University Press.

———. 1992. *Hermetica: The Greek Corpus Hermeticum and the Latin Asclepius in a New English Translation with Notes and an Introduction*. Cambridge: Cambridge University Press.

Copenhaver, Brian P., and Charles B. Schmitt. 1992. *Renaissance Philosophy*. Oxford: Oxford University Press.

Córdova, Pedro de. [1544] 1988. *Doctrina cristiana y cartas*. Santo Domingo, Dominican Republic: Fundación Corripio.

Creagh, J. 1907. "Benefice." In *The Catholic Encyclopedia*. New York: Robert Appleton Co., www.newadvent.org/cathen/02473c.htm.

Creamer, Winifred. 1987. "Mesoamerica as a Concept: An Archaeological View from Central America." *Latin American Research Review* 22(1): 35–62.

Cruz Soto, Irma Guadalupe. 1993. "Magdalena Papalo y Joseph Chicon: dos médicos nahuas del siglo XVI." BA thesis, History Department, Universidad Autónoma de México.

Damrosch, David, ed. 2009. *Teaching World Literature*. New York: Modern Languages Association of America.

Daston, Lorraine, and Katharine Park. 1998. *Wonders and the Order of Nature, 1150-1750*. New York: Zone Books.

Davies, Nigel. 1977. *The Toltecs: Until the Fall of Tula*. Norman: University of Oklahoma Press.

———. 1980. *The Toltec Heritage: From the Fall of Tula to the Rise of Tenochtitlán*. Norman: University of Oklahoma Press.

———. 1987. *The Aztec Empire: The Toltec Resurgence*. Norman: University of Oklahoma Press.

Davies, Owen. 1999. *Witchcraft, Magic, and Culture, 1736–1951*. Manchester, U.K.: Manchester University Press.

———. 2003. *Cunning-Folk: Popular Magic in English History*. London and New York: Hambledon and London.

———. 2009. *Grimoires: A History of Magic Books*. Oxford: Oxford University Press.

Davies, Owen, and Willem Blécourt, eds. 2004a. *Beyond the Witch Trials: Witchcraft and Magic in Enlightenment Europe*. Manchester, U.K.: Manchester University Press.

———. eds. 2004b. *Witchcraft Continued: Popular Magic in Modern Europe*. Manchester, U.K.: Manchester University Press.

Dehouve, Danièle. 1994. *Entre el caimán y el jaguar. Los pueblos indios de Guerrero*. México: Centro de Investigaciones y Estudios Superiores en Antropología Social.

———. 2008. "El venado, el maíz y el sacrificado." *Diario de Campo. Cuadernos de Etnología* 4: 1–39 (México: INAH).

———. 2010. "Un ritual de cacería. El conjuro para cazar venados de Ruiz de Alarcón." *Estudios de Cultura Náhuatl* 40: 299–331.

Del Río, Martín. 1991. *La magia demoníaca. Libro II de las Disquisiones mágicas*. Madrid: Hiperión.

———. 2000. *Investigations into Magic*. Edited and translated by P. G. Maxwell-Stuart. Manchester, U.K.: Manchester University Press.

Delumeau, Jean. 1977. *Catholicism between Luther and Voltaire: A New View of the Counter-Reformation*. London: Burns and Oates.

Díaz Balsera, Viviana. 2005. *The Pyramid under the Cross: Franciscan Discourses of Evangelization and the Nahua Christian Subject in Sixteenth-Century Mexico*. Tucson: University of Arizona Press.

———. 2007. "Nombres que conservan el mundo: los *nahualtocaitl* y el *Tratado sobre idolatrías* de Hernando Ruiz de Alarcón." *Colonial Latin American Review* 16(2): 159–78.

———. 2011a. "Tezcatlipoca neoplatónico y las correspondencias ocultas del amor." *Colonial Latin American Review* 20(3): 279–301.

———. 2011b. "Atando dioses y humanos: Cipactónal y la cura por adivinación en el *Tratado de supersticiones* de Hernando Ruiz de Alarcón." In *Estudios coloniales latinoamericanos del siglo XXI. Nuevos itinerarios*, edited by Stephanie Kirk, 331–49. Pittsburgh, Pa.: Instituto Internacional de Literatura Iberoamericana.

———. 2017. "Voicing Mesoamerican Identities on the Roads of Empire: Alarcón and the Nahualtocaitl in Seventeenth-Century Mexico" In *To Be* Indio *in Colonial Spanish America: Discourses and Practices*, edited by Mónica Díaz, 169–89. Albuquerque: University of New Mexico Press.

Diethelm, Oskar. 1970. "The Medical Teaching of Demonology in the 17th and 18th Centuries." *Journal of the History of the Behavioral Sciences* 6: 3–15.

Douglas, Eduardo. 2003. "Figures of Speech: Pictorial History in the Quinatzin Map of about 1542." *Art Bulletin* 85(2): 281–309.

Durán, Diego. 1971. *Book of the Gods and Rites and the Ancient Calendar.* Edited and translated by Fernando Horcasitas and Doris Heyden. Norman: University of Oklahoma Press.

———. 1994. *The History of the Indies of New Spain.* Translated by Doris Heyden. Norman: University of Oklahoma Press.

Duverger, Christian. 2007. *El primer mestizaje. La clave para entender el pasado mesoamericano.* México: Universidad Nacional Autónoma de México; Instituto Nacional de Antropología e Historia; Taurus; Consejo Nacional para la Cultura y las Artes.

Ebersole, Alvar V. 1978. Introduction to Ciruelo (1978), 119.

Ekholm, Gordon F., and Ignacio Bernal. 1971. *Archaeology of Northern Mesoamerica.* Vols. 10 and 11 of *Handbook of Middle American Indians.* Austin: University of Texas Press.

Eger Valadez, Susana. 1996. "Wolf Power and Interspecies Communication in Huichol Shamanism." In Schaefer and Furst 1996, 267–305.

Eliade, Mircea. 1972. *Shamanism: Archaic Techniques of Ecstasy.* Princeton, N.J.: Princeton University Press.

Feldman, Lawrence. 1974. "Tollan in Central Mexico: The Geography of Economic Specialization." In *Studies of Ancient Tollan: A Report of the University of Missouri Tula Archaeological Project,* edited by Richard A. Diehl, 150–89. University of Missouri Monographs in Anthropology 1. Columbia: University of Missouri.

Feliciano Velázquez, Primo, ed. and trans. 1992. *Códice Chimalpopoca. Anales de Cuauhtitlán y leyenda de los soles.* México: Universidad Autónoma de México.

Fellowes, William H. 1985. "Los tratados de Hernando Ruiz de Alarcón. A Commentary Upon *El conjuro para cazar venados. Tlalocan* 10: 457–87.

Ficino, Marsilio. 2002. *Three Books on Life.* Edited by Carol V. Kaske and John R. Clark. Tempe: Arizona Center for Medieval and Renaissance Studies; Renaissance Society of America.

Fields, F. Herbert. 1969. "*Rivea Corymbosa*: Notes on Some Zapotecan Customs." *Economic Botany* 23(3): 206–9.

Fisher, John. 1908. "Martin Anton del Rio." In *The Catholic Encyclopedia,* vol. 4. New York: Robert Appleton Co., www.newadvent.org/cathen/04701b.htm.

Flint, Valerie I. J. 1991. *The Rise of Magic in Early Medieval Europe.* Princeton, N.J.: Princeton University Press.

Florescano, Enrique. 1999. *The Myth of Quetzalcoatl.* Translated by Lysa Hochroth. Baltimore: Johns Hopkins University Press.

Foster, George M. 1944. "Nagualism in Mexico and Guatemala." *Acta Americana* 2(1–2): 84–103.

Foucault, Michel. 1973. *The Order of Things: An Archaeology of the Human Sciences.* New York: Vintage Books.

Freidel, David, Linda Schele, and Joy Parker. 2001. *Maya Cosmos: Three Thousand Years on the Shaman's Path.* New York: Perennial.

Furst, Jill Leslie McKeever. 1995. *The Natural History of the Soul in Ancient Mexico.* New Haven, Conn.: Yale University Press.

Furst, Peter T. 1967. "The Olmec Were-Jaguar Motif in the Light of Ethnographic Reality." In *Dumbarton Oaks Conference on the Olmec: October 28th and 29th, 1967*, edited by Elizabeth P. Benson, 143–78. Washington, D.C.: Dumbarton Oaks.

———. 1995. "Shamanism, Transformation and Olmec Art." In *The Olmec World: Ritual and Rulership*, 69–81. Princeton: Art Museum of Princeton University in association with Harry N. Abrams.

Galinier, Jacques. 1990. *La mitad del mundo. Cuerpo cosmos en los rituales otomíes*. México: Universidad Autónoma de México Centre d'Études Mexicains et Centre Américains, Instituto Nacional Indigenista.

García, Ciro. 2015. "La experiencia de Dios en el *Libro de la vida* de Santa Teresa de Jesús." *Scripta Theologica* 47(2): 419–39.

García de León, Antonio. 1969. "El universo sobrenatural de los nahuas de Pajapán, Veracruz." *Estudios de Cultura Náhuatl* 8: 279–311.

Garibay K., Ángel María. 1954. *Historia de la literatura náhuatl*. 2 vols. México: Porrúa.

———. 1958, ed. and trans. *Veinte himnos sacros de los nahuas*. México: Universidad Autónoma de México: Instituto Nacional de Historia.

———. 1965. *Teogonía e historia de los mexicanos. Tres opúsculos del siglo XVI*. México: Porrúa.

Gellman, Jerome. 2014. "Mysticism." In *The Stanford Encyclopedia of Philosophy*, edited by Edward N. Zalta, plato.stanford.edu/archives/spr2014/entries/mysticism.

Gerhard, Peter. 1972. *A Guide to the Historical Geography of New Spain*. Cambridge: Cambridge University Press.

Gibson, Charles. 1964. *The Aztecs under Spanish Rule: A History of the Indians of the Valley of Mexico, 1519–1810*. Stanford, Calif.: Stanford University Press.

Godbeer, Richard. 1992. *The Devil's Dominion: Magic and Religion in Early New England*. Cambridge: Cambridge University Press.

Gonçalves de Lima, Oswaldo. 1956. *El maguey y el pulque en los códices mexicanos*. México: Fondo de Cultura Económica.

González Martínez, José Luis. 2006. "Sincretismo e identidades emergentes. *El Manual de Jacinto de la Serna* (1630)." *Revista Dimensión Antropológica* (Instituto Nacional de Antropología e Historia) 38: 87–113, www.dimensionantropologica.inah.gob.mx/?p=437.

González Novalín, José Luis. 1963. "Historia de la reforma tridentina en la diócesis de Oviedo." *Hispania Sacra* 16: 323–46.

González Torres, Yolotl. 1995. *Diccionario de mitología y religión de Mesoamérica*. México: Larousse.

Graulich, Michel. 1997. *Myths of Ancient Mexico*. Translated by Bernard R. Ortiz de Montellano and Thelma Ortiz de Montellano. Norman: University of Oklahoma Press.

Gregory, John. 1999. *The Neoplatonists: A Reader*. London and New York: Routledge.

Greenleaf, Richard E. W. 1965. "The Inquisition and the Indians of New Spain: A Study in Jurisdictional Confusion." *The Americas* 22(2): 138–66.

———. 1978. "The Mexican Inquisition and the Indians. Sources for the Ethnohistorian." *The Americas* 34(3): 315–44.

———. 1991. "Historiography of the Mexican Inquisition: Evolution of Interpretations and Methodologies." In Perry and Cruz 1991, 248–76.

Griffiths, Nicholas, and Fernando Cervantes, eds. 1999. *Spiritual Encounters: Interactions Between Christianity and Native Religions in Colonial America*. Lincoln: University of Nebraska Press.

Gruzinski, Serge. 1993. *The Conquest of Mexico: The Incorporation of Indian Societies into the Western World, 16th–18th Centuries*. Translated by Eileen Corrigan. Cambridge: Polity Press.

Handley, Sasha. 2007. *Visions of an Unseen World: Ghost Beliefs and Ghost Stories in Eighteenth-Century England*. London: Brookfield.

Harvey, H. R. 1971. "Ethnohistory of Guerrero." In Ekholm and Bernal 1971, 11:603–18.

———. 1972. "The *Relaciones Geográficas*, 1579–1586: Native Languages." In Cline 1972, 12:279–323.

Haskett, Robert. 1991. "Our Suffering with Taxco Tribute: Involuntary Labor and Indigenous Society in Central New Spain." *Hispanic American Historical Review* 71(3): 447–75.

Hassig, Ross. 2001. *Time, History, and Belief in Aztec and Colonial Mexico*. Austin: University of Texas Press.

Hémond, Aline. 1996. "Pratiques cynégetiques et nouveaux discours écologiques chez les Nahuas du Balsas (Mexique)." *Journal d'agriculture traditionelle et de botanique appliquée* 38(2): 268–88.

Henningsen, Gustav. 1980. *The Witches' Advocate: Basque Witchcraft and the Spanish Inquisition (1609–1614)*. Reno: University of Nevada Press.

Henry, John. 1991. "Doctors and Healers: Popular Culture and the Medical Profession." In *Science, Culture, and Popular Belief in Renaissance Europe*, edited by Stephen Pumfrey, Paolo L. Rossi, and Maurice Slawinski, 191–221. Manchester, UK: Manchester University Press.

Hernández Bautista, Paulina, Herminio Farías Bautista, Pedro Silvestre, and José Barón Larios. 2004. "Chicomexóchitl. La leyenda del maíz." In Ruvalcaba Mercado, Pérez Zevallos, and Herrera, 369–78.

Holquist, Michael. 2002. *Dialogism: Bakhtin and His World*. London: Routledge.

Hornborg, Alf. 2006. "Animism, Fetishism, and Objectivism as Strategies for Knowing (or Not-Knowing)." *Ethnos* 71(1): 21–32. DOI: 10.1080/00141840600603129

Hornsby, Jennifer. "Illocution and Its Significance." In *Foundations of Speech Act Theory: Philosophical and Linguistic Perspectives*, edited by Savas L. Tsohatzidis, 187–207. London: Routledge.

———. 2006. "Speech Acts and Performatives." In *The Oxford Handbook of Philosophy of Language*, edited by Ernest Lepore and Barry C. Smith, 893–909. Oxford: Oxford University Press.

Howells, Edward. 2002. *John of the Cross and Teresa of Avila: Mystical Knowing and Selfhood*. New York: Crossroads.

Ingold, Tim. 2006. "Rethinking the Animate, Reanimating Thought." *Ethnos* 71(1): 9–20. DOI: 10.1080/00141840600603111

Ingold, Tim, and T. Kurttila. 2000. Perceiving the Environment in Finnish Lapland. *Body and Society* 6: 183–96.

Israel, Jonathan I. 1975. *Race, Class, and Politics in Colonial Mexico, 1610–1670*. London: Oxford University Press.

Jaffary, Nora. 2004. *False Mystics: Deviant Orthodoxy in Colonial Mexico*. Lincoln: University of Nebraska Press.

Jiménez Moreno, Wigberto. 1942. "El enigma de los olmecas." *Cuadernos Americanos* 1(5): 113–45.

Kamen, Henry. 1985. *Inquisition and Society in Spain in the Sixteenth and Seventeenth Century.* Bloomington: Indiana University Press.

Kartunnen, Frances E. 1983. *An Analytical Dictionary of Nahuatl*. Austin: University of Texas Press.

Kaske, Carol V., and John R. Clark, eds. 2002. Introduction to *Three Books on Life*, by Marsilio Ficino. Tempe: Arizona Center for Medieval and Renaissance Studies; Renaissance Society of America.

Keber, John. 1988. "Sahagún and Hermeneutics: A Christian Ethnographer's Understanding of Aztec Culture." In *The Work of Bernardino de Sahagún: Pioneer Ethnographer of Sixteenth-Century Mexico*, edited by José Jorge Klor de Alva, Henry B. Nicholson, and Eloise Quiñones Keber, 53–63. Albany: Institute for Mesoamerican Studies, State University of New York.

Kellogg, Susan. 2010. "Introduction—Back to the Future: Law, Politics, and Culture in Colonial Mexican Ethnographical Studies." In *Negotiation within Domination: New Spain's Indian Pueblos Confront the Spanish State*, edited by Ethelia Ruiz Medrano and Susan Kellogg, 1–17. Boulder: University Press of Colorado.

Klein, Cecilia. 1976. "The Identity of the Central Deity on the Aztec Calendar Stone." *Art Bulletin* 58(1): 1–12.

Kramer, Heinrich, and James Sprenger. 1971. *The Malleus Maleficarum of Heinrich Kramer and James Sprenger.* Translated by Montague Summers. New York: Dover.

Krickeberg, Walter. 1985. *Las antiguas culturas mexicanas*. Translated by Sita Garst and Jasmín Reuter. México: Fondo de Cultura Económica.

Lara Cisneros, Gerardo. 2015. *¿Ignorancia invencible? Superstición e idolatría en el Provisorato de Indios y Chinos del Arzobispado de México en el siglo XVIII*. México: Universidad Autónoma de México.

Larner, Christina. 1981. *Enemies of God: The Witch-Hunt in Scotland*. Baltimore, Md.: Johns Hopkins University Press.

Las Casas, Bartolomé de. 1967. *Apologética historia sumaria*. 2 vols. Edited by Edmundo O'Gorman. México: Universidad Nacional Autónoma de México; Instituto de Investigaciones Históricas.

Laughlin, Robert M. 2000. "Poetic License." In *The Flowering of Man: A Tzotzil Botany of Zinancatán*, edited by Dennis E. Breedlove and Robert M. Laughlin, 101–8. Washington D.C.: Smithsonian Institution.

León-Portilla, Miguel. 1963. *Imagen del México antiguo*. Buenos Aires: Editorial Universitaria de Buenos Aires.

Lerner, Isaías. 2003. Prologue to Mexía 2003, 11–25.

Levack, Brian P. 2006. *The Witch-Hunt in Early Modern Europe*. Harlow, UK: Pearson Longman.

Lewis, Laura. 2003. *Hall of Mirrors: Power, Witchcraft, and Caste in Colonial Mexico*. Durham, N.C.: Duke University Press.

Limón Olvera, Silvia. 2001. "El dios del fuego y la regeneración del mundo." *Estudios de Cultura Náhuatl* 32: 51–68.

Lipp, Frank J. 1991. *The Mixe of Oaxaca: Religion, Ritual, and Healing.* Austin: University of Texas Press.

Lisbona Guillén, Miguel. 1999. "Moradores de la montaña. Los zoques chima de Oaxaca." In *Configuraciones étnicas en Oaxaca: perspectivas etnográficas para las autonomías*, vol. 7, edited by Alicia Barabas and Miguel Bartolomé, 135–56. México: Instituto Nacional Indigenista; Consejo Nacional para la Cultura y las Artes; Instituto Nacional de Antropología e Historia.

Llaguno, José A., SJ. 1963. *La personalidad jurídica del indio y el III Concilio Provincial Mexicano (1585). Ensayo histórico-jurídico de los documentos originales.* México: Porrúa.

Lockhart, James. 1992. *The Nahuas after the Conquest: A Social and Cultural History of the Indians of Central Mexico, Sixteenth through Eighteenth Centuries.* Stanford, Calif.: Stanford University Press.

———, ed. and trans. 1993. *We People Here: Nahuatl Accounts of the Conquest of Mexico.* Berkeley: University of California Press.

Londoño Sulkin, Carlos D. 2005. "Inhuman Beings: Morality and Perspectivism among Muinane People (Colombian Amazon)." *Ethnos* 70(1): 7–30.

Longxi, Zhang. 2007. *Unexpected Affinities: Reading across Cultures.* Toronto: University of Toronto Press.

———. 2009. "What Is Literature? Reading across Cultures." In Damrosch 2009, 61–72.

López Austin, Alfredo. 1966. "Los temacpalitotique. Brujos, profanadores, ladrones y violadores." *Estudios de Cultura Náhuatl* 6: 97–117.

———. 1967a. "Cuarenta clases de magos del mundo náhuatl." *Estudios de Cultura Náhuatl* 7: 87–117.

———. 1967b. "Términos del *nahuallatolli*." *Historia Mexicana* 17: 1–36.

———, ed. 1969. *Augurios y abusiones.* México: Universidad Autónoma de México, Instituto de Investigaciones Históricas.

———. 1970a. "Conjuros médicos de los nahuas." *Revista de la Universidad de México* 24(11): 1–16.

———. 1970b. "Ideas etiológicas en la medicina náhuatl." *Anuario Indigenista* 30: 255–75.

———. 1988. *The Human Body and Ideology: Concepts of the Ancient Nahuas.* 2 vols., translated by Thelma Ortiz de Montellano and Bernard Ortiz de Montellano. Salt Lake City: University of Utah Press.

———. 1993. *The Myths of the Opossum: Pathways of Mesoamerican Mythology*, translated by Bernard R. Ortiz de Montellano and Thelma Ortiz de Montellano. Albuquerque: University of New Mexico Press.

———. 1997. *Tamoanchan, Tlalocan: Places of Mist*, translated by Bernard R. Ortiz de Montellano and Thelma Ortiz de Montellano. Niwot: University Press of Colorado.

Lupo, Alessandro. 2001. "Cosmovisión de los nahuas de la Sierra de Puebla." In *Cosmovisión, ritual e identidad de los pueblos indígenas de México*, edited by Johanna Broda and Félix Baez-Jorge, 335–89. México: Consejo Nacional para la Cultura y las Artes; Fondo de Cultura Económica.

Mackenna, Stephen, trans. 1916. *Plotinus. Psychic and Physical Treatises; Comprising the Second and Third Enneads*. 2 vols. Boston: Charles T. Branford.

Maffie, James. 2014. *Aztec Philosophy: Understanding a World in Motion*. Boulder: University Press of Colorado.

Maldonado Jiménez, Druzo. 2000. *Deidades y espacio ritual en Cuahnáhuac y Huaxtepec. Tlalhuicas y xochimilcas de Morelos. (Siglos XII–XVI)*. México: Universidad Nacional Autónoma de México; Instituto de Investigaciones Antropológicas.

Marcos Casquero, Manuel A., and Hipólito B. Riesco Álvarez. 1997. Introduction to *Pedro de Valencia. Obras completas*. Vol. 7: *Discurso acerca de los cuentos de brujas*, 9–221. León: Universidad de León.

Martínez González, Roberto. 2011. *El nahualismo*. México: Universidad Autónoma de México.

Mastache, Alba Guadalupe, Robert H. Cobean, and Dan M. Healan. 2002. *Ancient Tollan: Tula and the Toltec Heartland*. Boulder: University Press of Colorado.

Matos Moctezuma, Eduardo. 1997. "Tlaltecuhtli. Señor de la Tierra." *Estudios de Cultura Náhuatl* 27:15–40.

Maxwell-Stuart, P. G., ed. 2000. Introduction to *Investigations into Magic* by Martín del Río. Manchester and New York: Manchester University Press.

Menchú, Rigoberta. 2009. *I, Rigoberta Menchú: An Indian Woman in Guatemala*, edited by Elisabeth Burgos-Debray, translated by Ann Wright. London and New York: Verso.

Mendieta, Gerónimo. 1993. *Historia eclesiástica indiana*. México: Porrúa.

Mentzer, Raymond A. 1984. *Heresy Proceedings in Languedoc, 1500–1560*. Transactions of the American Philosophical Society, vol. 74, pt. 5. Philadelphia, Pa.: American Philosophical Society.

Mexía, Pedro. 2003. *Silva de varia lección*, edited by Isaías Lerner. Madrid: Castalia.

Mignolo, Walter. 2002. "José de Acosta's *Historia natural y moral de Indias*: Occidentalism, the Modern/Colonial World and the Colonial Difference." In *Natural and Moral History of the Indies*, by José Acosta, trans. by F. M. López-Morillas, 451–523. Durham, N.C.: Duke University Press.

Millen, Ron. 1985. "The Manifestation of Occult Qualities in the Scientific Revolution." In *Religion, Science and Worldview: Essays in Honor of Richard S. Westfall*, edited by Margaret J. Osler and Paul Lawrence Farber, 185–216. Cambridge: Cambridge University Press.

Miller, Mary Ellen. 1986. *The Art of Mesoamerica: From Olmec to Aztec*. New York: Thames and Hudson.

Mohar Betancourt, Luz María. 2004. *Códice Mapa Quinatzin. Justicia y derechos humanos en el México antiguo*. México: Porrúa, CIESAS.

Molina, Alonso de. 1992. *Vocabulario en lengua castellana y mexicana y mexicana y castellana*. México: Porrúa.

Monaghan, John. 1998. "The Person, Destiny and the Construction of Difference in Mesoamerica." *RES: Anthropology and Aesthetics* 33: 137–46.

Montaner, Alberto, and Eva Lara, eds. 2014. *Señales, portentos y demonios. La magia en la literatura y la cultura españolas del Renacimiento*. Salamanca: Sociedad de Estudios Medievales y Renacentistas.

Motolinía, Toribio de Benavente. 1951. *History of the Indians of New Spain*, translated by Francis Borgia Steck. Washington, D.C.: Academy of American Franciscan History.

Muchembled, Robert. 1985. *Popular Culture and Elite Culture in France, 1400–1750*. Baton Rouge: Louisiana State University Press.

Muñoz Camargo, Diego. 1979. *Historia de Tlaxcala. Crónica del siglo XVI*, edited by Alfredo Chavero. México: Innovación.

Musgrave-Portilla, L. Marie. 1982. "The Nahualli, or Transforming Wizard, in Pre- and Postconquest Mesoamerica." *Journal of Latin American Lore* 8(1): 3–62.

Myerhoff, Barbara G. 1974. *Peyote Hunt: The Sacred Journey of the Huichol Indians*. Ithaca, N.Y.: Cornell University Press.

Narby, Jeremy. 1998. *The Cosmic Serpent: DNA and the Origins of Knowledge*. New York: Jeremy P. Tarcher/Putnam.

Nesvig, Martin. 2009. *Ideology and Inquisition: The World of the Censors in Early Mexico*. New Haven, Conn.: Yale University Press.

Nicholson, Henry B. 1971. "Religion in Pre-Hispanic Central Mexico." In Ekholm and Bernal 1971, 10:395–446.

———. 1988. "The Provenience of the Codex Borbonicus: A Hypothesis." In *Smoke and Mist: Mesoamerican Studies in Memory of Thelma E. Sullivan*, edited by J. Kathryn Josserand and Karen Dakin, pt. 1, 77–97. Oxford: BAR.

———. 1991. "The Octli Cult in Late Pre-Hispanic Central Mexico. In *To Change Place: Aztec Ceremonial Landscapes*, edited by Davíd Carrasco, 158–87. Niwot: University Press of Colorado.

———. 2001. *Topiltzin Quetzalcoatl: The Once and Future Lord of the Toltecs*. Boulder: University Press of Colorado.

Nutini, Hugo G., and John M. Roberts. 1993. *Bloodsucking Witchcraft: An Epistemological Study of Anthropomorphic Supernaturalism in Rural Tlaxcala*. Tucson: University of Arizona Press.

Olivier, Guilhem. 2003. *Mockeries and Metamorphoses of an Aztec God: Tezcatlipoca, "Lord of the Smoking Mirror."* Translated by Michael Besson. Boulder: University Press of Colorado.

———. 2014. "Venados melómanos y cazadores lúbricos: cacería, música y erotismo en Mesoamérica." *Estudios de Cultura Náhuatl* 47: 121–68.

Olmos, Andrés de. 1990. *Tratado de hechicerías y sortilegios*, edited by Georges Baudot. México: Universidad Nacional Autónoma de México, Instituto de Investigaciones Históricas, Centro de Estudios Mexicanos y Centroamericanos.

O'Neil, Mary. 1984. "Sacerdote ovvero strione: Ecclesiastical and Superstitious Remedies in Sixteenth-Century Italy." In *Understanding Popular Culture: Europe from the Middle Ages to the Nineteenth Century*, edited by Steven L. Kaplan, 53–83. Berlin and New York: Mouton.

Ortiz de Montellano, Bernard R. 1990. *Aztec Medicine, Health, and Nutrition*. New Brunswick, N.J.: Rutgers University Press.

Pagden, Anthony. 1982. *The Fall of Natural Man: The American Indian and the Origins of Comparative Ethnology*. Cambridge: Cambridge University Press.

Pardo, Osvaldo F. 1999. "Contesting the Power to Heal: Angels, Demons, and Plants in Colonial Mexico." In Griffiths and Cervantes 1999, 163–84.

Parsons, Jeffrey R., and Andrew Darling. 1993. "A Reconsideration of Maguey in Mesoamerican Civilization." Paper Presented at the Thirteenth International Congress of Anthropological and Ethnological Sciences, México.

Parsons, Jeffrey R., and Mary H. Parsons. 1990. *Maguey Utilization in Highland Central Mexico: An Archaeological Ethnography.* Anthropological Papers 82. Ann Arbor: Museum of Anthropology, University of Michigan.

Paso y Troncoso, Francisco de. [1892] 1953. "Como introducción." In Serna 1953, 17–23.

Paz, Josef. 1995. "The Vicissitude of the Alter Ego Animal in Mesoamerica: An Ethnohistorical Reconstruction of Tonalism." *Anthropos* 90: 445–65.

Pérez, Joseph. 2005. *The Spanish Inquisition: A History.* Translated by Janet Lloyd. New Haven, Conn.: Yale University Press.

———. 2010. *Historia de la brujería en España.* Madrid: Espasa.

Pérez Puente, Leticia. 2005. *Tiempos de crisis, tiempos de consolidación. La catedral metropolitana de la Ciudad de México, 1653–1680.* México: Universidad Autónoma de México, CESU, Plaza y Valdés, El Colegio de Michoacán.

Perry, Elizabeth, and Anne J. Cruz. 1991. *Cultural Encounters: The Impact of the Inquisition in Spain and the New World.* Berkeley: University of California Press.

Peters, Edward. 2015. "The Medieval Church and State on Superstition, Magic and Witchcraft: From Augustine to the Sixteenth Century." In *Superstition and Magic in Early Modern Europe: A Reader,* edited by Helen Parish, 52–90. London: Bloomsbury.

———. n.d. *The Cornell Witchcraft Collection. Literature on Demonology,* http://ebooks.library.cornell.edu/w/witch/peters4.html.

Pike, Nelson. 1992. *Mystic Union: An Essay in the Phenomenology of Mysticism.* Ithaca, N.Y.: Cornell University Press.

Pitt-Rivers, J. 1970. "Spiritual Power in Central America: The Naguals of Chiapas." In *Witchcraft Confessions and Accusations,* edited by Mary Douglas, 183–206. London: Tavistock.

Platz, Conrad Wolffgang. 1565. *Kurtzer, Nottwendiger, und Wollgegrundter bericht, Auch Christenliche vermanung, von der Grewlichen, in aller Welt gebreuchlichen Zauberey, Sünd dem Zauberischen Beschwören und Segensprechen.* N.p.

Pohl, John. 1998. "Themes of Drunkenness, Violence, and Factionalism in Tlaxcalan Altar Paintings." *Res: Anthropology and Aesthetics* 33: 184–207.

Pool, Christopher A. 2007. *Olmec Archaeology and Early Mesoamerica.* New York: Cambridge University Press.

Poole, Stafford. 1987. *Pedro Moya de Contreras: Catholic Reform and Royal Power in New Spain, 1571–1591.* Berkeley: University of California Press.

Porta, Giambattista della. [1658] 1957. *Natural Magick.* New York: Basic Books.

Quezada, Noemí. 1980. "Hernando Ruiz de Alarcón y su persecución de idolatrías." *Tlalocan* 8: 323–54.

———. 1991. "The Inquisition's Repression of Curanderos." In Perry and Cruz 1991, 37–57.

Quiñones Keber, Eloise. 1989. "Central Mexican Pictorial Manuscripts. Mayahuel and Maguey: Sustenance and Sacrifice in an Aztec Myth. *Latin American Indian Literatures Journal* 5(2): 72–83.

———, ed. 1995. *Codex Telleriano-Remensis: Ritual, Divination, and History in a Pictorial Aztec Manuscript.* Austin: University of Texas Press.

———. 2002. "Painting Divination in the *Florentine Codex.*" In *Representing Aztec Ritual: Performance, Text, and Image in the Work of Sahagún,* edited by Eloise Quiñones Keber, 251–76. Boulder: University Press of Colorado.

Rabasa, José. 1998. "Franciscans and Dominicans under the Gaze of the Tlacuilo: Plural-World Dwelling in an Indian Pictorial Codex." New Faculty Lecture Series. Berkeley: Doe Library, University of California.

———. 2011. *Tell Me the Story of How I Conquered You: Elsewheres and Ethnosuicide in the Colonial Mesoamerican World.* Austin: University of Texas Press.

Raby, Dominique. 2006. "Mujer blanca y dolor verde: uso de los colores, del género y de los lazos de parentesco en el *Tratado* de Ruiz de Alarcón." *Estudios de Cultura Náhuatl* 37: 293–315.

Read, Kay Almere. 1998. *Time and Sacrifice in the Aztec Cosmos.* Bloomington: Indiana University Press.

Redondo Goicoechea, Alicia. 1987. "Adiciones a la introducción de Ángel Rosenblatt." In *Amadís de Gaula*, by Garci Rodríguez de Montalvo, 1–10. Madrid: Cátedra

Ricard, Robert. 1991. *La conquista espiritual de México. Ensayo sobre el apostolado y los métodos misioneros de las órdenes mendicantes en la Nueva España de 1523–1524 a 1572.* Translated by Ángel M. Garibay. México: Fondo de Cultura Económica.

Río, Martín del. [1599] 1991. *La magia demoníaca. Libro II de las Disquisiciones mágicas.* Translated by Jesús Moya. Madrid: Hiperión.

———. 2000. *Investigations into Magic.* Translated by P. G. Maxwell-Stuart. Manchester and New York: Manchester University Press.

Rodríguez López, María Teresa, and Pablo Valderrama Rouy. 2005. "The Gulf Coast Nahua." In Sandstrom and García Valencia 2005, 158–86.

Rosenblatt, Ángel. 1987. Introduction to *Amadís de Gaula*, by Garci Rodríguez de Montalvo, ix–xv. Madrid: Cátedra.

Ruggiero, Guido. 1993. *Binding Passions: Tales of Magic, Marriage, and Power at the End of the Renaissance.* New York: Oxford University Press.

Ruiz de Alarcón, Hernando. 1892. "Tratado de las supersticiones y costumbres gentílicas que oy viuen entre los indios naturales desta Nueva España, escrito en México año de 1629." *Anales de Museo Nacional de México* 6: 125–223.

———. 1982. "The Treatise on Superstitions by Hernando Ruiz de Alarcón." In *Aztec Sorcerers in Seventeenth-Century Mexico*, edited and translated by Michael D. Coe and Gordon Whittaker. Albany: Institute for Mesoamerican Studies, State University of New York at Albany.

———. 1984. *Treatise on the Heathen Superstitions and Customs That Today Live Among the Indians Native to This New Spain, 1629.* Edited and translated by J. Richard Andrews and Ross Hassig. Norman: University of Oklahoma Press.

Ruvalcaba Mercado, Jesús, Juan Manuel Pérez Zevallos and Octavio Herrera, eds. 2004. *La Huasteca, un recorrido por su diversidad.* México: Centro de Investigaciones y Estudios Superiores en Antropología Social, Colegio de San Luis, Colegio de Tamaulipas.

Sáenz de Santa María, Carmelo. 1969. "Un formulario mágico mexicano: el 'Manual de ministros de indios' del doctor Jacinto de la Serna." *Revista de Indias* 29: 531–79.

Sahagún, Bernardino de. 1950–82. *Florentine Codex: General History of the Things of New Spain.* 12 vols. Translated by Arthur J. O. Anderson and Charles E. Dibble. Salt Lake City: University of Utah Press.

———. 1986. *Coloquios y doctrina cristiana.* Edited and translated by Miguel León-Portilla. México: Instituto de Investigaciones Históricas, Universidad Nacional Autónoma de México, Fundación de Investigaciones Sociales.

———. 1989. *Historia general de las cosas de la Nueva España. Primera versión íntegra del texto en castellano del manuscrito conocido como Códice Florentino*. 2 vols. Edited by Josefina García Quintana and Alfredo López Austin. México: Consejo Nacional para la Cultura y las Artes, Alianza Editorial Mexicana.

Sanders, William T., Jeffrey R. Parsons and Robert R. Santley, eds. 1979. *The Basin of Mexico: Ecological Processes in the Evolution of a Civilization*. New York: Academic Press.

Sandstrom, Alan R. 1991. *Corn Is Our Blood: Culture and Ethnic Identity in a Contemporary Aztec Indian Village*. Norman: University of Oklahoma Press.

Sandstrom, Alan, and E. Hugo García Valencia, eds. 2005. *Native Peoples of the Gulf Coast of Mexico*. Tucson: University of Arizona Press.

Sandstrom, Alan R., and Arturo Gómez Martínez. 2004. "Petición a Chicomexóchitl: un canto al espíritu del maíz, por la chamana nahua Silveria Hernández." In Ruvalcaba Mercado, Pérez Zevallos, and Herrera 2004, 343–67.

Schaefer, Stacy B., and Peter T. Furst, eds. 1996. *People of the Peyote: Huichol Indian History, Religion, and Survival*. Albuquerque: University of New Mexico Press.

Schwaller, John F. 1987. *The Church and Clergy in Sixteenth-Century Mexico*. Albuquerque: University of New Mexico Press.

Scribner, Robert W. 1984. "Ritual and Popular Religion in Catholic Germany at the Time of the German Reformation." *Journal of Ecclesiastical History* 35: 47–77.

———. 1987. *Popular Culture and Popular Movements in Reformation Germany*. London: Hambledon Press.

Searle, John. 1976. "A Classification of Illocutionary Acts." *Language in Society* 5(1): 1–23.

Seler, Eduard. 2014. "Los cantos religiosos de los antiguos mexicanos (primera parte, cantos del 1 al 10)." *Estudios de Cultura Náhuatl* 47: 254–336.

Serna, Jacinto de la. 1892. "Manual de ministros de indios para el conocimiento de sus idolatrias y extirpacion de ellas." *Anales del Museo Nacional de México* 6: 264–480.

———. 1953. "Manual de ministros de indios para el conocimiento de sus idolatrías y extirpación de ellas." In *Tratado de las idolatrías, supersticiones, dioses, ritos, hechicerías y otras costumbres gentílicas de las razas aborígenes de México*, vol. 1, 46–368. México: Ediciones Fuente Cultural.

Sharpe, James. 1996. *Instruments of Darkness: Witchcraft in Early Modern England*. Philadelphia: University of Pennsylvania Press.

Sigal, Pete. 2011. *The Flower and the Scorpion: Sexuality and Ritual in Early Nahua Culture*. Durham, N.C.: Duke University Press.

Smith, Michael E. 2012. *The Aztecs*. Malden, Mass.: Wiley-Blackwell.

Smith, Michael E., and Francis F. Berdan. 2003. "Postclassic Mesoamerica." In *The Postclassic Mesoamerican World*, edited by Michael E. Smith and Francis F. Berdan, 3–13. Salt Lake City: University of Utah Press.

Solaguren, Celestino. 1970. Introduction to Agreda [1655–60] 1970, xi–cv.

Somolinos D'Ardois, Germán. 1960. "Vida y obra de Francisco Hernández." In *Obras completas de Francisco Hernández*, vol. 1, 97–316. México: Universidad Nacional Autónoma de México.

Sosa, Francisco. 1877. *EGl episcopado de México. Galería biográfica ilustrada de los Illmos. Señores Arzobispos de México desde la época colonial hasta nuestros días*. México: H. Triarte y S. Hernández.

Spranz, Bodo. 1973. Los dioses en los códices mexicanos del Grupo Borgia. Una investigación iconográfica. México: Fondo de Cultura Económica.

Staller, John E., and Brian Stross. 2013. *Lightning in the Andes and Mesoamerica: Pre-Columbian, Colonial, and Contemporary Perspectives*. Oxford: Oxford University Press.

Stone, Rebecca. 2011. *The Jaguar Within: Shamanic Trance in Ancient Central and South American Art*. Austin: University of Texas Press.

Stresser-Peán, Guy. 2011. *El Sol-Dios y Cristo: la cristianización de los indios de México vista desde la Sierra de Puebla*. México: Fondo de Cultura Económica, Consejo Nacional para la Cultura y las Artes, Centro de Estudios Mexicanos y Centroamericanos.

Stross, Brian. 1998. "Seven Ingredients in Mesoamerican Ensoulment: Dedication and Termination in Tenejapa." In *The Sowing and the Dawning: Termination, Dedication, and Transformation in the Archaeological and Ethnographic Record of Mesoamerica*, edited by Shirley Boteler Mock, 31–39. Albuquerque: University of New Mexico Press.

Sullivan, Thelma D. 1982. "Tlazolteotl-Ixcuina: The Great Spinner and Weaver." In *The Art and Iconography of Late Post-Classic Central Mexico: A Conference at Dumbarton Oaks, October 22nd and 23rd*, edited by Elizabeth H. Boone, 7–36. Washington D.C.: Dumbarton Oaks.

Szőnyi, György E. 2004. *John Dee's Occultism: Magical Exaltation through Powerful Signs*. Albany: State University of New York Press.

Taggart, James M. 1983. *Nahuat Myth and Social Structure*. Austin: University of Texas Press.

Tate, Carolyn E. 2012. *Reconsidering Olmec Visual Culture: The Unborn, Women, and Creation*. Austin: University of Texas Press.

Taube, Karl. 2003. "Ancient and Contemporary Maya Conceptions about the Field and Forest." In *The Lowland Maya Area: Three Millennia at the Human-Wildland Interface*, edited by Arturo Gómez-Pompa, Michael F. Allen, Scott L. Fedick, and Juan J. Jiménez-Osorio, 461–92. New York: Food Products Press.

Tavárez, David E. 1996. "The Interplay of Orality, Writing, and Performance: Ruiz de Alarcón's Incantations as a Nahua Oral Genre." *Chicago Anthropology Exchange* 22: 50–78.

———. 1999. "La idolatría letrada: un análisis comparativo de textos clandestinos rituales y devocionales en comunidades nahuas y zapotecas, 1613–1654." *Historia Mexicana* 49(2): 197–252.

———. 2011. *The Invisible War: Indigenous Devotions, Discipline, and Dissent in Colonial Mexico*. Stanford, Calif: Stanford University Press.

Taylor, René. 1967. "Architecture and Magic: Consideration on the Idea of the Escorial." In *Essays in the History of Architecture Presented to Rudolf Wittkower*, edited by Douglas Fraser, Howard Hibbard, and Milton J. Lewine, vol. 2: 81–109. London: Phaidon.

Taylor, William B. 1979. *Drinking, Homicide, and Rebellion in Colonial Mexican Villages*. Stanford, Calif.: Stanford University Press.

———. 1996. *Magistrates of the Sacred: Priests and Parishioners in Eighteenth-Century Mexico*. Stanford, Calif.: Stanford University Press.

Tedlock, Barbara. 2001. "Divination as a Way of Knowing: Embodiment, Visualisation, Narrative, and Interpretation." *Folklore* 112(2): 189–97.

Tedlock, Dennis, ed. 1985. *Popol Vuh: The Mayan Book of the Dawn of Life*. New York: Simon and Schuster.

Thévet, André. 1905. "Histoyre du Mexique, manuscrit français inédit du XVIe siècle." Edited by Édouard du Jonghe. *Journal de la Societé des Américanistes*, new ser. 2:1–41.

Thomas, Keith. 1971. *Religion and the Decline of Magic*. New York: Charles Scribner's Sons.

Thompson, E. Sydney. 1939. "The Moon Goddess in Middle America, with Notes on Related Dieties." *Contributions to American Anthropology and History* 29: 122–73.

Todorov, Tzvetan 1984. *Mikhail Bakhtin: The Dialogical Principle*. Manchester: Manchester University Press.

Torquemada, Juan. 1943. *Monarquía indiana*. 3rd ed., vol. 2. México: Salvador Chávez Hayhoe.

Toussaint, Manuel. 1931. *Tasco: su historia, sus monumentos, características actuales y posibilidades turísticas*. México: Fondo de Cultura Económica.

Traslosheros, Jorge E. 2002. "El tribunal eclesiástico y los indios en el Arzobispado de México, hasta 1630." *Historia Mexicana* 51(3): 485–516.

Tyler, Peter. 2013. *Teresa of Ávila: Doctor of the Soul*. London: Bloomsbury.

Vespucci, Amerigo. [1503] 1916. Mundus Novus: Letter to Lorenzo Pietro di Medici. Translated by George Tyler Northrup, 1–13. Princeton, N.J.: Princeton University Press, www.encyclopediavirginia.org/Mundus_novus_1503

Villela F., Samuel. 2001. "El culto a los cerros en la Montaña de Guerrero." In Broda, Iwaniszewski, and Montero García 2001, 331–51.

Viveiros de Castro, Eduardo B. 2004. "Exchanging Perspectives: The Transformation of Objects into Subjects in Amerindian Ontologies." *Common Knowledge* 10(3): 463–84.

———. 2012. *Cosmological Perspectivism in Amazonia and Elsewhere*. Masterclass Series 1. Manchester, U.K.: HAU Books.

Vogt, Evon A. 1969. *Zinacantan: A Maya Community in the Highlands of Chiapas*. Cambridge, Mass.: Harvard University Press.

Walker, Daniel P. 1975. *Spiritual and Demonic Magic: From Ficino to Campanella*. Notre Dame, Ind.: University of Notre Dame Press.

Wallace, W. A., J. A. Weisheipl, and M. F. Johnson. 2003. "St. Thomas Aquinas." In *New Catholic Encyclopedia*, 13–29. Washington, D.C.: Catholic University of America, Gale.

Walsham, Alexandra. 2008. "The Reformation and the 'Disenchantment of the World' Reassessed." *Historical Journal* 51(2): 497–528.

Wasson, Gordon. 1980. *The Wondrous Mushroom: Mycolatry in Mesoamerica*. New York: McGraw-Hill.

Yates, Frances. 1964. *Giordano Bruno and the Hermetic Tradition*. Chicago: University of Chicago Press.

Zaballa Beascoechea, Ana. 2005. "Jurisdicción de los tribunales eclesiásticos novohispanos sobre la heterodoxia indígena. Una aproximación a su estudio." In *Nuevas perspectivas sobre el castigo de la heterodoxia indígena en la Nueva España: siglos XVI–XVIII*, edited by Ana Zaballa Beascoechea, 57–78. Bilbao: Servicio Editorial de la Universidad del País Vasco.

Zambelli, Paola. 2007. *White Magic, Black Magic in the European Renaissance: From Ficino, Pico, Della Porta to Trimethius, Agrippa, Bruno*. Boston: Brill.

Zamora Calvo, María Jesús. 2014. "Tratados reprobatorios y discursos antisupersticiosos en la España del Renacimiento." In Montaner and Lara 2014, 185–200.

Index

Page numbers in *italic* type refer to illustrations.